Give Us This Day

A Devotional Guide for Daily Living

Cover/interior: Koechel Peterson & Associates

Brownlow Publishing Company, Inc.
6309 Airport Freeway, Fort Worth, Texas 76117

A SPECIAL GIFT

at your retirement

for:

Toni

from:

Beth   Escoto

date:

6 / 4 /98

To My Grandsons

John Paul Brownlow

and

Andrew Brownlow

Give Us This Day

A Devotional Guide for Daily Living

Leroy Brownlow

Brownlow

Brownlow Publishing Company, Inc.

BROWNLOW GIFT BOOKS

INTRODUCTION

Give Us This Day was written for all ages and all peoples in every situation and condition of life. This book is for my grandsons, for my family and your family, for the young, for those in middle life and for those in their golden years.

All of us need strength. And there is no more effective way to get it than on a daily basis. For life is a growth, which is a daily process. This volume is my third book of daily meditations, the first two being *Today Is Mine* and *Living with the Psalms*.

Each person is what he thinks, and as he reads he thinks. Thus it is exceedingly imperative that each has a little time every day for uplifting meditation.

An effort has been made to make this volume profound, readable in simple language, interesting, and at times humorous, and most of all—helpful. An attempt has been made to present the deep meaning and ever possibility of life, to give lines that penetrate the heart for practical benefits. May these daily messages furnish guidance in times of difficulty, counsel in moments of perplexity, rest for the weary, courage for the threatened, cheer for the despondent, comfort for the afflicted, power for the struggling, cure for the blues, hope for the fainthearted, and vision for all to see the fuller, more exhilarating and more jubilant life.

Inasmuch as humanity's needs are ever present and basically the same, this book—except in minor points—should always be up-to-date. Its suggestiveness and helpfulness should be as relevant tomorrow as today.

Now the hope is cherished that you and all readers may find these pages, day by day, the stepping stones to higher ground.

Leroy Brownlow

A New Beginning

· ·

Add year to year.

ISAIAH 29:1

Happy New Year!

The old one is behind us. Forever! Some things God gives often, but He gives time only once. The flowers of spring return again and again. The trees burst into a new foliage year after year. But time does not come twice to anyone.

We enter the new year with high hopes. Every new year holds a brighter hope than the last, and we are ever ready to shake off bad habits and to give life a new start and a new effort. Such thinking has possibilities, for every improvement begins with a thought. This was the power that turned the feet of the ancient Psalmist, who said, "I thought about my ways, and turned my feet to Your testimonies" (Psalm 119:59). The trouble has been we have allowed some conflicting thoughts to grab us and change the direction of our feet.

❧ *So our first resolution is to keep our thoughts working for us.* No person is better, bigger or stronger than his or her thoughts.

❧ *Second, let us be grateful for the many blessings of last year.* We are not worthy of more if we are ungrateful for what we have.

❧ *Third, may we determine to be sympathetic toward all less fortunate persons than ourselves.* Having a heart is a big accomplishment.

❧ *Fourth, let us resolve to place the best reasonable construction on the words and deeds of others.*

❧ *Fifth, let us build life on the good foundation of loving God and our fellowmen.*

GIVE US THIS DAY

. . . .

Let me go, for the day breaks.
GENESIS 32:26

On what is commonly called The Lord's Prayer we are taught to pray, "Give us this day." It is a sacred gift. Definitely a gift. Sacred because it is God-given. It is a gift worthy of petition and we pray for its continuance.

Ralph Waldo Emerson said:

A Day is a miniature Eternity.

This day is a whole world within itself. It can make a world of difference in the life God has given each of us. In these twenty-four hours one can plot a course that will shape one's life and destiny. In these 1,440 minutes there are blessings to be received: bread to sustain life (but much more), opportunities to be used, challenges to be accepted, internal peace to quiet nerves, joy to give buoyancy, vision to look ahead, ability to struggle, time to make amends, and will power to make dreams come true. *Today.* Too much cannot be said in its behalf. Without it, the tent has been folded and the pilgrim has gone home. With it, the world beckons.

Today. Let me grab it, seize it, use it, live it, enjoy its every second. It is more valuable than money—no amount of money will buy another today. Treasure it as if your entire life depended upon it...and it very well could.

This day is nothing unless appreciated, used and enjoyed. What are books, health, wealth, travel, security, if we have not today?

A BETTER YEAR

. . . .

Behold, now is the accepted time.

2 CORINTHIANS 6:2

When Thorwaldsen was asked, "Which is your greatest statue?" he replied, "The next one."

It has been said that Cromwell wrote in his Bible, "If I cease to become better, I shall cease to be good." Even the best may be bettered. Indeed, it must be bettered if it is not to become worse.

Nothing remains static very long. It is meant for us to advance on our past. Whatever we gain each year is not meant to be a level on which to stop but a plateau on which to ascend. This means that we need to resolve and plan to go on to better things and greener pastures. For this reason, good resolutions are more than a duty; they are a necessity.

Let us thoughtfully meditate on the following lines:

I will start afresh each new day from petty littleness freed;
I will cease to stand complaining of my ruthless
neighbor's greed;
I will cease to sit repining while my duty's call is clear;
I will waste no moment whining, and my heart shall
know no fear.

I will not be swayed by envy when my rival's strength
is shown;
I will not deny his merit, but I'll try to prove my own;
I will try to see its beauty spread before me, rain or shine;
I will cease to preach your duty and be more concerned
with mine.

Now let us thoughtfully pursue a better day, a better year, a better life.

LOOK TO THIS DAY

. . . .

Moses had said,
"Consecrate yourselves today to the Lord,...
that He may bestow upon you a blessing this day."

EXODUS 32:29

Most people miss the best of today, because they plan to get the best tomorrow. And then when tomorrow comes it is no better than today. So all their tomorrows become only dusty dreams. But by saluting the dawn we make today our blessing and tomorrow our hope.

Look to this Day

For it is life, the very breath of life.
In its brief course lie all the verities and
Realities of your existence;
The Bliss of Growth,
The Glory of Action,
The Splendors of Beauty;
For yesterday is already a dream
And tomorrow is only a vision.
But today, well lived,
Makes every yesterday a dream of happiness
And every tomorrow a vision of hope.
Look well, therefore, to this day!

FROM THE SANSKRIT

It is the stuff of which real living is made!

HOW TO BE HAPPY THIS YEAR

. . . .

I must walk today, and tomorrow, and the day following.

LUKE 13:33

❧ *Learn to forget.* Bury the miseries of the dead past. Let them stay buried. If God forgets, why shouldn't we? The only use of bygones is to prepare us to meet by*comes.* One of the secrets of success and happiness is letting go of that which absorbs our energies and hinders our progress.

❧ *Make your conscience a source of peace and joy.* Conscience is the voice of approval or condemnation in the soul. Do what you believe is right and the voice will approve and give you an appreciation of self.

❧ *Cultivate contentment.* Every discontented person is unhappy. Furthermore, it decreases his or her level of efficiency. Many people are unhappy because they spend their time looking at other people and thinking how happy they could be if they were in their place. The truth is, those people are looking at you and thinking the same thing. Blessed is the person who can say, "I have learned, in whatever state I am, to be content" (Philippians 4:11).

❧ *Be helpful.* To be happy we must be helpful. Happiness cannot be obtained without giving it away. When you lift another's burden, you lighten your own.

❧ *Be trusting.* All that I *have seen* teaches me to trust God for all that I *cannot see.* If God can control the universe, He can help me and *will*—not always as I wish, but always in my eventual welfare.

BRAVER THAN A BEAR

Be strong and of a good courage, do not fear,
nor be afraid of them; for the Lord your God,
He is the One who goes with you.
DEUTERONOMY 31:6

Our little town was too small to have a picture show, and at that time there were no radios or televisions. This made it very inviting for tent shows to come for a one- or two-night stand.

One of the traveling shows had a big bear trained to wrestle. The show people would put gloves on the bear's paws and feet and a guard over his head. This was to protect the man who wrestled him from being cut and chewed to pieces. If a man ever prayed in his life, it was when he stepped into the ring to battle that bear!

To draw a crowd, they wanted a well-known man of the community to wrestle the bear. My father accepted the challenge. I shall never forget it. The match was some contest, and my father came away unhurt—braver than a bear and a hero.

A few years passed, and he got older and I got grown. He became a Christian and I admired him more than ever.

Everybody appreciates bravery. Wrestling a bear, however, is just one kind of heroism. During the last eight years of his life he was painfully ill, but day after day he showed a new kind of courage, more valiant than meeting the bear.

Though their bravery is unsung, multitudes are going through trials and hardships—physical, mental, social, economic—that make them heroes in their own right.

Because God is with us, we can all be brave.

NEVER SAY FAIL

· ·

Indeed we count them blessed who endure.

JAMES 5:11

ohn and Mary are climbing to the top. Happy, too. The
reasons are obvious. They miss a step occasionally, but
they won't say *fail*.

Among the millions of youth destined to reach a bright
future there is no such word as *fail*.

The ability of man to dignify and elevate his life is found
in his refusal to utter one word, *fail*.

Never say *fail*. If at first you don't succeed, try, try, again.

If our poor performance is not in our stars (and it's not),
why quit? We can change ourselves and keep on struggling.

Keep pushing—'tis wiser
Than sitting aside,
And dreaming and sighing,
And waiting the tide.
In life's earnest battle
They only prevail
Who daily march onward
And never say fail!

In life's early morning,
In manhood's firm pride,
Let this be your motto
Your footsteps to guide;
In storm and in sunshine,
Whatever assail,
We'll onward and conquer,
And never say fail!

A DETERMINED BURRO

· ·

Yes, you shall be steadfast, and shall not fear.

JOB 11:15

A city man spent his vacation on a cattle ranch and learned some very interesting lessons. He rode with the cowboys on a roundup. It was thrilling—and even more, it was a school within itself.

There was one wild steer over in the breaks that didn't want to be driven to the corral. He wouldn't drive. Neither would he be pulled. When roped, he would lie down and twist and roll. He was the wildest, meanest thing that ever walked on four hoofs. Whirling, turning, charging, ever watching with blood-stained, glassy eyes and breathing out a vapor of murder, he was saying he wouldn't be tamed. But the old cowboys knew better. They knew what to do. They tied that unbroken beast close to a little Mexican burro. When they turned them loose, that big angry steer threw the pint-sized burro ten ways to the veterinarian. And he kept doing it. But every time that burro got up, he got up one step closer home. He wanted to go home.

About ten days later the steer and burro arrived at the corral. And the steer was the tamest thing anyone had seen. Persistence and steadfastness had won.

Sometimes it's not how big we are but how steadfast we are that gets us where we wish to go. The grit to continue when the going gets rough has a way of coming out on top. It is fatal to enter any endeavor of struggle without the will to win. Persevering people begin their success at the very point where others end in failure.

LISTEN TO LOGIC

. . . .

Now hear my reasoning, and heed the pleadings of my lips.

JOB 13:6

A teacher asked her pupils, "Which is more helpful to us, the moon or the sun?"

Jimmy replied, "The moon."

"Why?" asked the teacher.

Jimmy answered, "The moon gives us light at night when we need it, but the sun gives us light only in the daytime when we don't need it."

We laugh at the child's reasoning, but it's no laughing matter that some of us don't do much better.

Logic is a process used for cutting down our mistakes. Whatever characteristics we have, logic should be one of them. We do so many foolish things because we either don't use logic or our logic is faulty. We should not throw to the wind such logic as:

"A man who has friends must show himself friendly" (Proverbs 18:24). "A gift in secret pacifies anger: and a reward in the bosom, strong wrath" (Proverbs 21:14). "Confidence in an unfaithful man in time of trouble is like a broken tooth, and a foot out of joint" (Proverbs 25:19). "Where no wood is, there the fire goes out: so where there is no talebearer, the strife ceases" (Proverbs 26:20). "Where there is no vision, the people perish" (Proverbs 29:18). "By their fruits you shall know them" (Matthew 7:29). "For whatever a man sows, that shall he also reap" (Galatians 6:7).

Each of these statements is common-sense reasoning that is unquestionably right.

OF THE SAME CLAY

. . . .

I returned, and considered all the oppressions
that are done under the sun.

ECCLESIASTES 4:1

There are many oppressions, hardships and burdens of every kind. Whatever our fellowman's oppression may be, we should be considerate and compassionate in dealing with him. Unless we have walked in his steps we don't know what he has been through.

Do Not Judge Too Harshly

Pray do not find fault with the man that limps
Or stumbles along the road, unless you have
worn the shoes he wears,
Or struggled beneath his load.

There may be tacks in his shoes that hurt,
though hidden from view,
Or the burdens he bears placed on your back—
Might cause you to stumble, too.

You may be strong, but still the blows that were his,
If dealt to you in the selfsame way at the
selfsame time—
Might cause you to stagger, too.

We should be considerate of each other for all of us belong to the same family, having been made of the same clay. But there is a relationship in addition to blood. Human need and pity relate us all to each other. Our needs vary, but all have them.

THE TOUCH OF A LOVING HAND

. . . .

Jesus, moved with compassion,
put out His hand, and touched him.

MARK 1:41

There is an interesting and helpful story to learn from a five-year-old girl. She was fascinated by the story of "The Three Little Pigs." Understandably, she requested her father to read the story night after night.

While it became boring to the father, it continued to be gripping to the daughter. Seeking relief, the father simply made a tape of the story, and when his daughter asked for it, he switched on the recording.

This worked for three nights, but the following evening the child handed the storybook to her father.

"Now, sweetheart," he said, "you know how to turn on the recorder."

"Yes," said the little girl, "but I can't sit on its lap."

Aloofness makes cool strangers of us all, but touch has a magnetic pull that unites and makes us friends. Even beasts respond to the touch of a loving hand. How much more do we!

Touch speaks the message that words cannot utter. We must all learn the art of it for the most effective communication.

AND THEN SOME

. . . .

And whoever compels you to go a mile,
go with him two.

MATTHEW 5:41

An executive once stated that the secret of every success-ful person he had ever known was in three little words: "And then some."

This is the second-mile philosophy: it is following in the steps of God, who does not think in terms of least amounts but rather does "exceedingly abundantly above all that we ask or think" (Ephesians 3:20).

Our world is a competitive one. To get ahead we can't stop at the minimum. It is absolutely necessary to give more, to outdo and outlast others—to do our duty "and then some." Anyone who works with the view, "I'm going to do the least I can to hold a job," is not going to get pro-moted. In merchandising it is better to give an ounce than to take an ounce, and to give a pint of gasoline than to short the customer a pint. In school you will receive no awards if you are satisfied just to pass.

If it's your philosophy that you are not going to do any-thing for anybody you don't have to do, then mankind will never overflow your basket. "*Give* and it shall be given to you; good measure, pressed down, and shaken together, and running over, shall men give into your bosom" (Luke 6:38). Give to your fellowman and he will respond by giving you good measure and running over. Duty—"and then some!" Therein is success!

TWO BURDENS WE CANNOT BEAR

. . . .

Sufficient for the day is its own trouble.

MATTHEW 6:34

There are two burdens no one can bear—yesterday's and tomorrow's. No person gives way beneath the burdens of today. It's the ones of yesterday and the ones of tomorrow that break us. Too much for any human to bear. The wolves that howled at us yesterday are already gone, and the roaring lions we see for tomorrow may be only friendly kittens.

❧ *One way* to eliminate worry from our lives is to forget the things that are behind. This was the psychology the Apostle Paul followed in his own life. He said:

Forgetting those things which are behind, and reaching
forward to those things which are ahead,
I press toward the goal.

PHILIPPIANS 3:13-14

Dragging a lengthening chain of regrets from the dead past is like the life of a prisoner with a ball and chain around his ankle.

❧ *Another way* to prevent ulcer-creating apprehension is to live in the present rather than the future. Fear is the dread of trouble to come and a feeling of inability to handle it. But if I admit no evil which I cannot surmount with God's help, then I shall not be afraid as each day dawns. As Gertrude Bower Webster has written,

When storms swoop down, and torrents roar,
And troubles crowd your day,
Be robust, brave, and undismayed
For troubles pass away.

All ills are transients that afflict
And cumber life's brief way.
They flee before eternal things
That never pass away.

A DOG NAMED SUNSHINE

· ·

How long, O Lord? Will You forget me forever?
How long will You hide Your face from me?

PSALM 13:1

To the majority, life presents problems that often perplex and discourage. Then it is easy to question our lot and the God who supports us.

Several years ago I visited an old woodcutter in his one-room cabin. His face bore the lines of hardship, and the contents of his cabin signaled privation. His life had consisted of only bare necessities. No comfort or luxury had ever entered his door, except maybe one—his dog. It was a big dog he called *Sunshine.*

In all of his loneliness, privation and suffering he had been able to find a little sunshine, even if it was only a dog. Here is an example for us.

In the course of our conversation, he stated that he had been through the wringer of disappointment, suffering and sorrow. For a short time his faith had weakened, and it was then that he questioned God's care for him. But not anymore. He stated that time had given the events a different perspective, and he was now a better and more sensitive man because of what had happened to him.

Indeed, some pages in life's book *are* hard to understand, but we know that pain can sweeten and ennoble human character. This is the reason the Apostle Paul could say, "We also rejoice in our sufferings" (Romans 5:5). And this we further know: what looks topsy-turvy to us is clear and untoppled before the eyes of Him whom we serve.

DREAM A LITTLE

· ·

I must also see Rome.

ACTS 19:21

$\mathcal{F}$or a man nineteen hundred years ago—in Paul's situation and that far away, as distance was measured in that day—to dream of going to Rome was considered mere fantasy by most people.

We can learn from Paul. No one should ever stop reaching for new lands to conquer and for new goals to reach. To rise above earth's common ground we must dream a little. Dream of a star and hitch ourselves to it.

The world is filled with dreamers, but the ones who really profit from it are the ones who dream when they are awake.

Those who dream by day are cognizant of many things which escape those who dream only by night.

EDGAR ALLAN POE

The dreamers are the lonely pioneers of human progress. Our society is blessed by the fortunate visions of its open-eyed dreamers.

Humanity cannot afford to forget its dreamers. It must not let their ideas wither and die, for every great reality was once only a dream. Dreams are the seeds of realities. Illustrious accomplishments rise from little dreams just as mighty oaks sprout from little acorns.

Don't quit dreaming. As long as you dream you are alive. Cease to dream and life loses its zest and ebbs away.

Maybe in your own soul there is a vision that is beginning to stir. Not a material one. A spiritual one. A vision of a fuller life that will glorify your Maker. The dream you have of yourself—*that* you will become.

What Makes a Strong Nation?

· ·

And God said,
"Let us make man in Our image, after Our likeness."
GENESIS 1:26

As seen from the above passage, man was created and designed by a wise Creator to rule over creation, *not* to be held in any form of bondage.

Unquestionably, among all races and nations there are various degrees of talent, but equality gives each person the right to develop his own endowment.

Hugh Black has forcefully stated that America must not fail on the proposition of equal opportunity:

"Faith in the people rests on the belief—in spite of ignorance and folly and mob passion, and all the rest of the indictment which we know so well—that the average man is honest and fair and wants to do right. I do not see how you can be a real democrat on any other basis.

"We make an appeal too often to the baser side of man, to prejudice and self interest. The better side of man is the stronger side, if we would believe it seriously and apply the faith unflinchingly....

"America is a great political adventure, dedicated to the incredible proposition that men are born equal. I know all the criticism of that in fact and logic, but if America fails here she fails entirely."

BE STRONG AND PREVAIL

Be strong, and do not let your hands be weak,
for your work shall be rewarded.

2 CHRONICLES 15:7

Be Strong

Be strong!
We are not here to play, to dream, to drift;
We have hard work to do, and loads to lift;
Shun not the struggle—face it; 'tis God's gift.

Be strong!
Say not, "The days are evil. Who's to blame?"
And fold the hands and acquiesce—oh, shame!
Stand up, speak out, and bravely, in God's name.

Be strong!
It matters not how deep entrenched the wrong,
How hard the battle goes, the day how long;
Faint not—fight on! Tomorrow comes the song.

MALTBIE DAVENPORT BABCOCK

When I, barely seventeen, went away to college my mother said, "Son, be strong." Three words, but they carry a world of instruction and warning.

Be strong enough to know you're weak. Be strong enough to be your own person. Be strong in resisting temptation. Be strong in wholesome associations. Be strong in worthy friendships. Be strong in honor. Be strong in the defense of right. Be strong in the pursuit of truth. Be strong in respect of the elderly. Be strong in facing difficulties. Be strong in Bible reading. Be strong in prayer.

Yes! Be strong! Be strong! Be strong!

THANKFUL FOR TEARS

· ·

She weeps bitterly in the night,
and her tears are on her cheeks.

LAMENTATIONS 1:2

Life on this earth consists of sorrows and joys, tears and smiles. There is a time for each. Solomon said, "A time to weep, and a time to laugh." When the time comes for either, let us give ourselves to it. Shakespeare said, "If you have tears, prepare to shed them now."

Those who weep are cognizant of many things which escape the ones who only smile; and they receive a deeper blessing, though it's grievous, than those who have never known the depth of such sorrow. As John Cheney once said, "The soul would have no rainbows had the eyes no tears."

There are four things for which we can be thankful concerning tears:

❧ *First, we have emotions that can be stirred.* We are not robots. "My eye wastes away because of grief" (Psalm 6:7).

❧ *Second, God sees our tears.* "Thus says the Lord...I have heard your prayer, I have seen your tears, surely I will heal you" (2 Kings 20:5).

❧ *Third, after sorrows and tears come joys and smiles.* "Those who sow in tears shall reap in joy" (Psalm 126:5).

❧ *Fourth,* we have the assurance that in another land on a faraway strand "*God shall wipe away all tears* from their eyes; and there shall be no more death, neither sorrow, nor crying" (Revelation 21:4).

IF THE LION EATS DADDY

. . . .

There is a way which seems right to a man,
but its end is the way of death.

PROVERBS 14:12

A father took his little boy to a zoo, where they saw a caged lion. Greatly impressed with the lion's ferocity, the child said, "Daddy, if that lion gets out and eats you up, which bus do I take to get home?"

The situation seems a little incongruous to us, but when the child faced the possibility of a crisis, his thoughts turned toward home.

It should be a part of the vital training of every youth to go home. Home is a place of refuge to which we return. And our boys and girls need a curfew. It is more evident every day that the street with its establishments is not a place of safety.

Home should be one of the first and most sacred thoughts of the child. Blessed is the child who has this feeling and carries it throughout childhood, then through youth and adult life. All of us need a magnetic pull back to the rallying point of home. There we bind our wounds, dry our tears, bend our knees, and read the Scriptures, rewind our energy, renew our quest and rekindle our hope.

'Mid pleasure and palaces though we may roam,
Be it ever so humble, there's no place like home.

Some young people with their contempt for the old standards and proven ways, seeking a life of no restraint of thrills and spills, catch a bus going to disaster, disappointment, dismay, failure, misery, even to prison. Wherever we wish to go, we'll have to take the bus that's going there. We just have to remember, not all buses go to the same place.

REVIVE US AGAIN

. . . .

Though I walk in the midst of trouble,
You will revive me.

PSALM 138:7

The long-winded preacher preached and preached. After about an hour of shouting and whispering and pounding the podium, he stopped and asked, "What hymn shall we sing?"

One elderly brother appropriately responded, "Revive Us Again."

It nearly broke up the service.

So many times we need to be recharged. The possibilities are there but need rekindling. This is why churches have revivals, why schools have pep rallies, the reason political parties have conventions, and the reason the individual needs motivational helps.

Revival. This is something everybody needs at times. Human spirits lag and need renewing. Enthusiasm runs down and needs winding up.

Because of this universal need, we occasionally sing in worship services the renowned hymn, "Revive Us Again." Even the Psalmist at times was in need of spiritual revival. He openly admitted it: "As for me, my feet were almost gone; my steps had well-nigh slipped" (Psalm 73:2). And then he told us how long his need lasted and what revived him: "until I went into the sanctuary of God" (verse 17)— until he went *to the Temple* to be near to God. Bringing it up-to-date, going to church can revive us, too.

LET YOUR LIGHT SHINE

. . . .

Let your light so shine before men,
that they may see your good works,
and glorify your Father who is in heaven.

MATTHEW 5:16

Man once used a candle for light. It was hailed as a revolutionary discovery, a big improvement over the burning torch. However, the candle flickered, gave off odor, and the least puff of wind would blow it out.

Then came the kerosene lamp. It too was applauded as a jump of progress in the field of illumination. But it had problems: The bowl had to be filled with kerosene. The wick had to be trimmed and sometimes did not reach the fluid. The globe became smoky and had to be cleaned.

Another improvement was the Coleman gasoline lamp or lantern. We had one when I was a boy, and one of my jobs was to keep it going. It required gasoline, mantles, and had to be kept pumped up.

Then, thanks to Mr. Edison, came the incandescent light. When connected to the power source and if the globe was good, it produced light very efficiently.

What kind of light are we? Just a candle that quivers and emits odor? Or just a kerosene light with a short wick and a smoky globe? Or just a gasoline light that won't shine at all unless someone is there to keep us pumped up all the time? Or an efficient incandescent light, connected to the great source of light, that shines and shines and shines?

One of the greatest compliments ever paid mortal man was given by the Apostle Paul to the Philippians. He told them, "You shine as lights in the world" (Philippians 2:15). A darkened world needs our light. Let us *shine!*

THE HIGH COST OF FREE ADVICE

Whoever guards his mouth and his tongue,
keeps his soul from troubles.

PROVERBS 21:23

There are some shortages in the world. But there is one thing in overflowing abundance—advice. Furthermore, it's free. Unless you take it. And if you do, you may find it costly.

So much "free" advice goes like this:

§ *"Why don't you get a new car?"* But the advisor doesn't know your finances, your obligations, your job security, your plans for the future, your priorities, etc. So it's advice from ignorance.

§ *"You should get a new suit,"* or *"new dress,"* or *"a new hairstyle,"* or *"new shoes."* But the advisor is not aware of your plans, problems or preferences.

§ *"You should paint your house."* Again, the self-appointed counselor lacks all the personal information you possess.

Many, many more examples could be cited. But why? It is better to stop the flow of free advice by asking, "Who is this who darkens counsel by words without knowledge?" (Job 38:2).

While I have been a counselor for many years, I freely say that it is not wise to give advice unless it is requested. Even Jesus taught against teaching or counseling those who don't want it. He called it casting "pearls before swine" who may later turn and rend you (Matthew 7:6).

There are exceptions, of course, to nearly all rules, including this one on giving advice. There are some friends and relatives with whom you are close enough to offer a little counsel, provided you don't appear superior or dictatorial. But generally speaking, refrain from it unless asked.

TURNING CLOUDS INSIDE OUT

. . . .

But as for you, you meant evil against me;
but God meant it for good, to bring to pass,
as it is this day, to save many people alive.

GENESIS 50:20

*J*oseph's brothers did him an awful injustice, but it turned out to be a cloud with a silver lining. It became the means whereby he rose to the second-highest office in Egypt, and thus enabled him to save the multitudes from seven years of famine, including his own people.

When our plans are frustrated and we are saddled with pressing burdens, there is always the possibility of becoming bitter and rebellious. Grumbling so often follows disappointment. A scoffer is usually a person whose expectations and hopes have been dashed. He saw a cloud but not its silver lining. It is highly imperative, therefore, that we turn our clouds inside out so that we can see bigger hopes and brighter dreams.

> *The inner side of every cloud is bright and shining;*
> *I therefore turn my clouds about*
> *And always wear them inside out*
> *To show the lining.*

ELLEN THORNCROFT FOWLER

One of the most trying tests of life is how we meet adverse circumstances. I like the way the great Paganini met it. When his favorite violin was broken, he accepted the loss as a challenge and got another one. He said, "I will show them the music is in me and not in any instrument."

It is much easier to put back together the broken pieces of a dream when you learn to say, as Paul said, "My God shall supply all [my] needs," and when you have the grit to say, as Paul said, "I can do all things through Christ who strengthens me."

THE WORLD AS SOME SEE IT

. . . .

See, your house is left to you desolate.

MATTHEW 23:38

- *The center of things*—the place where I am.
- *Good ideas*—those that agree with mine.
- *Bad ideas*—those that oppose mine.
- *Sinful pleasures*—the things others like to do.
- *Innocent pleasures*—the things I like to do.
- *A sensible person*—one who heeds what I say.
- *Benevolence*—everyone giving handouts to me.
- *Humility*—everyone bowing to my whims.
- *Patience*—everyone bearing with me.
- *Cooperation*—everyone working with me.
- *Hospitality*—everyone entertaining me.
- *Encouragement*—everyone bragging on me.
- *Unity*—everyone going along with me.
- *Sympathy*—everyone identifying with me.
- *Meekness*—everyone stepping aside for me.
- *A contentious person*—one who disagrees with me.
- *Visitation*—everyone coming to visit me.

Such a person can't see because he has too much "I" in his eye. This blinds him to the better and fuller life. It leaves his own little house desolate.

HANDLING ANNOYANCES

. . . .

And her rival also provoked her severely,
to make her miserable.

1 SAMUEL 1:6

A minister was asked if a man who was taking trumpet lessons on Sunday would go to heaven. The preacher's short reply with hidden meaning was, "Oh, I suppose so. But it's doubtful if the man next door will!"

We all need to handle the annoyances smoothly and victoriously. There are so many things to ruffle us and grate on our nerves. Just had a flat. The postman put the long-awaited check in a box down the street. The paperboy failed to throw the paper. Ready to fix breakfast and out of coffee. The neighbor's cat spends too much time in our yard. The car ran out of gasoline. The children next door knock the ball through our window. Bought tickets to go see a sister, but when the day comes the airline is on strike.

What can we do about it?

First, accept the fact that life has annoyances as well as buoyances.

Second, decide that we are bigger than any annoyance that confronts us. That we can handle it.

Third, through soul searching, prayer and determination, grow into a calmer person with a longer fuse. One of the qualifications of a bishop or elder is "not soon angry." This is an ideal to which all should strive.

LIKE THE GENTLE RAIN FROM HEAVEN

· ·

For judgment is without mercy
to the one who has shown no mercy.

JAMES 2:13

In ages past, a king called his servants to give an account. One owed ten thousand pieces of money. Unable to pay, he pleaded for mercy, promising to pay. The king had compassion and forgave him.

Then that servant went out and found a fellow servant who owed him only a hundred pieces of money, and he took him by the throat and said, "Pay up." The debtor, not having the payment, pleaded for leniency, promising to pay. Now the very one who had asked for mercy and received it was unwilling to grant it to another. He ordered the poor man to be cast into prison and left there till he paid.

When the news got back to the king, he was angry and reminded that cruel servant of the grace he had received but that he was unwilling to grant it in a much smaller amount to another. The king then commanded the unmerciful servant to be sent to prison and tormented till he paid.

This is a good and apt story. I know it is. For it was given by Jesus Christ.

Unmerited clemency will do more than severity. Mercy purifies the soul, but vengeance lets it rot with rancor. Humanity is too imperfect not to be in dire need of mercy.

Shakespeare stated that mercy twice blesses—the one who gives and the one who receives. This should make it free and unrestrained.

The quality of mercy is not strained;
It droppeth as the gentle rain from heaven
Upon the place beneath: it is twice blest;
It blesseth him that gives and him that takes.

GET ACQUAINTED WITH YOURSELF

. . . .

I thought about my ways,
and turned my feet to Your testimonies.

PSALM 119:59

A renowned example of seeking solitude is Jesus. "Now in the morning, having risen a long while before daylight, He went out and departed to a solitary place; and there He prayed" (Mark 1:35).

Solitude lends itself to many blessings, including prayer, self-examination, a reflection of one's past and present, and the formation of plans for the future. Free from the distractions of a fast-moving, hard-pressing world, we should ask: From whence have I come? Where am I now? Where am I going?

In a talk to young men, Robert Burdette said: "Get away from the crowd for awhile, and think. Stand on one side and let the world run by, while you get acquainted with yourself and see what kind of a fellow you are.

"Ask yourself hard questions about yourself. Ascertain if you are really the manner of man you say you are; and if you are always honest; if you always tell the whole, perfect truth in business details; if your life is as good and upright at twelve o'clock at night as it is at noon; if you are as good a temperance man on a fishing excursion as you are on a Sunday School picnic; if you are as good when you go out of town as you are at home; if, in short, you are really the sort of man your father hopes you are and your sweetheart believes you are.

"Get on intimate terms with yourself, my boy, and, believe me, every time you come out of one of those soul-searching sessions you will be a stronger, better, purer man."

THE STUFF OF WHICH LIFE IS MADE

. . . .

So teach us to number our days,
that we may apply our hearts unto wisdom.

PSALM 90:12

Since time is brief and uncertain, it behooves us all to live in the present and appropriate our days to the fullest. For the person who squanders time wastes the very thing out of which life is made. Thus by killing time one commits suicide tick by tick.

The Clock of Life

The clock of life is wound but once
And no man has the power
To tell just where the hand will stop—
At late or early hour.

Now is the only time you own!
Live, love, toil with a will;
Place no faith in "tomorrow" for
The clock may then be still.

Time deals kindly with those who use it rightly and harshly with those who use it wrongly. Just a minute of time is a minute of life and is not to be scorned.

Just a Minute

I have only just a minute,
Just sixty seconds in it;
Forced upon me—can't refuse it,
I must suffer if I lose it,
Give account if I abuse it;
Just a tiny little minute,
But eternity is in it.

Time works wonders, so *use it.*

PEACE, PERFECT PEACE

· ·

To be spiritually minded is life and peace.

ROMANS 8:6

If we would know peace, let us:

❧ *Be thankful for life,* because it gives us the opportunity to work and to play and to live and to look into the heavens. "He gives to all life, and breath, and all things" (Acts 17:25).

❧ *Affirm that our faith is stronger than our difficulties and that we will conquer them.* "This is the victory that overcomes the world, even our faith" (1 John 5:4).

❧ *Constantly keep our goal before us.* Let's never give up our dreams. "I press toward the mark" (Philippians 3:14).

❧ *Live unselfishly, thinking of others.* The self-centered person can never get enough of himself or herself or the favors of others to find peace. "Look not every man on his own things, but every man also on the things of others" (Philippians 2:4).

❧ *Be satisfied with our possessions.* Then what we have, *we have*—not what we have has us. "There is a severe evil which I have seen under the sun: riches kept for their owner to his hurt" (Ecclesiastes 5:13).

❧ *Stamp out negative thoughts with positive thoughts.* No one gets up the Mount of Happiness in reverse gear. "Whatever things are true, honest, just, pure, lovely, of good report; if there be any virtue, and if there be any praise, think on these things" (Philippians 4:8).

❧ *Put our trust in God,* in good times and bad, fully confident that we are in the hollow of His hand. "The Lord is my rock, and my fortress, and my deliverer; my God, my strength, in whom I will trust" (Psalm 18:2).

WHAT DO YOU SEE?

. . . .

Hear now this, O foolish people, without understanding,
who have eyes, and see not,
and who have ears and hear not.

JEREMIAH 5:21

*P*oor Henry. He never beheld anything but defeat, failure and disaster. Most of his years were spent in reverse. He wore the invisible crown of pessimism (or was it invisible?). Perhaps more people saw that cloud of gloom encircling his head than he thought. For he had a way of showing it. He came in late at the club meeting and abruptly spoke out, "I don't know what you're talking about, but I can see it's wrong."

One thing that determines what we see is the kind of eyeglasses we wear. If our glasses are blue, the world looks blue; if brown, the world appears brown; if green, the world seems green. Sometimes it's our glasses that need attention, not the world.

This is the difference between an optimist and a pessimist: an optimist sees an opportunity in every difficulty; a pessimist sees a difficulty in every opportunity. They look through different glasses.

But history—and our own past—teaches the brighter view. Sometimes it just takes awhile for it to develop. Moses was eighty years old before he was prepared to become the great leader of God's people. Maybe you, too, are now training for a greater service, and the best is yet to come. By looking for something better, we're more apt to find it. For what a person finds depends largely on what he looks for.

There is ever a sun somewhere, my dear;
Though the skies are dark, in time it'll break here.

GRANDPA WAS NOT FOOLED

. . . .

But solid food belongs to those who are of full age,
that is, those who by reason of use have their senses
exercised to discern both good and evil.

HEBREWS 5:14

Grandpa had some very interesting stories to tell. All made sense. All had a point.

One of them concerned his inspection of a farm for sale. After arriving at the farmer's house and the customary greetings, they began to walk over the place. After the owner learned that Grandpa was a preacher, he thought a naive lamb had come his way, ready for the fleecing.

While walking through some bottom land, bordered by a little river, Grandpa noticed some mud and debris up waist high on the trees. It prompted him to ask, "Does this river ever overflow and flood this land?"

"Oh, no. Never," replied the farmer.

"Well, what's the mud and debris doing on the trees?" inquired Grandpa.

"What mud? I don't see any mud. Oh, you mean that mud over there on those trees? The hogs did that. They get muddy and rub up against the trees."

They continued their inspection, circling back toward the house. Then the anxious farmer asked, "Parson, would you like to buy my farm?"

"No, I guess not," said Grandpa. "But I tell you what, I really *would* like to get a start of those hogs."

Be discerning, for not everything that's told is right. Keep your head when others try to turn it.

THINGS COULD BE WORSE

. . . .

And now I urge you to take heart,
for there will be no loss of life among you,
but only of the ship.

ACTS 27:22

*P*aul and 275 others were caught in a tempest at sea. There was neither sun nor stars for many days. The situation was so desperate that in an effort to lighten the ship, they cast the freight and tackling overboard. For fourteen days they fasted. The ship was wrecked, but all the passengers and crew were saved. The calamity was severe and frightening, but it could have been worse; there could have been no survivors.

Nearly every reverse, mishap or disaster could have been worse.

An old story is very illustrative: A doctor called a man and said, "I have the reports on your tests. I wish you would come to the office. I would like to talk to you." In thirty minutes the patient was there. The doctor said, "I have bad news and worse news. The bad news is you're going to live only twenty-four hours." The patient interrupted, "Doctor, that's terrible! That's awful! Only twenty-four hours to live. What could be worse than that?" The doctor replied, "I tried to call you yesterday."

May God give us the grace to see that our trials, setbacks, failures and disasters could be worse, and to be thankful that we are as well off as we are. Life could be worse. So, instead of sighing over how hard circumstances are, take a look around you and see the blessings that bloom on every hand.

LAUGHING AT OURSELVES

Bear with me that I may speak,
and after I have spoken, keep mocking.

JOB 21:3

A preacher friend of mine had a world of friends. Not because of superior ability as a pulpit man but because of his blessed talent in getting along with people. One of his remarkable traits was his freeness in laughing at his own quirks. He could stand criticism. Even better, he could joke about it.

Here is one of the stories he used to tell: After a Sunday sermon a man said, "Brother, you have a special talent; come to think of it, three talents: I believe you can stand the stillest, speak the longest, and say the least of any man I've ever heard."

He could laugh at himself. To stand ten feet tall after you've been cut down is a major accomplishment. The preacher's amusement in repeating the criticism shows that he was not possessed with a feeling of insecurity that demanded everyone's plaudits. However, some people have to have such. They won't even admit to themselves that they may be weak on any point.

When we acknowledge our peculiarities and weaknesses, people love us and want to help us. But when someone dares to suggest that we might be wrong, our feigned perfection and bristling manner alienate and make enemies.

There is a kind of greatness that doesn't depend upon superior fortune. It's our superior *touchableness*. Not being too sensitive, we haven't built a barrier that cuts off accessibility to us and closeness with us.

TRY IT AGAIN

. . . .

Then he took his staff in his hand, and he chose for himself
five smooth stones from the brook....

1 SAMUEL 17:40

$\mathcal{D}$avid, in going to fight the giant Goliath, picked five smooth stones. If the first failed, he could try again. This took courage.

Three Kinds of Courage

There's the courage that nerves you in starting to climb
The mount of success rising sheer;
And when you've slipped back there's the courage sublime
That keeps you from shedding a tear.

These two kinds of courage, I give you my word,
Are worthy of tribute—but then,
You'll not reach the summit unless you've the third—
the courage to try-it-again.

ROY FARRELL GREENE

Try-it-again is the stuff of which success made.

The farmer's crop was hailed out. Did he quit? No. He planted again. The cowboy mounted the bucking bronc. He got thrown, but he tried him again. The baseball player struck out. He didn't quit. When his turn came, he went to bat again. A man seeking employment got turned down. But the world didn't end. He applied elsewhere.

It is comforting that God lets us try again. This is evident from the Prayer of Example. The prayer includes, "Forgive us our debts, as we forgive our debtors." However, we are not to pray this only once in a lifetime but often, indicating that we have erred, failed and are in need of forgiveness. He forgives and lets us start again.

LEARNING TO PRAY

Be anxious for nothing, but in every thing by prayer
and supplication with thanksgiving let your requests
be made known to God.

PHILIPPIANS 4:6

A tear-stained, emotionally bereft man came into my office. His mother had died the day before, and her funeral was to be conducted the next day. Aware of all this, my heart went out to him. In broken speech he said, "My mother lies cold in death and I can't even pray."

I assured him: "It's not hard; it's only a natural outpouring of the heart. First, *address it to God* as Jesus showed us when He prayed, 'Our Father which art in heaven.' Second, *use hallowed expressions,* for prayer is no place for flippant language. Jesus prayed, 'Hallowed be Your name.' Third, just *express your feelings openly,* freely and sincerely. You can be absolutely yourself, free from all pretensions and shams, for you couldn't fool God if you wished. You can thank Him for past and present blessings and pray for future help. Fourth, in closing, you can *pray in Jesus' name,* for He said, 'If ye shall ask anything in my name, I will do it' (John 14:14)."

On this basis and in this framework we prayed. It dried his tears and soothed his aching heart. He left a fortified man. He came with worry and left with assurance.

Prayer is a simple exercise of turning our thoughts heavenward. And God's ears that hear are more efficient than our lips that pray. Once we have found relief from stress and worry on our knees at the feet of Jesus, maybe we will choose to remain there forever.

APPLES OF GOLD

· ·

A word fitly spoken is like apples of gold
in pictures of silver.

PROVERBS 25:11

Two men who had not seen each other in four or five years met at a sales meeting in another state.

"How is your wife?" one of them asked his old friend.

"She's in heaven," was the reply.

"Oh, I'm sorry." Then he realized that didn't sound right, so he added, "I mean, I'm glad." Now that sounded even worse. He finally blurted out with, "Well, I'm surprised."

Choosing the right words for the right moment is an art, so much so that colleges give degrees in it. A word can cut more than a sword or heal more than an ointment. Thus, "a word spoken in due season, how good is it!" (Proverbs 15:23). Speaking the right word at the right time can change the world. Job expressed it this way, "How forcible are right words!" (Job 6:25).

Hot words inflame human relationships, but cool words never scald a tongue or burn a listener. Words! Words! Words! Sometimes they come by the gallon while the thoughts come by the spoonful.

For words to be fitly spoken they must come from fit thinking. Therefore, *think before you speak*; and if you do, sometimes you may not speak at all.

And if your mouth should misfire, be careful about reloading.

ABIDE WITH ME

. . . .

And, lo, I am with you always, even unto the end of the world.

MATTHEW 28:20

Francis Lyte was born in Kelso, Ireland, in 1793. His father died when he was a child, and he and his mother moved to Dublin. There Francis was educated, and at age twenty-two he answered the call for ministerial services.

In 1819 he went to Lymington, where he overtaxed his strength and developed tuberculosis. Hoping to regain his health, he accepted the fishermen's parish of Brixham-on-Sea. But the tuberculosis continued to worsen.

In the late summer of 1847 his doctors decided that he should retire and spend the winters in southern France, for he was becoming weaker. Thus arrangements were quickly made. The last Sunday came, and in emotional language he bid his congregation farewell. Among the simple fisher-folk there was scarcely a dry eye. Later he strolled into the garden and sat down on a bank overlooking Torbay, the sea below, the sky above, some clouds in the distance. He asked God to help him leave something to help humanity. Then he went indoors, suffering the anguish of leaving a people he loved, and wrote:

> *Abide with me; fast falls the eventide;*
> *The darkness deepens, Lord, with me abide;*
> *When other helpers fail, and comforts flee,*
> *Help of the helpless, O abide with me!*
>
> *Swift to its close ebbs out life's little day;*
> *Earth's joys grow dim, its glories pass away;*
> *Change and decay in all around I see;*
> *O Thou who changest not, abide with me!*

The next morning he left for France and died there less than three months later, but the hymn he wrote will never die.

WHY DO THEY HATE ME?

. . . .

A lying tongue hates those who are crushed by it,
and a flattering mouth works ruin.

PROVERBS 26:28

A bothered man with a personal problem came to me for counseling. He stated that a fellow worker didn't like him and that it was very visible. He then explained, "I've never done him a wrong in my life. Not by word. Not by deed. I can't see why he dislikes me."

"Let me ask you a question," I stated. "Has he ever done you any special wrong?"

"Yes. Two years ago he lied on me and blocked my getting a promotion on the job. He wanted it but didn't get it."

"Now that's it," I continued. "He hates you not because of what you've done to him, but because of what he's done to you. After lying on you, his mind got busy and started making you into an awful creature that deserves the worst. This was done to try to justify the wrong he perpetrated. Since he did you wrong, he thought you wouldn't like him; so his mind reacted, 'You don't like me, so now I don't like you.' Of course he could have apologized but he didn't. He chose the course of multiplying evil. As hatred renews itself, it gets worse."

No faculty of the human mind is so perverted and persistent as *hate*. Hate can usually find something wrong. If only a little, it can enlarge it. If nonexistent, it can manufacture it.

I flinch at the thought of anyone's doing me wrong. Not that I can't take the punishment. I can. Not that I can't forgive. I can. It's because that person, unless he or she repents, will always be my enemy; and not because of what I've done to the person, but because of what that one has done to me.

PUT MAN BACK TOGETHER

· ·

Then the Lord saw that the wickedness of man
was great in the earth....

GENESIS 6:5

Sometime ago there was a touching story of a father who
noticed a map of the world in a daily newspaper. He tore
the page out of the paper, cut it into small pieces and told
his young son to put the world together. The boy returned in
a few short minutes and announced, "Dad, I've done it!"

The father was amazed. "So soon?" he said. "How did
you do it?"

The boy replied, "I turned the page over and there was a picture of a man. I just put the man together, and the world was
right."

Here is a lesson for us: *put man together and the world
will be right.* Man has trouble with man (and there are a
thousand ways for it to occur), because first of all he has
trouble with himself. Our society is fragmented because
man is fragmented, and hurts because man hurts. Man has
ripped and torn himself up with selfishness, hate, envy, jeal-
ousy, laziness, irresponsibility, unforgiveness, dishonesty,
untruthfulness, inconsideration, cruelty, vengeance, strife,
covetousness, lust, pride and unthankfulness (not that *all*
have split into such pieces of waywardness, but many have).

The only way we can put him back together is to rid him
of what tore him apart in the first place. This can be done.
The Ephesians did. The Apostle Paul said of them, "For you
were once darkness, but now you are light in the Lord"
(Ephesians 5:8). This revolutionary change occurred
because they were redeemed (1:7) and Christ dwelt in their
hearts by faith (3:17).

PASS IT ON

. . . .

Therefore, as we have opportunity, let us do good to all,
especially to those who are of the household of faith.

GALATIANS 6:10

To receive a blessing and pass it on is like the running,
pure water of a river. But to receive and hoard is like the
dead, stagnant water of a pool that receives and keeps what
it gets. In time the dead pool stinks, and so does the all-get-
never-give person.

If you have received a smile, pass it on; a kind word, pass
it on; a helping hand, pass it on; a visit when ill, pass it on;
encouragement when ready to faint, pass it on; a lift when
you fell, pass it on; forgiveness when you blundered, pass it
on; direction when you went astray, pass it on; sympathy
when you heart was heavy, pass it on; or financial assistance
when you were down-and-out, pass it on.

Life needs to be lived on a reciprocal basis.

Pass on more than empty words, for empty words feed
with an empty spoon. Pass it on without fanfare. Pass it on
freely, unselfishly, with no hooks attached. Pass it on—not
out of vanity but out of true commitment.

Have you had a kindness shown?
Pass it on!
'Twas not given to you alone!
Pass it on!
Let it travel down the years,
Let it wipe another's tears,
Till in Heaven the deed appears;
Pass it on!

HENRY BURTON

WHAT ABOUT THE BOX?

· ·

And do not be conformed to this world:
but be transformed by the renewing of your mind.
ROMANS 12:2

A certain soap maker who ran out of superlatives to describe the perfection of his product came up with a novel way to attract customers. He stated: "As we couldn't improve our product, we improved *the box*."

We can't improve the gospel, but we can improve the box—ourselves. The gospel has no need to be improved or changed, although the methods of advocating it can be changed and the box can be made more appealing.

The gospel is carried in earthen boxes—humans. "But we have this treasure in earthen vessels" (2 Corinthians 4:7). These vessels if defiled will be stumbling blocks; "judge...that no man put a stumbling block or an occasion to fall in his brother's way" (Romans 14:13). In a reflection on the unattractiveness of a gospel container, a man once said to another, "I can't hear what you *say* because I see what you *do*." The world is getting its idea of the preaching by observing the practicing.

The importance of the container is seen in businesses. An attractive building makes the merchandise it houses more salable. A finer and more elegant decor in a restaurant pleases the diners. Likewise, the gospel carried by those who live it is impressive. Example is a lesson that all can read. What do people read in us?

A beautiful tribute is paid to Christian wives who influence their husbands by their righteous living: "if any [husbands] obey not the word, they also may without the word be won by the conversation [behavior] of the wives" (1 Peter 3:1). It is the box that gets them interested in the contents.

NO LONGER A CHILD

· ·

When I was a child, I spoke as a child,
I understood as a child, I thought as a child:
but when I became a man, I put away childish things.

1 CORINTHIANS 13:11

The ability to handle the various affairs of life in an effective way is called *maturity*. The world's hard knocks are too much for babyish people. A mature person takes his job seriously and does the best he can as long as he is on the job, regardless of pay. Maturity can't be bought with money. A mature person stays with a task until it's finished. It's hard to get a child to finish a job.

A mature person doesn't become frightened at every opposition or adversity. Children scare easily. A mature person is too big to act little. A child acts little because he is immature. A mature person doesn't enjoy feeling that he has been mistreated. A child does.

A mature person doesn't have to have his way about everything. The child says, "If you don't play my way, I'll pick up my marbles and go home." A mature person doesn't have to head the list and be first in everything. But a child that doesn't get to be first will often pout. A mature person is responsible. A child is not.

A mature person is more discerning, can better distinguish fact from fancy whereas a child believes anything you tell him. A mature person is flexible and adaptable. But a child finds it difficult to change his plans. A mature person can take the stress and strain of life. A child will soon break under stress.

The best place to find help in maturing is the Bible. It talks about growing. It develops responsible people with a whole new concept of living.

LINCOLN'S SPEECH LIVES

. . . .

The memory of the just is blessed:
but the name of the wicked shall rot.

PROVERBS 10:7

President Abraham Lincoln's speech at the Gettysburg Battlefield, November 19, 1863, has been lauded as one of the greatest pieces of human literature. This is the address:

"Fourscore and seven years ago our fathers brought forth on this continent a new nation, conceived in liberty and dedicated to the proposition that all men are created equal. Now we are engaged in a great civil war, testing whether that nation, or any nation so conceived and so dedicated, can long endure.

"We are met on a great battlefield of that war. We have come to dedicate a portion of that field as a final resting place for those who here gave their lives that that nation might live. It is altogether fitting and proper that we should do this. But in a larger sense we cannot dedicate, we cannot consecrate, we cannot hallow this ground. The brave men, living and dead, who struggled here have consecrated it far above our power to add or detract.

"The world will little note nor long remember what we say here, but it can never forget what they did here. It is for us, the living, rather to be dedicated here to the unfinished work which they who fought here have thus far so nobly advanced. It is rather for us to be here dedicated to the great task remaining before us, that from these honored dead we take increased devotion to that cause for which they gave the last full measure of devotion; that we here highly resolve that these dead shall not have died in vain, that this nation, under God, shall have a new birth of freedom, and that government of the people, by the people, and for the people shall not perish from the earth."

GIVE THE BUG A CHANCE

. . . .

Everyone helped his neighbor,
and said to his brother, "Be of good courage!"

ISAIAH 41:6

Abraham Lincoln, with that ready wit, deep insight, country style and homely sincerity, touched the hearts of millions of Americans who have given him a foremost place in their affections. He was so earthy and attendant to the little things of life as well as to the big things that build a worthy nation.

Mr. Lincoln was walking with a friend about Washington. When he saw a beetle that had gotten on its back, legs sprawling in the air and vainly trying to turn himself over, the president turned aside to help him. The friend expressed surprise that the burdened president should find time to assist a bug.

"Well," said Lincoln, "if I had left that bug struggling there on his back, I wouldn't have felt just right. I wanted to put him on his feet, and give him an equal chance with all the other bugs of his class."

The statement has great merit and practicality because it applies to nations, to men and women, and boys and girls. We need to help our fellowmen get up on their feet and have an equal chance with all others of their class.

In our age much is being said about the value of exercise in strengthening the heart, and there are many kinds of exercise. The best, however, is to reach down and lift people up.

The Bible says, "Bear one another's burdens" (Galatians 6:2); it does not say, "Bear down on them."

LANGUAGE OF THE HEART

. . . .

Many waters cannot quench love,
neither can the floods drown it.

SONG OF SOLOMON 8:17

Valentine's Day is a day devoted to love. Love is not fantasy. It is not a topic just for poets and philosophers. It is not just an idealistic longing for those who roam the silvery heavens. It is a state of the heart for now and *here*, and its need is universal.

It is the secret sympathy,
The silver link, the silken tie,
Which heart to heart and mind to mind
In body and in soul can bind.

SIR WALTER SCOTT

Love has been the thrilling theme of the sweetest eloquence through the centuries. The dearest words, however, have neither been spoken by orators nor penned by poets. They have been uttered in broken, unrhythmic language and lived in deeds by millions of unschooled people whose hearts overflowed with it. They knew the meaning of love. They learned it in the schoolroom of their own heart. Love utters a heart language, and no one group has the exclusive possession of that kind of heart.

Love is a powerful feeling that lets each speak it and demonstrate it in his own way, and that is the loveliest poetry and the grandest elocution. As Shakespeare said, "All hearts in love use their own tongues."

WHY ARE WE HERE?

What is man that You are mindful of him,
or the son of man that You take care of him?
You made him a little lower than the angels;
You crowned him with glory and honor.

HEBREWS 2:6-7

While teaching her little boy on unselfishness, a mother concluded, "We are in this world to help others."

After musing the matter, he asked her, "Well then, what are the others here for?"

The problems of many people stem from their not knowing why they are here. With no knowledge of why they are here or faith in the higher role of man, they have only a meager conception of the real meaning of life—its origin, its purposes, its opportunities, its potentials, its joys, its sorrows, its hopes and its destiny.

§ *We are here because God put us here and ordered man to multiply.* We are the product of His command.

§ Also, *we are here to be free,* to occupy God's free earth, to breathe His free air, to stand up and be an ideal person and to live in keeping with our divine image.

§ Besides, *we are here to be in charge of God's creation.* May we be capable and worthy stewards.

§ Additionally, *we are here to give a hand to the fallen,* a word to the weary, a lift to the burdened, an example to the erring, drink to the thirsty, food to the hungry, and a light to those in darkness. Our humanity demands it.

THAT CLOSED THE CASE

· ·

Men listened to me and waited,
and kept silence for my counsel.

JOB 29:21

It is reputed that five women living in the same apartment house in Chicago got into a brawl of such severity that it resulted in their being hauled into court. When the case was called, they all rushed to the bench and began making bitter indictments of each other. Confusion had the floor.

The poor judge sat dumfounded as accusations and counter accusations filled the charged air. Then, struck with a thought, he rapped for order. When the verbal noise subsided, he gently said, "Now, I'll hear the oldest first."

Not one woman responded. The case was closed.

Have you ever noticed how quiet it becomes when the subject of age comes up? But, of course, there should be other reasons for silence at appropriate times.

Never talk *if*:

§ *you have nothing to say.*

§ *your words would come out heated.*

§ *what you'd say would hurt another.*

§ *your words would kindle strife.*

§ *you would be repeating a rumor.*

§ *what you'd say were untrue.*

§ *talking would do no good.*

§ *you don't know what you're talking about.*

Sometimes it shows more knowledge to say nothing. There is no wisdom like it. Even silence can have an eloquent tongue.

A SORT OF DIVINITY

. . . .

Ointment and perfume delight the heart,
and the sweetness of a man's friend does so
by hearty counsel.

PROVERBS 27:9

Friendship is more precious than gold. There is no man so poor that he is not rich if he has a friend, and there is no man so rich that he is not poor without a friend.

Friendship is not the product of a fanciful imagination and vain words, but rather the golden strand linking lives forged from untarnished mettle. It is like the rope mountain climbers use to bind themselves for safety and progress.

Real friendship is abiding. Like love, it suffers long and is kind. It is not proud. It pursues the even tenor of its way, unaffrighted by ill report. It is loyal in adversity and the shining jewel of happy days.

Friendship—in sunshine *or* shadow—is true. Wealth may crumble like some building shaken by an earthquake, but friendship remains. Disaster and defeat may strike us and, like a storm, hide our star. Our ambitions may turn to vanity on our lips. But friendship comes with warmth, rekindling and fanning into life the hope which had almost fled.

Friendship is an antidote for despair, the panacea of hope, the tonic for depression.

Friendship is a gift, but it is also an acquirement.

It is a sort of divinity that hovers over two hearts.

DAILY HEROISM

· ·

Be of good courage, and He shall strengthen your heart,
all you who hope in the Lord.

PSALM 31:24

Heroes are found in many fields besides the battlefield. We see them in day-to-day living. They keep a forward pace—no turning from the goal, no holding back in fear. We see them as they seek better things and hope for the road's last turn to be the best.

Let me but live my life from year to year,
With forward face and unreluctant soul;
Not hurrying to, nor turning from the goal;
Not mourning for the things that disappear
In the dim past, nor holding back in fear
From what the future veils: but with a whole
And happy heart that pays its toll
To Youth and Age, and travels on with cheer.

So let the way wind up the hill or down,
O'er rough or smooth, the journey will be joy;
Still seeking what I sought when but a boy,
New friendship, high adventure, and a crown,
My heart will keep the courage of the quest,
And hope the road's last turn will be the best.

HENRY VAN DYKE

LIVE WITH LIFE

. . . .

I know your works, that you are neither cold nor hot:
I could wish you were cold or hot. So then because you are
lukewarm, and neither cold nor hot,
I will spew you out of My mouth.

REVELATION 3:15-16

How sad! Many people are bored to frustration! But they weren't born bored. Boredom is a state they have allowed to develop. Somewhere along life's way they lost their enthusiasm. Like the thought in Revelation 3:15-16, they are in the sad fix of being neither cold nor hot. The gusto for life is gone.

How glad we are to be around people whose zeal spills all over us! One of my acquaintances who is physically weak and who has been through the wringer of trials has an eager spirit that flashes like a revolving beacon. Just to be around him five minutes lets one see that he is a man who enjoys himself. And that's not a bad definition of enthusiasm: the trait of simply enjoying oneself.

Enthusiasm is a generator of power. Power over self. Power over others. Napoleon said, "Men of imagination rule the world."

One of the secrets of success is enthusiasm. Without it no book is written, no church grows, no religion is propagated, no business flourishes, no battle is won, no empire is founded. The men and women of victory have been the ones who have kept the fires of fervency burning while other flames have dwindled into smoky half-heartedness or the gray ashes of despair.

The warmth of wholeheartedness is a winning trait. We cannot kindle a fire in others unless it is burning within us.

THE BUCK STOPS HERE

. . . .

So then every one of us
shall give account of himself to God.

ROMANS 14:12

The mother was away from home one evening, but she had planned for the meal to go on as usual. She appointed little Mary to sit in her place at the dinner table. You guessed it—the slightly older brother was not fond of the arrangement. In his dissatisfaction, he sneeringly said, "All right, now you're the mother tonight. How much is four times seven?"

Mary unhesitatingly and nonchalantly replied, "I'm busy. Go ask your daddy."

President Harry Truman had this plaque sitting on his desk: "The buck stops here."

Actually, the buck stops at each of us. We may try to pass it; but it won't pass, for the simple reason that each of us is a responsible, accountable being. We just can't put the monkey on somebody else's back.

Responsibility is the price we pay to be a human being. Irresponsibility puts one in a jungle world. How dreadful! In the jungle, irresponsible people walk with tigers they're afraid to stroke and crawl with snakes. They keep their distance and dare not go to sleep. In sharp contrast, responsible people fully accept their humanity and fully account for it.

For a human being, every talent is a responsibility, every duty an obligation and every opportunity a challenge. The moment duty or opportunity appears, that very moment man (as opposed to animals) should arise with this assertion, "Here is where I come in."

WATCH THE BUGS

Nevertheless we made our prayer unto our God, and set
a watch against them day and night, because of them.

NEHEMIAH 4:9

politician was speaking at a Fourth of July celebration
with gripping and enchanting effectiveness. There were
bugs—thousands of bugs—flying around the bright light
over his head. The bugs buzzed around him like jets, but he
remained unperturbed and undistracted, and continued his
speech with force and eloquence. Every time he inhaled, the
audience thought surely he would suck in a bug. Finally the
expected happened. He did. The people flinched. "What'll he
do?" they asked themselves. He swallowed hard, coughed a
little, caught his breath and said, "That bug got what was
coming to him. He should have watched where he was going!"

Many an intellectual man at the height of his oratory has
been a bug eater.

Diligent watch prevents misfortune. Watchfulness has
been a part of man's life since time immemorial. Eternal vigilance is the price of freedom.

*The condition
upon which God hath given liberty to man
is eternal vigilance, which condition if he break,
servitude is at once the consequence of his crime
and the punishment of his sin.*

JOHN PHILPOT CURRAN

Constant vigilance is also the price of spiritual welfare.
"Be watchful in all things, endure afflictions...fulfill your
ministry" (2 Timothy 4:5). Paul's advice to young Timothy
is just as necessary for us all.

THE FATHER OF OUR COUNTRY

· ·

As the man is, so is his strength.

JUDGES 8:21

It was a reflective experience to stand at the grave of George Washington. As I stood there I told myself that he is *not* dead. Truly, his beneficial works follow after him, though two centuries have passed. His struggles and sacrifices in behalf of freedom continue to live in a free and grateful people. His words, in times of peace and war, still ring in the speeches of countless numbers.

While history says he lost more battles than he won, yet he won the *last* one...the battle that really counts.

Though invisible, yet potent, Washington is a favorite for politicians to stand behind. They know that the very mention of his name in the midst of political turbulence has a winning appeal. It is magic. Hence he is often quoted in public gatherings of every sort, at schools, clubs, businesses, political rallies and in the halls of Congress.

Let us find direction and inspiration from the fact that Washington—patriotic, courageous, determined, modest, a simple man—stands today above fearful misgivings, selfish purposes, petty ambitions, the turmoil of civil strife. His words speak to the scrambling throngs and bid us all to be manly, brave, thoughtful and considerate, not "like dumb driven cattle, but heroes in the strife." He is still saying:

Happily the Government of the United States,
which gives to bigotry no sanction, to persecution
no assistance, requires only that they who live
under its protection should demean themselves
as good citizens in giving it on all occasions
their effectual support.

THE BUTTONS ARE BEHIND ME AND I'M IN FRONT

. . . .

But they hearkened not, nor inclined their ear,
but walked in the counsels and in the imagination
of their evil heart, and went backward, and not forward.

JEREMIAH 7:24

Little Naomi was trying to dress herself. After a long while she asked, "Mother, will you help me? I guess you'll have to button my dress. The buttons are behind me and I'm in front."

Quite a predicament!

This amusing little story is a big enlightenment on many failures in all endeavors of life. Doing things backward. Going at it the wrong way. Misdirected effort. It tells us much.

Reminds me of the man who went deer hunting. He followed the deer tracks for a whole day before he discovered that he was following them backward. Movement, activity; it's not enough. Even the backslider is moving, but downward. No matter how fast we go, if we're going in the wrong direction we are not making progress. Regardless of how hard we try, if we're doing something the wrong way we will not succeed.

We have seen individuals, businesses, and churches go backward and not forward. In most cases the reason was not so much a lack of effort as it was the result of poor counsel and vain imagination. In the majority of failures enough energy was expended to succeed, if only it had been channeled into productive areas.

Half the way is to *know the way.*

ENTWINED THEY STAND

You, being rooted and grounded in love,
may be able to comprehend with all saints
what is the breadth, and length, and depth and height.

EPHESIANS 3:17-18

One of the wonders of the world is the Redwood Forest in California. Some of the trees are the oldest, largest, and tallest living things in all the world. Some of the trees are more than three hundred feet tall and more than twenty-five hundred years old. Think of that! Their existence goes back hundreds of years into B.C. They have weathered the ravages of time, holding up against all the combative elements. They stand tall in spite of opposing forces.

Unknowledgeable people immediately jump to the conclusion that the redwoods have a deep root system. To the contrary, their roots are shallow. What holds them? What supports them? Their root system entwines and locks each tree to the trees around it. They stand together, and that is the secret to their herculean strength. When wind and hail and upheaval threaten, no tree stands alone but rather is strengthened and supported by the others. Each is needed for the support of the whole grove. The redwoods can truly say, "United we stand, divided we fall."

How true of us! *We need the help of others.* Even pigs in a litter lie close together to stay warm. Of course a man is grander and finer than a pig, but it is still a cold world out there for him if he's standing alone. One of the blessings of the church is its fellowship in which we have the entwining of each other and of the Lord. Locked together we can withstand the storms of life. Unquestionably, "two are better than one" (Ecclesiastes 4:9).

MISERABLE COMFORTERS

. . . .

I have heard many such things;
miserable comforters are you all.

JOB 16:2

*P*oor Job was a man desperately in need of comfort. His children had been stricken in death, his property destroyed, his body afflicted with boils from head to toe. His irreverent wife gave tragic advice, and to cap it all, his friends were miserable comforters.

It is commendable to want to comfort the troubled, the perplexed, the suffering, the sorrowing. However, some who would like to help just don't know *how*. In trying to help, they actually hurt; and in attempting to encourage, they discourage.

To do a first-rate job of comforting:

§ *Avoid acting superior.* This was one of the disgusting faults of the Pharisees. A person with a hurt doesn't need to have his intelligence insulted.

§ *Refrain from being judgmental.* Such a spirit is evident in the expression, "God is punishing you. You're getting what you deserve." But hardship is not necessarily rough treatment from God. It certainly wasn't in Job's case, even if his friends thought it was.

§ *Never try to outdo the sufferer's woes*—for instance, "You don't have any real problems; let me tell you about mine."

§ *Do not frighten*—for instance, "You haven't seen anything yet; just wait another two weeks!"

§ *Sympathize.* Enter into the sufferer's feelings and let him know that you are standing with him, ready to help. This lets another shoulder carry part of the load.

TODAY IS OUR DAY

. . . .

Come now, you who say,
"Today or tomorrow we will go to such and such a city,
spend a year, and buy and sell, and make a profit."

JAMES 4:13

One of the most tragic things about life is missing so much of it by being too related to the past or the future instead of the present. It robs us of the *now*.

We tend to put off living. While we dream of a magic rose garden free from all thorns across yonder hill, we neglect to enjoy the fragrant roses just outside our window.

Today is our day to act. When tomorrow arrives it will be today. When the far distant future gets here it will be today. We don't have to deal directly with anything but *today*.

We must rid ourselves of self-pity, criticism and blame. Bury all excuses. Tomorrow is the fool's paradise. Today is ours. Let's take up every today, one by one, with clean hands and a pure heart and see what we can do with it.

Time—page writ, no returning line,
The vanished hour, no longer thine.
One hour alone is in thy hands,
The NOW on which the shadow stands.

IT COULD HAVE BEEN DIFFERENT

My son, if sinners entice you, do not consent.

PROVERBS 1:10

My phone rang one evening and a woman with whom I was not acquainted was the caller. It was evident she was emotionally disturbed. In broken, tearful speech she asked me if I would conduct the funeral for her son. I assured her that I would if I had no conflicting appointments.

Then she said, "But he isn't dead yet." After a pause she continued, "He's to be electrocuted in the penitentiary just after midnight. Will you still do the funeral?"

"Yes," I said. "I will still do it." I never ask for merit in serving human needs, because God loves all.

That night I woke up about midnight, the fatal hour, and these thoughts weighed heavily on me: A young man who murdered a citizen while attempting to rob him will soon pay with his life. What happened? What wrong turns did he take? What can I say?

The next morning I made a personal visit to the mother's home. I learned that she, a widow, had been compelled to go into a competitive, unsympathetic world to earn a living for her family. While she worked to support her children, there were evil forces up and down the streets and alleys working to destroy them. There had not been enough counteractive spiritual influences. At the most critical time when the family should have been in church *they weren't.*

As church attendance has gone down, the crime rate has gone up.

I Didn't Go to School

. . . .

Wisdom is the principal thing; therefore get wisdom:
and in all your getting get understanding.

PROVERBS 4:7

When my grandfather died my grandmother was left at age forty-one with six children at home. The family lived on a farm of 140 acres, and their living had to come from it. No savings, no salary, no Social Security, no pension, no food stamps. It was up to Grandma, her children and God. But that made a winning team.

Grandmother was not bitter. Neither did she feel sorry for herself. Her philosophy was, "What is *is* and must be accepted." She was practical. She knew she had to play the game of life according to the hand that had been dealt her. It was more profitable to be thankful for what she had than to complain about what she didn't have. I can still hear her humming and singing as she went about her work.

She got along exceptionally well. After the children had married, she kept the farm but also bought a home in town. She did so well, in fact, that she was able to finance farms for other people to buy.

One day a businessman asked her, "How is it that you have managed so well and accumulated what you have?"

Her explanation was simple: "Being I didn't go to school very much, I just had to use my head. I figured that if I had more coming in than I had going out, it would leave me a surplus. And it worked." (Grandma had a sense of humor.) She used her head. We call it *wisdom*.

LOVE IS NOT POSSESSIVE

. . . .

Love...does not seek its own.

1 CORINTHIANS 13:4-5

Love grants freedom. It is not possessive. One of the most convincing manifestations of pure love is the freedom it grants another.

One woman in speaking of another said, "I can't afford to become a close friend of hers. She wouldn't let me have other friends. I would have to be with her constantly. She gives no freedom." Love doesn't draw a circle that small.

Demanding that our friends cut off all other friendships (even members of the family) and shower all the attention on us is not true love. It is only a distortion of love that reverts back to selfish childhood.

I am acquainted with a woman who nags and persecutes her husband when he goes fishing or golfing, which is not often. She feels neglected. She harps on the idea that if he loved her he wouldn't do it. Her love of self permits no latitude for him.

Then there is the man who resents his wife's mixing in various social circles during the day. He says she ought to stay home. He would imprison her if he could.

But love is no browbeating, domineering quality. It is no choking process. It does not restrict all freedom and smother all dignity. On the contrary, it is a big, soft kind of consideration that frees one to respond naturally to the lover.

WHEN NEITHER SUN NOR MOON SHINES

· ·

A friend loves at all times,
and a brother is born for adversity.

PROVERBS 17:17

There are many so-called friendships that are not born for adversity. Adversity is the stormy wind that separates the true from the pretended, the genuine from the feigned.

The Shadow once said to the Body: "Do you have another friend like me? I follow you wherever you go. In sunlight and moonlight I never forsake you."

"That's true," answered the Body. "You do go with me in sunlight and in moonlight. *But where are you when neither sun nor moon shines upon me?*"

A true friend is faithful when storms rage and the light of the sun is blotted out.

To be a friend we must:

- *be concerned.*
- *be free of exploitation.*
- *never pick a friend to pieces.*
- *learn to close one eye to faults.*
- *never act superior.*
- *keep our heart a little softer than our head.*
- *be helpful.*

When a friend makes a fool of himself, accept it as only a temporary deficiency.

Be loyal when adversity comes. See your friend through when others think he is through.

To have friends, *one must be a friend!*

THE TRAGEDY OF FORGETTING

. . . .

Only take heed to yourself,
lest you forget the things your eyes have seen.

DEUTERONOMY 4:9

An older preacher, in praising the beauty and influence of motherhood, stated: "The happiest days of my life were spent in the arms of another man's wife—*my mother*."

A young preacher in the audience liked the novelty and force of the point. Thought it was a clever attention-grabber. In his next sermon he decided to use the shocking technique. Being young and inexperienced, he was nervous. All went well until he got to the end of the story. He said, "The happiest days of my life were spent in the arms of another man's wife." Suddenly he suffered a memory blockage. He just couldn't remember the rest of it. He hesitated, backed up and started again: "The happiest days of my life were spent in the arms of another man's wife." Again he'd forgotten the punch line. He paused, gulped and said, "For the love of me, I can't remember who she was!"

All of us are threatened with the danger of forgetting matters much more important than the climax of a story. May I keep my memory fresh and never forget:

۶ *the God* who has given me life, breath and all things.

۶ *who I am* and my duties in life.

۶ *my parents,* who sacrificed so much in my behalf.

۶ *the people who stood by me* and helped to make me what I am.

So I say in the language of Rudyard Kipling:

> *Lord God of Hosts, be with us yet,*
> *Lest we forget—lest we forget.*

HE'S STILL IN THERE

. . . .

But He knows the way that I take;
when He has tested me, I shall come forth as gold.
JOB 23:10

The father had promised to take the children to the park on Sunday afternoon. They could hardly wait. But they had a problem. The father had lain down for a little rest and was enjoying the relaxation so much that he began to play possum. The youngsters tried to rouse him. They begged and pulled his arm, all to no avail. Finally the six-year-old daughter pried open one of his eyelids, looked carefully and said, "He's still in there."

Their dad was tired, but he was still in "the earthly house of this tabernacle." Therein is hope.

᠑ Life is a race. Let's *stay in there,* refusing to be encumbered with excess baggage that would weigh us down. It makes sense to "lay aside every weight, and the sin which so easily besets us, and...run with patience the race that is set before us" (Hebrews 12:1).

᠑ Life is warfare. Let's *stay in there.* "This charge I commit to you...that you may wage the good warfare" (1 Timothy 1:18). "Endure hardness as a good soldier." We have to keep up the fight, for much is at stake.

᠑ Life is bearing fruit. Let's *stay in there.* "Even so, every good tree bears good fruit; but a bad tree bears evil fruit.... Therefore by their fruits you shall know them" (Matthew 7:17-20).

As long as we are in the flesh may others say of the race we run, the warfare we wage and the fruit we bear, "They're still in there."

POOR BUT RICH

. . . .

There is one who makes himself rich, yet has nothing;
and one who makes himself poor, yet has great riches.

PROVERBS 13:7

A man poor in money—not poor, just poor in money—
once met a multimillionaire. The wizard of wealth
worked hard every day at getting more money. The man of
little means said to him, "I'm really richer than you are."

"What kind of mathematician are you to figure that?"
asked the man, who was nearly as rich as Fort Knox.

"Because *I have as much money as I want,*" said the mon-
etarily poor man, "but *you don't.*"

No matter how big a fortune the lover of money amasses,
he's never satisfied. The covetous person has a bottomless
purse that can never be filled.

It is highly appropriate, therefore, that we identify The
Richest People according to the Scriptures:

֍ *The rich in spirituality.* "Though he was rich, yet for
your sakes he became poor, that you through his poverty
might be rich" (2 Corinthians 8:9).

֍ *The rich in faith.* "Rich in faith, and heirs of the kingdom" (James 2:5).

֍ *The rich in good works.* "They that be rich in good
works" (1 Timothy 6:18).

֍ *Those who have a big bank account in heaven.* "Lay up
for yourselves treasures in heaven" (Matthew 6:20).

Material wealth does not make one rich but busy, burdened and troubled. It is the heart that makes a person rich
indeed.

WHEN DISASTER STRIKES

. . . .

For you do not know what a day may bring forth.

PROVERBS 27:1

The devastating quakes of 1985 that struck Mexico City, the largest city in the world, and the surrounding area left a death toll of at least ten thousand and many more thousands injured and maimed. There is no way to assess the human suffering and misery. The lives crushed out. The injuries. The horror. The destruction. The chaos. The homeless. The orphans. The jobless. The threat of more quakes. The threat of disease. The bereavement. Tragedy immeasurable! Immeasurable!

How sobering! What a teacher of priorities! Many heroic stories came out of the catastrophe. One is of a mother who gave her life to save her infant daughter only a few days old. Eight days after the quake, when crumblings and debris were removed, there lay a dead mother bent over her baby in protective form. The baby was alive. A mother's way!

And it's only one of many brave and moving deeds.

The hearts of people throughout the world were touched. We take courage that humanity is sensitive and tenderhearted.

Relief efforts of food, medicine, and professional help poured in. American engineers, French firefighters, British helicopter pilots, Canadian paramedics and many others rushed to be included in the relief effort.

Their response speaks well for the human race. It is more than a humanitarian spirit. Man must be possessed with a spark of divinity. How great is mankind!

THE MOUSE HAD A CHURCH DAY

Arise, go to Nineveh, that great city,
and preach to it the message that I tell you.

JONAH 3:2

The audience had trouble holding back the giggles while the preacher was preaching. No, it was neither the preacher's wit nor his boners that made them shake with laughter. The cause was a little mouse that had climbed the latticework of flowers next to the podium.

After awhile the pulpiteer spotted the little, four-legged nuisance that had turned out to be a better attention-getter than he. With theological fervor but without mercy, he rolled up his sermon manuscript and whacked that mouse with it. But the mouse was unharmed and just ran away. At this point a brother spoke out, "Preacher, that sermon you're holding there is too weak to slow even a mouse!"

The audience gave way to loud laughter. If a sermon isn't solid enough to affect a mouse, it's mighty soft and flimsy.

Paul told the young preacher Timothy to "Preach the word." That is, preach it solidly, not that preachers should tell people where to get off but rather where to *get on*. They're to preach the Word without adding to it or taking from it, a principle commanded by God (Deuteronomy 4:2).

Of course some audiences would be too weak to take a strong sermon. Paul dealt with the reality of the situation when he stated that some were too babyish and undeveloped for the meat of the Word and thus needed the *milk* of the Word instead. As a result, we may hear sermonettes because of Christian-ette listeners.

FACE VALUE

. . . .

A merry heart makes a cheerful countenance,
but by sorrow of the heart the spirit is broken.

PROVERBS 15:13

Some of the pithiest observations have been stated in just a few words:

- A *smile* has face value in every land.
- Progress is built on *smiles*, not frowns.
- There is magnetic power in a *smile*.
- A *smile* is one of the very best relaxation exercises.
- A person without a *smiling* face must not open a shop.
- It is better to forget and *smile* than to remember and be sad.
- A salesman has to *smile*; it comes with the territory.
- A *smile* is one of the world's most cherished scenes.
- *Smile* and you can go another mile.
- A pleasant *smile* is sunshine in the house.
- Nobody ever died of *smiling*.
- *Smiling* is a tranquilizer with no ill effects.
- *Smile*, if you are wise.

If we don't learn to smile at trouble, we are going to have more trouble—trouble that troubles even trouble.

DO THE BEST YOU CAN

Nevertheless the men rowed hard to bring the ship
to the land, but they could not, for the sea continued
to grow more tempestuous against them.

JONAH 1:13

Life is not always smooth sailing. Sometimes we have to
sail in tempestuous seas. In those times, let's row hard
and do the best we can.

For life is great to every man
Who lives to do the best he can.

Rowing against boisterous winds in a turbulent sea tests
character and builds muscle. If we are unable to handle our
boat, a strong resolve still lets us handle ourselves, and that
is our main victory and chief success.

Think not of failure. Think of success. Don't think *why*
we can't. Think *how* we can. Some say, "It can't be done,"
but we say, "It will be done because it must be done."

We can be thankful if we are faced with a challenging
problem or have a job harder than we like. Great character
does not emerge from a life of ease, just as a skyscraper does
not rise from a feather pillow.

About the only things that come to us without effort are
sunshine, rain, air, flabbiness, wrinkles, gray hair, old age
and death. Everything else we have to work for.

No effort, no result; little effort, little result; big effort,
big result. That's how simple it is.

INGENUITY FINDS A WAY

· ·

Then the king answered and said, "Give the first woman
the living child, and by no means kill him; she is his mother.

1 KINGS 3:27

In the context of the above Scripture, two women both claimed to be the mother of the same child. They asked Solomon to decide between them. He simply commanded that the child be cut in two and each woman be given half. Immediately one exclaimed, "Oh my lord, give *her* the child!" Solomon said, "Give the first woman [who unselfishly spoke out to save the baby] the living child, and by no means kill him; *she* is his mother." Solomon's ingenuity settled the matter and added to his fame.

§ *Ingenuity solves the problem.* A young mother was perturbed about her eight-year-old son. She was at her wit's end. No matter how much she pleaded, exhorted or rebuked, he went around with his shirttail hanging out. Nothing she said or did got through to him. However, her neighbor had two boys, and she observed that their hair might be ruffled, their faces and hands dirty, but one thing was sure—they always kept their shirttails in. This difference in the boys alarmed her. Finally the young mother asked her neighbor to tell her the secret.

"Oh, it's easy," she answered, "I just sew a band of lace around the bottom of all their shirts."

§ *Ingenuity is the child of thought.* Thinking makes the difference in people.

§ *Ingenuity is the greatest time-saver of all.* It gets busy and then we have inventions.

Don't be afraid to think. I never knew a person to kill himself thinking. But I *have* known many who didn't think to kill themselves by degrees.

IF I COME THROUGH IN THE MORNING

You do not know what will happen tomorrow.
For what is your life? It is even a vapor, that appears
for a little time, and then vanishes away.

JAMES 4:14

My father had seen many doctors, and they said there was no hope for him; death was just a matter of time. Due to arteriosclerosis there was almost a complete blockage of the aorta. Because the blood was not getting to his foot, a part had already been amputated.

But he heard about two heart specialists in Houston who'd just begun to perform an unusual type of operation. They were taking the aorta from a dead person and transplanting it in a patient. So I took Dad to them.

The night before the surgery, members of the family stayed with him past the visiting hours. After prayer, and as we were getting ready to leave his room, he asked me to stay a little longer. He wanted to discuss some business and personal matters. Then when I was again ready to depart, he took me by the hand and with a firm grip and an intensive look said, "Son, if I come through in the morning, it will be just wonderful. If I don't, it will still be all right."

While he'd never had much formal education, I consider his statement one of the most profound philosophies I have ever heard or read. "If I come through in the morning, it will be just wonderful," for *life is precious*. It will give me another opportunity. It will provide another day to achieve and to enjoy. "If I don't, it will still be all right," for *there is another life*. Death is the end of this one and the beginning of the new one. Dad did survive that operation, and he lived seven more wonderful years.

OUR KIND OF A MAN

· ·

Now prepare yourself like a man.

JOB 38:3

Our kind of a man is:

❧ *a lover of liberty, as* expressed by Patrick Henry: "As for me, give me liberty or give me death."

❧ *uncompromising, as* stated by Abraham Lincoln: "Important principles may and must be inflexible."

❧ *truthful, as* voiced by George Washington: "Father, I cannot tell a lie, I did it with my little hatchet."

❧ *honest, as* verbalized by Robert Burns: "An honest man's the noblest work of God."

❧ *a devotee of enlightenment, as* phrased by Thomas Jefferson: "Enlighten the people generally, and tyranny and oppressions of body and mind will vanish."

❧ *a lover of his children,* as sobbed out by David: "Would God I had died for thee, O Absalom, my son, my son!"

❧ *compassionate,* as demonstrated by the Good Samaritan who aided the half-dead man lying by the wayside.

❧ *a doer,* as worded by Sir Winston Churchill: "It is better to be making the news than talking it; to be an actor rather than a critic."

❧ *a servant of God,* as spoken by Joshua: "As for me and my house, we will serve the Lord."

Truly, our kind of a man is no ordinary man. He is superior.

LEARNING TO FORGIVE

You ought rather to forgive and comfort him,
lest perhaps such a one should be swallowed up
with too much sorrow.

2 CORINTHIANS 2:7

There is an old story about a convict who went before the governor of a state to get a pardon. The governor recognized him as a steamboat mate under whom he had served as a cabin boy. The governor said, "I want you to promise me that you will never again take a stick and drive a sick boy out of his berth on a stormy night. Someday that boy may be governor, and you may want him to pardon you for a different crime. I was that boy. *Here* is your pardon."

In addition to teaching the merciful spirit of forgiveness, the story also teaches the need to be good to children, for you never know what they may grow up to become.

"Oh yes, I forgave her," said a woman who felt bighearted, "but I was cool to her for several days. I wanted her to know how I felt about what she did."

Another interesting story concerns a man who thought he was going to die. He expressed his forgiveness of a neighbor who, in his view, had injured him. "But," he added, "if I get well, the old grudge still stands."

Forgiveness is not really forgiveness when it retaliates. Forgiveness cannot come from the surface. Neither will it stay at arm's length. Forgiveness must come from the heart, and as it comes it finds an eager, kind, sweet and compassionate way to help.

EXPERIENCE IS THE BEST TEACHER
. . . .

I have been young, and now am old; yet I have not seen
the righteous forsaken, nor his seed begging bread.

PSALM 37:25

The writer had learned from experience. One of the advantages in being old is experience, which has no substitute.

A city boy went to visit his country cousin. Being from what he thought was a privileged situation—among tall buildings, concrete slabs, traffic jams, push and shove, big school buildings, dusty libraries, polluted air, chemically treated water and artificial parks—he felt mentally superior to what he thought was an underprivileged, short-of-brains cousin. He even condescended enough to offer his philosophy on how to treat forest animals. "Just be friendly to them and they'll be friendly to you."

The country boy could hardly keep from laughing as he thought of the lesson coming up for Cousin Inexperience. The next day he and his city cousin went into the woods and came across a skunk. Country Cous said, "Hold up!"

But City Cous just said, "I'll show you how to be friendly to him," not realizing that the animal he was approaching was a skunk. Well, it took just about two weeks (all his vacation) to get the odor off him.

In dealing with a skunk, four-legged or two-legged, experience will soon teach you to keep your distance.

The burned child is afraid of fire. The scalded dog fears even cold water. He knows the current best who has swum the river.

Experience costs a lot, but I don't know how to get it without paying the price.

WHERE IS HAPPINESS?

Blessed is every one who fears the Lord, who walks
in His ways. When you eat the labor of your hands,
you shall be happy.

PSALM 128:1-2

*F*irsthand witnesses can testify to where happiness is *not*
found:

❧ *Not in unbelief,* because Voltaire, one of the most vocal
infidels, said, "I wish I had never been born."

❧ *Not in education,* because the learned Solomon wrote,
"In much wisdom is much grief: and he that increases
knowledge increases sorrow."

❧ *Not in pleasure,* because Lord Byron, who sought it
madly, wrote in disappointment, "The worm, the canker
and the grief are mine."

❧ *Not in fame and possession,* because Lord Beaconsfield
(Disraeli) had both, yet he wrote, "Youth is a mistake, manhood a struggle, old age a regret."

❧ *Not in military glory,* because Alexander the Great con-
quered the world of his day and then wept because, as he
said, "There are no more worlds to conquer."

❧ *Not in money,* because Jay Gould was so wealthy his
name is still used in this sense, yet when dying he said, "I
suppose I am the most miserable man on earth."

❧ *God has placed happiness in simple things:* in conscience void of offense, in peace with ourselves, in love of
others and in being loved, in giving ourselves to a cause bigger than ourselves, in kind words and helping hands that
make others rejoice, in a memory that forgets the wrongs we
suffer, and in a realization that the gift of life is wonderful.
Happiness is not a destination reached, but a journey.

ROAST PREACHER

. . . .

And why do you look at the speck in your brother's eye,
but do not consider the plank in your own eye?

MATTHEW 7:3

As the family sat down for their Sunday dinner, they had more than roast beef. They had *roast preacher*. The father said, "The sermon this morning was very boring."

"What tore me up was that he kept repeating himself," commented the mamma.

Aunt Jane added, "He's hard to follow."

Next, Cousin Mary said, "'Twas a mighty poor sermon topic."

But it was little Johnny who shook them up with his expressed perception: "I thought it was a pretty good show for a quarter!"

After a few hard swallows the father said, "Why that preacher can't see his mistakes, I don't know." Then he put hypocrisy's thickest icing on the cake by saying, "I think I could see my mistakes, *if I had any.*"

Really, if a person had no faults of his own, he wouldn't get so much joy from pointing out the faults of others. Critics are like peas in a pod; they all look alike and smell like spoiled leftovers. And the paradoxical thing is that while they think they know how to do everything perfectly, they're usually failures. In most cases they're faultier than the ones they fault.

BABY

. . . .

And when she saw that he was a beautiful child,
she hid him three months.

EXODUS 2:2

When Moses was born the Egyptians were killing all Hebrew baby boys, so his mother hid him for three months. Only for three months because baby wouldn't wait; he'd grown too noisy to be safe from the Egyptians. Then she put him in a waterproof basket and placed it in the river, hoping his life would be spared. In God's plan, her plan worked.

Baby won't wait. A few tomorrows and our babies stand as tall as we do. Whatever joy we derive from the child's babyhood and whatever early shaping of the mind we intend to do, we must hurry. "As the twig is bent, so grows the tree."

Baby is a mutual ownership, belonging half to mother and half to father. Furthermore, he or she is half of mother and half of father.

This precious little one is a helpless creature who lies, sits, crawls and wobbly walks. Which way are we leading and pointing our own children? They are little lives with lots of potential for good. May their future not be thwarted.

Baby has no appreciation of time, so he or she may get days and nights mixed up. Rest assured, the parents will know.

Infant babe, so little, makes hands busier, nights longer, days shorter, clothes shabbier, eyes sleepier and purses lighter; *but*, love stronger, happiness greater, closeness tighter, hope brighter, play better and singing sweeter.

If You Run With the Goats

. . . .

Do not be deceived:
"Evil company corrupts good habits."

1 CORINTHIANS 15:33

When our son Paul was a little boy, he had some special friends. One of them lived on a little acreage where the happy children could play in the great outdoors. Another special attraction this friend had was some goats and a little wagon for the goats to pull.

There were times when the goats chose to be unruly and butted the children off their feet, but each time those two boys got back up. What a lesson! Life has its blows, jolts and kicks that flatten us; but as long as we can get back up, we're still in the struggle and still in reach of victory.

One day Paul came home smelling like a goat, and that's *not* a savory odor. I said, "Son, if you *run* with the goats you'll *smell* like a goat." He was too young then to comprehend the full import of what I'd said, but later he learned and heeded the message. Now, with two sons of his own, he understands even more fully the power of association and influence.

Jesus truly wants us to learn this lesson on influence. I know He does. For He told us what a little leaven could do to three measures of meal (Matthew 13:33). Since we're all creatures of influence, we'll find protection and elevation in associating with righteous, honorable people.

Whatever others do or say
Can lead you aright or astray.

RID YOUR BURDEN BY FORGIVING

. . . .

Bearing with one another, and forgiving one another,
if anyone has a complaint against another;
even as Christ forgave you, so you also must do.

COLOSSIANS 3:13

At a morning service in an evangelistic meeting a lady went forward during the invitation song. She sat down on the front pew, directly in front of a lady on the second pew. Apprehension and nervousness ran through the audience. You could see it. You could feel it. The respondent had gone forward to confess her sins, ask for the prayers of the church, and to be restored to the fellowship of God and the church.

After the service was dismissed, the woman on the second pew walked around and took her hand and said, "I'm so glad you came. I hold nothing against you. May God bless you."

Later I learned that the poor respondent woman's son had murdered the other woman's husband and son. It was reported that the murderer had been under investigation by the grand jury for bootlegging and that he'd warned the man and his son to skip the country and not testify against him. When they refused, he shot them.

Then there were the murder trials. Naturally the families (members of the same church) were pitted against each other. The trials ended with a death sentence and the prodigal son's having to die in the electric chair. From that terrible time until this evangelistic meeting, his brokenhearted mother had not been in church.

Later in the afternoon the woman who'd lost her husband and son and yet had welcomed the other woman back in the spirit of love and forgiveness said, "I feel that a great burden has been lifted from my back. I feel better now than I have felt in years."

POLITENESS OPENS DOORS

. . . .

"How do you advise me to answer these people?"
And they spoke to him saying, "If you are kind to these people, and please them, and speak good words to them,
they will be your servants for ever."

2 CHRONICLES 10:6-7

A gracious lady gave Jimmy an orange. His reaching for it without saying *Thank you* prompted his mother to ask, "Now what do you *say* to the lady, Jimmy?"

"*Peel it,*" said Jimmy.

Everyone should learn to say *Thank you..., I appreciate..., I'm grateful..., It was nice of you..., Excuse me..., I beg your pardon...* and *I'm sorry....*

Politeness is simply an expression of good will and kindness. It comes easily when it springs from good nature, love and excellent training.

Courtesy is a part of true religion and thus should be an urgent part of religious training. We must learn to be civil in dealing with each other. Our fellowmen, because they are the offspring of God, are sacred and should be treated with respect.

Courtesy gives a person extra help in handling exchanges, connections and relationships with others. Contrariwise, the smartest tongue is handicapped when it wags in rudeness. Impoliteness—the ugly spirit—can be expressed in many ways, one of which is to shoot from the lip.

GIVE FULL MEASURE

. . . .

You shall have a perfect and just weight,
a perfect and just measure,
that your days may be lengthened
in the land which the Lord your God is giving you.

DEUTERONOMY 25:15

When I was a boy working in my father's store, we weighed many items at the time of purchase: beans, sugar, etc. One day my father noticed that I was trying to guess the exact amount before putting the bag on the scales. Later he suggested, "Son, don't do it that way. Seldom ever will you guess it exactly. Half the time you will have too little, and half the time you will have too much. When you have too much and have to take out some, the customer will say to himself, 'You tightwad, why didn't you leave it in there?' Be sure you don't have enough, and then take the scoop and keep pouring until you bring it to the mark. That way you'll create the true impression that the customer is getting everything that's coming to him. We want that reputation."

The reputation for honesty is no empty echo in the community; it sounds and sounds and sounds, and the people listen. Though your reputation is not necessarily what you are, only what people think you are, still it is to be sought.

Business can't thrive where honesty is questioned. Integrity is the absolute essential of every worthwhile endeavor.

Indeed, honesty is more than the best policy, it is the manifestation of *you*—the *real you*. Hence, you will never obtain a full life from giving short measures, for it shrinks the *you*.

BIG RESULTS FROM LITTLE BEGINNINGS

. . . .

For what you had before I came was little,
and it is now increased to a great amount.

GENESIS 30:30

The other morning I had breakfast with a friend who mentioned that some six or seven weeks ago he had turned a key in a very special lock for the last time. Turning that key was a hard thing for him to do because it closed a jewelry store that he had opened forty-two years ago. He said, "I opened that business with one counter of jewelry. That was the beginning of the whole chain." The chain now consists of more than two hundred large department stores.

Big results, both good and bad, can emerge from little beginnings. The break in the dam and the flooding of the town downstream began with the oozing through of one drop of water. The execution of John the Baptist had its beginning in one rash promise—a promise to give a girl anything she wished. And the fate of Lot, Abraham's nephew, was also determined by what seemed an insignificant matter: he merely pitched his tent overlooking the wicked city of Sodom. But eventually he moved into that city, and there he lost his family. This powerful nation of ours began with a few determined settlers.

There is power in little things and little beginnings. No matter how little we may think we are, God can lift us up and make us powerful. He can kindle a fire within us.

Thus out of small beginnings
greater things have been produced by His hand
that made all things of nothing, and gives being to all things
that are; and, as one small candle may light a thousand,
so the light here kindled hath shone unto many,
yea in some sort to our whole nation.

WILLIAM BRADFORD

AN ISLAND OF BUTTER

. . . .

The Lord is my shepherd; I shall not want.

PSALM 23:1

The Psalmist was optimistic—from personal experience—when he wrote, "The Lord is my shepherd; I shall not want."

We need optimism, the expectant and victorious view, for all the circumstances of life; and the gloomier the situation is, the more we need a bright outlook.

Have you heard the story of the two frogs that fell into a churn of milk? One frog was a pessimist. Thinking there was no hope, he made no effort to stay afloat. He went down. The other was an optimist. Believing something good would happen, he kept kicking and in time an island of butter floated by. He crawled onto it and jumped out of the churn.

In making my morning coffee, I heat water in a teakettle. I have observed that when it's up to its neck in hot water, that kettle keeps right on singing.

When I was a boy growing up, we had a dog that was the most optimistic creature I ever saw. He was the very ultimate optimist. He never sounded a discouraging bark, yet I assure you he did have just cause to be discouraged. He chased scores of rabbits and never caught a one in his life. Did he ever get discouraged? Never. That optimistic dog was always ready to try again, evidently thinking this time he would win.

The right mental attitude is one of the prerequisites of success. No optimism, no victory. Expecting to win helps us to fulfill our own expectations. And if we don't, we still have won for trying.

IF HE HAD KNOWN

. . . .

But if you had known what this means,
"I desire mercy and not sacrifice,"
you would not have condemned the guiltless.

MATTHEW 12:7

*T*here is the story of two cowboys who were visiting in Colorado. While they were out walking, a bull spotted them and gave chase. After setting new track records, one of them scrambled up a tree. The other one ran into a cave. But just as quickly, he ran out again. The bull made a lunge, and he sprang into the cave. This darting in and shooting out continued for an awfully long time.

Finally the man in the tree yelled, "You nitwit, why don't you stay in there? If you stay in there, after a while the bull will go away." The in-and-out-of-the-cave man shouted back, "There's a *bear* in this cave!"

What we don't know often gets us into trouble.

Not until we've walked in another fellow's shoes are we fully prepared to criticize his limp; it just might be that the shoes are too tight or there are holes in the soles.

We wouldn't have criticized the nodding man at church of a lack of interest in worship if we had only known he'd been up most of two nights with his sick wife. If the teacher had known the child's transient parents had moved him from school to school every few weeks, she wouldn't have been so quick to mark him off as a slow learner.

The Scripture says, "If you had *known*...you would not have condemned."

LIKE A TREE

. . . .

And he shall be like a tree planted by the rivers of water,
that brings forth its fruit in its season....

PSALM 1:3

In Psalm 1:3 the upright man is likened to a tree, and in verse 4 the evil person is compared to chaff. The contrast is interesting. A bad man is like chaff—with no roots, no substance, no life, no value and no future! But the good man is like a tree.

Why is he like a *tree*?

❧ *He is a fixed person.* "Planted by the rivers," his roots are deep. One of his laudable traits is stability. He's steadfast and immovable. Not wishy-washy. Not blown about by the fickle winds of popularity and temporary gain. A person can deal with him.

❧ *He is a growing individual.* "Planted by the rivers of water," he has nutriment. God intended the spiritual part of man to grow and keep on growing. When the outward part of a man reaches its prime and begins to weaken, the inward part is renewed and becomes stronger day by day.

❧ *He is a fruitful being.* "Brings forth his fruit." He's successful. Productive. Fruitful of golden deeds. "In his season." Winter is sure to find out what summer has laid up. For his family and fellowmen to have fruit, he must produce.

❧ *He is a beautiful, living creature.* "His leaf also shall not wither." He retains his attractiveness, just as a tree holds its foliage. No ugly withering. Few objects in nature are as pleasing to the eye as a handsome tree. But even more attractive is a righteous, fruit-bearing life.

I Trust in Thee

· ·

What time I am afraid,
I will trust in You.

PSALM 56:3

Lightning flashed. Thunder roared. Black clouds rolled. The rain was torrential. And the train was traveling fast. Tension and fear among the passengers was most evident.

But one little boy, who sat all by himself, seemed unaware of any danger.

One of the passengers said to him, "Aren't you afraid to travel alone on such a stormy night?"

The lad looked up and answered with a smile, "No, ma'am, I'm not afraid. My daddy's the engineer."

It was a wise resolve the Psalmist stated in Psalm 56:3 above. We don't know the future, but we do know the One who holds the future. We *have seen* enough to teach us to trust God for what we *have not seen*.

I will not doubt though all my ships at sea
Come drifting home with broken masts and sails.
I will believe the Hand which never fails
From seeming evil worketh good for me.
And though I weep because those sails are tattered,
Still will I cry, while my best hopes lie shattered,
"I trust in Thee."

LEARN FROM THE ANT

Go to the ant,... consider her ways,
and be wise: which having no guide, overseer,
or ruler, provides her meat in the summer,
and gathers her food in the harvest.

PROVERBS 6:6-8

One of the traits to attain is *drive*. It's the first lesson to be learned from the ant. And I've noticed that get-aheaders have it, too, as well as the almost indefatigable energy that impels them toward their objectives. Drive is one of the reasons the "old boys with no chance" make it to the top. They come from the backwoods, the plains, the villages, the cities. But it's not where they're from that makes the difference, but what's *in* them—drive.

The second lesson to learn from the ant is *togetherness*; the ant works with others. "Two are better than one" (Ecclesiastes 4:9). If we cannot work with others, we're doomed to a life of lonely mediocrity.

And the third lesson is *thrift*. The ant stores meat in the summer so that it has food for the winter. While the grasshopper is playing and living only for the moment, the ant is toiling and filling its cupboard. This lesson was not given to make misers of us. Rather it was given to teach us a basic principle of survival—that we can't have by wasting. This self-preserving principle should not be scorned as a social crime. The lesson is divinely given.

By following the ant, Joseph preserved himself and his country through seven years of drought.

So our most painful sting is not from the ant, but from our failure to follow it. That sting comes from ourselves.

GET OFF THE MERRY-GO-ROUND

Simon Peter said to them, "I am going fishing."
They said to him, "We are going with you also."
They went out and immediately got into the boat,
and that night they caught nothing.

JOHN 21:3

When I was a boy my father took me into town to a carnival filled with attractions, and I stared at them with awed curiosity. Dad assisted me in getting on a wooden horse on the merry-go-round, and round and round I went with that carnival music blaring its allurement. After it stopped and we walked away, he said, "Son, there was a lot of motion and sound on that merry-go-round, but you didn't go anywhere."

That was some more of my father's deep insight and down-to-earth philosophy that has stuck with me and directed me. It has been one of the rules by which I have measured my activities: *am I getting anywhere?* Frankly, I am not constituted to be satisfied with defeat or stalemate.

Our God believes in progress. When He created the earth and the heavens, He did something productive every day for six days and then rested on the seventh (Genesis 1-2).

It is imperative that we constantly check our activities for results. Unless we discipline ourselves to stay with the pay-offs, we'll be diverted by the little merry-go-rounds of comparatively unimportant matters. On them we can actually slave without any worthwhile gain at all.

It's not enough to be *busy.* We have to be *productive.*

THE SHEPHERD HYMN

. . . .

The Lord is my shepherd, I shall not want. He maketh me to lie down in green pastures; He leadeth me beside the still waters. He restoreth my soul: He leadeth me in the paths of righteousness for His name's sake. Yea, though I walk through the valley of the shadow of death, I will fear no evil; for Thou art with me: Thy rod and Thy staff, they comfort me. Thou preparest a table before me in the presence of mine enemies: Thou anointest my head with oil: My cup runneth over. Surely goodness and mercy shall follow me all the days of my life: and I will dwell in the house of the Lord for ever.

PSALM 23

It was David, the shepherd boy who became king, who pictorially expressed the hope of frail man in the eloquent and immortal Twenty-third Psalm.

For hundreds of years, on every shore and in every clime, it has dried the tears and healed the hearts of countless numbers who helplessly stood by and watched as husband or wife, son or daughter, father or mother, brother or sister, slipped down through the valley of the shadow of death.

Its words have been upon the trembling lips of millions who slowly turned from the flower-decked mound where the earthly frame they loved so dearly was laid in hallowed ground.

And later, when time stood still in mournful shadows, while they tried to put back together a broken heart, they found peace in the way of life and death provided by the Good Shepherd.

Our needs are no different today. And the "Shepherd Hymn" is still a balm for hearts that ache and bleed and break.

HE DOES WHAT HE MUST

I must work the works of Him who sent me, while it is day;
the night is coming when no one can work.

JOHN 9:4

As seen in John 9:4, Jesus had the dedication and courage to face and do what He had to do. This attitude is ever relevant and ever descriptive of the ideal person. *He does what he must.*

He girds himself with determination and fights his daily battles out of true convictions, never-failing love and undying loyalty. He couldn't do otherwise and be himself. Our hats are off to him.

His business falls apart and has to be closed. Old doors close behind him, and now he must open some new ones. Because he is a giant among men, he *does.*

His investments fail and his plans shatter, yet he trusts God to see him through.

His wife is ill, bills are pressing, house payments due. To stay solvent, he takes on two jobs...and does it without a whimper.

Moral questions arise on the job. Right seems to be out of vogue. But he doesn't worry about the flow of popularity, because he knows popularity floods and dries up according to the whims and fancies of man. It's more important to him to live with the approval of his conscience.

He's knocked down again and again, yet he stays in the ring. In every round he is determined to score. The world can't beat a man that won't stay down. He rises and does what he must. "He alone is great, who by a life heroic conquers fate."

A LION IN THE STREET

. . . .

The slothful man says, "There is a lion outside,
I shall be slain in the streets."

PROVERBS 22:13

The fellow in Proverbs 22:13 didn't want to work, so he said there was a lion in the streets. When an excuse is needed, a friendly kitten can be pictured as a devouring lion.

Excuses! Excuses! Excuses! How *freely* you come! How *worthless* you are!

One Sunday morning, two men were out on the lake fishing. About 10:30 one of them looked at his watch and was reminded of where he ought to be. Feeling a twinge of conscience, he remarked, "Hubert, we really oughta be in church."

Hubert replied, "I couldn't have gone. My wife's sick."

Offering an excuse when we fail is a way to keep the ego inflated. We don't like to admit failure or wrong. Everybody has made an excuse at one time or another. I have, and you have. Sure, it seemed to give a little temporary relief from pain. But in the long run it is most injurious to refuse to see and face ourselves as we really are. It keeps us from correcting our mistakes and from improving our character.

The world doesn't accept excuses. Neither does the Lord. We're going to be judged now and later by our performance, not by excuses.

SHALL WE LIVE AGAIN?

Therefore we do not lose heart.
Even though our outward man is perishing,
yet the inward man is being renewed day by day.
2 CORINTHIANS 4:16

In his declining years, Victor Hugo (the French poet, novelist and dramatist) expressed some eloquent and encouraging thoughts on immortality. They continue to echo in many hearts the world over, and they're as relevant as man himself, who lives and dies.

"I feel in myself the future life. I am like a forest once cut down; the new shoots are stronger and livelier than ever. I am rising, I know, toward the sky.

"You say the soul is nothing but the resultant of the bodily powers. Why, then, is my soul more luminous when my bodily powers begin to fail? Winter is on my head, but eternal spring is in my heart. I breathe at this hour the fragrance of the lilacs, the violets and the roses, as at twenty years. The nearer I approach the end the plainer I hear around me the immortal symphonies of the world which invite me. It is marvelous yet simple. It is a fairy tale, and it is history.

"For half a century I have been writing my thoughts in prose and in verse: history, philosophy, drama, romance, tradition, satire, ode and song; I have tried all. But I feel I have not said the thousandth part of what is in me. When I go down to the grave I can say like many others, 'I have finished my day's work.' But I cannot say, 'I have finished my life.' My day's work will begin again the next morning. The tomb is not a blind alley; it is a thoroughfare. It closes on the twilight; it opens on the dawn."

AND THAT IS DYING

. . . .

Blessed are the dead who die in the Lord from now on.
Yes, says the Spirit, that they may rest from their labors;
and their works follow them.

REVELATION 14:13

*I*t adds joy and zest to life to have a hope that takes the sting out of the thought of dying. We do not want to go now, but we do want to know that all will be well when our time to go arrives.

We like to think of dying as the completion of our pilgrimage to the distant land, and that those who have preceded us are enjoying the love of there much more than the love of here, and that they are waiting to welcome us. That hope is expressed well in the following lines:

I am standing upon the seashore.
A ship at my side spreads her white sails
to the morning breeze and starts for the blue ocean.

She is an object of beauty and strength, and I stand
and watch her until at length she is only a ribbon of white cloud
just where the sea and sky come to mingle with each other.
Then someone at my side says:

"There! She's gone!"

Gone—where? Gone from my sight—that is all.
She is just as large in mast and hull and spar as she was
when she left my side and just as able to bear her load
of living freight—to the place of destination.

Her diminished size is in me, not in her,
and just at the moment when some one at my side says:
"There! She's gone!" other voices are ready to take up
the glad shout, "Here she comes!"

And that is dying in the Lord.

NEARER, MY GOD, TO THEE

Then God appeared to Jacob...
So Jacob set up a pillar in the place
where He talked with him,
a pillar of stone.
GENESIS 35:9-14

The inspiring hymn, "Nearer, My God, to Thee," was written by Sarah Fuller Adams, who was born in 1805. She wrote many lyrics, but her claim to fame is found in the authorship of this one hymn.

One night she had a dream in which she saw herself standing by the mounds in Bethel where Jacob once pitched his tent. There she saw Jacob, an exile to whom God had revealed Himself. She awoke feeling that God was with His people everywhere, no matter how desolate the place was. At once she wrote the words of the hymn.

This hymn has been emotionally associated with the Titanic disaster. As the ship was sinking, taking more than a thousand down to a watery grave, it has been stated that the band played the tune of the hymn and passengers and crew joined in the singing. The hymn that comforted them has comforted millions.

Nearer, my God, to Thee,
Nearer to Thee!
E'en though it be a cross
That raiseth me;
Still all my song shall be,
Nearer, my God, to Thee,
Nearer to Thee.

WHEN THE END COMES

. . . .

For we know that if our earthly house, this tent, is destroyed,
we have a building from God, a house not made
with hands, eternal in the heavens.

2 CORINTHIANS 5:1

When Earth's last picture is painted,
And the tubes are twisted and dried,
When the oldest colors have faded,
And the youngest critic has died,
We shall rest—and, faith, we shall need it—
Lie down for an aeon or two,
Till the Master of All Good Workmen
Shall set us to work anew!

And those that were good shall be happy;
They shall sit in a golden chair;
They shall splash at a ten-league canvas
With brushes of comet's hair;
They shall find real saints to draw from—
Magdalene, Peter and Paul;
They shall work for an age at a sitting
And never get tired at all!

And only the Master shall praise us,
And only the Master shall blame;
And no one shall work for money,
And no one shall work for fame;
But each for the joy of the working,
And each in his separate star
Shall draw the thing as he sees it
For the God of Things As They Are.

THE MASTER IS THERE

. . . .
Yes, though I walk through the valley of the shadow of death
I will fear no evil; for You are with me.

PSALM 23:4

There is a comforting story of a Christian physician who was caring for one of his patients in the patient's home. This was years ago. As the physician was leaving, the sick man asked, "Doctor, am I going to get well?" The doctor hesitated, then said, "I don't always know, but I do know you're a pretty sick man."

Then the man took his physician by the hand and said, "I don't want to die. Tell me what's on the other side."

The doctor replied, "I wish I could tell you, but I don't know."

They talked for a while about the mystery of life and death, and then the doctor prepared to leave. As he opened the door to go, a dog sprang into the room and happily leaped on him. Turning to his patient, the good physician remarked: "Did you see what happened here? This is my dog. He's never been here before. He didn't know what was inside your front door. He knew nothing except that I was here, and so he jumped through the door. He wasn't afraid. I cannot tell you what's on the other side of death, but I know that the Master is there. That's all anyone needs to know. When my Master opens the door, I expect to go through it without fear. And I shall dwell in His house forever."

WITH YOU ALWAYS

. . . .

And, lo, I am with you always, even to the end of the world.

MATTHEW 28:20

*J*esus promised His presence with us *all our days,* "even to the end of the world":

❧ *In days of loneliness,* which come to all. There can be the loneliness of the rich as well as of the poor, the king as much as the peasant. At times all suffer a loneliness hard to share—that is, except with the God who created us. We can share everything with Him in the communion of our spirit with His Eternal Spirit.

❧ *In days of sadness.* There are days when the singer has no song and the musician has no music. Occasions arise that sadden the most buoyant and dampen the hope of the most optimistic. But the promise "I am with you always" lifts the spirit of the sorrowful and encourages the downhearted.

❧ *In days of monotony.* Many people find their daily routines slavishly monotonous. In days of danger, opposition, threat or persecution, they rise to valor; but in easier days they find the humdrum experiences of life boring. But the knowledge of the Lord's presence should give our ordinary living a new appeal. He can help us through the common days.

❧ *In days of struggle.* The sea of life is not always smooth, nor is the wind always favorable. It takes hard rowing. But when the sailing is the harshest, inspired by the One who promised to be with us, we can say:

> *List not to the angry waters*
> *Of life's ever restless sea;*
> *Believers of the Lord, remember,*
> *"As thy days, thy strength shall be."*

HOUSE OF MANY MANSIONS

We know that if our earthly house, this tent,
is destroyed, we have a building from God,
a house not made with hands, eternal in the heavens.

2 CORINTHIANS 5:1

Moving from one house to another does not end the life of the tenant. When these old houses—your body and mine—shall have broken down, we shall move into fairer dwellings made for eternity.

The Tenant

This body is my house—it is not I;
Herein I sojourn till, in some far sky,
I lease a fairer dwelling, built to last
Till all the carpentry of time is past.
(In a new house away from) this lone star,
What shall I care where these poor timbers are?
What, though the crumbling walls turn dust and loam—
I shall have left them for a larger home.

FREDERICK LAWRENCE KNOWLES

Fashioned by a mighty hand that does all things well, our new bodies, made to last world without end, shall never know harassment and hurt, sickness and sorrow, despair and death; for the Great Giver shall design them to be like His own glorious body. For the Bible, in speaking of our Lord, says, "Who shall change our vile body, that it may be fashioned like His glorious body, according to the working whereby He is able even to subdue all things unto Himself" (Philippians 3:21).

THE GOOD BOOK

All Scripture is given by inspiration of God,
and is profitable for doctrine, for reproof, for correction,
for instruction in righteousness, that the man of God
may be complete, thoroughly equipped for every good work.
2 TIMOTHY 3:16-17

An unknown author once said of the Bible:

"This old book contains the mind of God, the state of man, the way of salvation, the doom of sinners, and the happiness of believers. Its doctrines are holy, its precepts are binding, its histories are true, and its decisions are immutable.

"Read it to be wise, believe it to be safe, and practice it to be holy.

"It contains light to direct you, food to support you, and comfort to cheer you. It is the traveler's map, the pilgrim's staff, the pilot's compass, the soldier's sword, and the believer's charter. Here paradise is restored, heaven opened and the gates of hell disclosed. Christ is its grand object, our good its design, and the glory of God its end.

"It should fill the memory, rule the heart, and guide the feet.

"It is a mine of wealth, a paradise of glory, and a river of joy. It is given you in life, will be opened at the judgment, and will be remembered forever. It involves the highest responsibilities, will reward the greatest labor, and will condemn all who trifle with its sacred contents."

If our society regarded the Scriptures with reverence as it once did, this world would be a better place.

HIGHLY EXAGGERATED

. . . .

And they gave a bad report of the land saying,
"There we saw the giants and we were like grasshoppers
in our own sight."

NUMBERS 13:32-33

Greatly exaggerated!

Evangelist Billy Sunday was always plain but unique. At the close of one of his sermons a woman approached him and asked, "I wonder if you can help me. I have an awful habit of exaggerating."

"Certainly, madam," replied Sunday. "Just call it lying."

The rumor was out that Mark Twain had passed away. A sympathizer went to the home to pay his condolences. He knocked on the door and Mark Twain answered. The startled man blurted, "I heard you were dead." The humorist replied, "I would say the report was greatly exaggerated."

The love of exaggeration is a love to enhance, improve and make a better story. There are people who really enjoy spilling news, for it puts them in the spotlight; they have a scoop! And the bigger the story, the bigger they feel.

Still, it is incredible that a person would pursue attention and limelight at the risk of losing credibility. How much more one is respected when he follows this straight principle of unadornment, "I am what I am; and what I say is, *is*."

HOW TO OVERCOME TENSIONS

· ·

When you lie down, you will not be afraid;
yes, you will lie down and your sleep will be sweet.

PROVERBS 3:24

*A*nxiety and tension are normal reactions when our safety and well-being are threatened. But, sometimes we become too anxious and tense. We should learn to deal with our difficulties without overreacting. Here are some suggestions:

❧ *Talk it out.* Don't bottle up your bother. Talk opens the high-pressure valve and allows tension to escape. Be cautious, however, in your choice of a listener.

❧ *Leave it for awhile.* It's helpful to escape from problems long enough to regain your balance. Then go back to the difficulty; it won't be as overwhelming.

❧ *Be not self-willed.* Life is made up of give and take. Compromise truth? *Never!* Compromise opinions? *Yes!* Remember, you could be wrong.

❧ *Take one day at a time.* The load you already carry will become too heavy if you attempt to bear the weight of all the potential and real burdens of the months and years ahead.

❧ *Expect realistic accomplishments.* Some people expect too much of themselves. We don't have to be supermen, just good people who use their talents.

❧ *Be able to take criticism.* The best people get criticized. What people say about you does not change who you are and what you are like.

GOD'S GARDEN

. . . .

She has done what she could.

MARK 14:8

All that can be expected of anyone is one hundred percent performance.

A grand little lady in New England came up with a novel way to serve the Lord and attain fulfillment in life. Next door to her humble house she had a vacant lot that had been growing weeds and creating worries. She decided to turn the liability into an asset. She planted a vegetable garden and raised all the kinds of vegetables that could thrive in the New England climate. She called her project "God's Garden," and the name was appropriate. A tiny portion of the vegetables met her own needs. Another portion went to needy people. And the rest were sold, and the money was given to the church.

Then one night she went home to be with her Lord. She had been at church and was as cheerful as ever, because doing for others always brings satisfaction and happiness. Afterward she had gone home to bed, and the next day neighbors found that she had fallen asleep in Jesus. The time had come for her to move into another garden—one more beautiful and meaningful than earth has ever known, a garden cultivated by One who said, "I go to prepare a place for you."

The people in the Northeast still remember the little, old lady who tilled "God's Garden." Frosts of many winters have cut down the vegetables, but the memories she planted in human hearts continue to live.

INVISIBLE AND ETERNAL
· ·

While we look not at the things which are seen,
but at the things which are not seen:
for the things which are seen are temporal;
but the things which are not seen are eternal.

2 CORINTHIANS 4:18

The Cathedral of Milan greets the visitor with some deep, self-examining philosophy. There are three inscriptions on the arches over the triple doorway.

One is a beautifully carved wreath of roses, and beneath it is the pronouncement, *"All that pleases is but for a moment."* Another is a sculptured cross with these encouraging words below it: *"All that troubles is but for a moment."* But the main entrance bears this masterpiece: *"That only is important which is eternal."*

Pleasures are fleeting, troubles are momentary, and man who knows both is soon carried away on the pale horse. Everything in the earth shall bow to death and pass away. Nothing material can withstand the ravages of time. One day even the earth itself "shall pass away with a great noise and the elements shall melt with fervent heat."

But God shall keep on living. He is from everlasting to everlasting. His word shall never pass away. It has been maliciously sentenced to death by foolish men, but it is indestructible. And the spirit of man lives on and on. Things eternal!

So, what *are* the major values? The answer is simple: they are the invisible things that defy time and answer not to death's call. They, and they only, can be considered the most important.

THE DONKEY IN THE LION'S SKIN

. . . .

For if anyone thinks himself to be something,
when he is nothing, he deceives himself.

GALATIANS 6:3

There is helpfulness in an age-old fable about a donkey that found a lion's pelt and put it on. Disguised as a lion, the donkey went into the pastures and threw the flocks and herds into a dreadful panic.

At last the donkey lion met its owner, who saw the long, donkey ears sticking out from under the lion's pelt. The owner took a stick and hit the donkey over the head, bringing it back to its senses.

Notwithstanding the donkey was dressed in a lion's pelt, it was still a donkey.

The lesson is, *People should be what they seem to be.*

The fable points out the vain pretense of putting on airs and assuming to be wiser, richer, more learned and of higher rank than one really is. Such persons are ever in danger of being found out; and when they are, they're liable to suffer the ridicule and humiliation of the donkey in the lion's skin.

In all conditions of life, the really honest person will show himself in his true garb and in his own character. He will not for temporary gain pretend to be something he is not. He will not pretend to be better than he is to impress people. Furthermore, he will not condescend to do anything below his own standards. He will act in the spirit of the proverb, "Be the same thing you would be called."

TOO SLOW

. . . .

And Jonathan cried out after the lad,
"Make haste, hurry, do not delay!"
So Jonathan's lad gathered up the arrows
and came back to his master.

1 SAMUEL 20:38

After the woman's husband was laid to rest, she was the only mourner to get into the big funeral limousine. She had no children and no relatives. On the way home from the cemetery the funeral director said, "Mary, I want to tell you something, and I don't want you to be offended. I mean it as a compliment. I've been secretly in love with you for all these years. That's why I have never married. Because of John I wouldn't say anything about it, but now he's gone. All of my life I've been too slow about everything, but this time I'm coming in early. So Mary, if you should ever think of marrying again, just remember I asked you first."

"Tom, I appreciate what you've told me," she replied, "but the doctor has already asked me to marry him."

Don't you feel sorry for Tom? Always a foot behind and a minute late.

Too slow. That's the best description of some people. They're always running behind. Late for work, late for church, late for every appointment. They need to reset their timing and rewind themselves.

In the everyday affairs of life we have to run fast just to stand still. But we can hasten without being in a breakneck hurry. *Hasten slowly.* There's a vast difference between rashness and haste. A prudent haste is great protection against loss and waste. Certainty is better than haste, but when we are certain we should hasten.

HE FAINTED AT CHURCH

. . . .

For consider Him who endured much hostility
from sinners against Himself, lest you become weary
and discouraged in your souls.

HEBREWS 12:3

While the man was sitting on a pew at church he keeled over in a dead faint. There was no purpose in preaching to him. He couldn't listen. No need to call him to sing. He couldn't sing. Nor could you call him to pray. He couldn't pray. Nor was there any point in passing him the contribution plate. He couldn't give.

The poor fellow was incognizant, unconscious, and had to be carried out. He was unable to accomplish anything, for he was in a faint. In this comatose state, he only breathed. This is true of those who faint spiritually. While they may breathe in the church, their heart is in some other world.

Here are some safeguards against fainting in business, at home and at church:

❧ First, *we shouldn't expect a life free of all hardships.* If we do, we will not be conditioned to face them when they come.

❧ Second, *we need to renew our strength.* This is accomplished by waiting on the Lord. Then we can rise with the wings of an eagle, run and not become weary, walk and not faint.

❧ Third, *we can count our blessings,* and then we'll realize how many more things are good than bad.

❧ *Fourth,* by increasing our faith and trust in God, we'll *build up our courage* to stay in there and keep going.

❧ *Fifth, we need to pray and meditate on God's Word.* I have never known a praying, Bible-reading person to faint spiritually. Prayer and the Bible put us in touch with the Higher Power.

THE GHOST OF PROCRASTINATION
· ·
And now why are you waiting?
ACTS 22:16

*P*utting off an easy thing today makes it hard tomorrow, if not impossible. Procrastination is the world's cruelest thief. It steals what people cannot afford to lose: opportunity, accomplishment and success.

At first there was just a little grass and weeds in the farmer's wheat field. A few tomorrows later the weeds took over and the crop was lost. At first there was only a tiny leak in the roof. A few tomorrows later the house was flooded.

If we do our duty today, we will have far less trouble tomorrow. Today is cash in hand. Tomorrow is only a promissory note.

Tomorrow
He was going to be all that a mortal should be
Tomorrow.
No one should be kinder or braver than he
Tomorrow.
A friend who was troubled and weary he knew,
Who'd be glad of a lift and who needed it, too;
On him he would call and see what he could do
Tomorrow.

The greatest of workers this man would have been
Tomorrow.
The world would have known him, had he ever seen
Tomorrow.
But the fact is he died and he faded from view,
And all that he left here when living was through
Was a mountain of things he intended to do
Tomorrow.

EDGAR A. GUEST

RUN, RABBIT, RUN!

· ·

In all labor there is profit,
but idle chatter leads only to poverty.

PROVERBS 14:23

A group of men and women stood on a hillside watching a dog chase a rabbit. They shouted, "Run, rabbit, run! Run for your life! Run! Run! Run!"

After circling in the chase two or three times and as the people shouted again, the poor rabbit yelled back, "Ladies and gentlemen, I appreciate your words of encouragement, but why doesn't someone chase off the dog?"

The shouters didn't say too much, but they did too little. They were vain talkers. Clouds without water. Rivers that were dry. A disappointment.

Talking comes cheap, so cheap that some talk when they have nothing to say. And the only reason some others listen is because they know it will be their turn to talk next.

Some think help is only a one-way street; all assistance should come their way and none go back to the givers. That was the view of the self-centered woman who arose one morning and said, "I wonder what nice thing somebody can do for me today." It had never dawned on her that she, like everybody else, is here to help others. Instead, she thought she was here for others to help.

It is a practical law of nature for us to help one another. Not just talk, but help. The Apostle Paul commanded, "Bear one another's burdens" (Galatians 6:10).

OLD JIGGS

. . . .

Where there is no wood, the fire goes out;
and where there is no talebearer, strife ceases.

PROVERBS 26:20-21

Old Jiggs. That was the name of our dog. I liked that dog and he liked me. Furthermore, he had jobs to do, just as I did, and he always did them faithfully and well.

My father's store had wood floors. Nearly all floors were made of wood back in that day. Customers would sometimes drop a cigarette on the floor. And this was a potential fire hazard—a dropped cigarette on a wood floor sometimes strewn with bits of paper and cardboard.

Now back to Jiggs. We trained Jiggs from the time he was a pup to put out cigarettes and burning paper. He was our firedog in that store, and one that could catch the scent of burning better than we could. He wouldn't hurt anybody, but he was death to cigarettes and little fires. His whiskers were scorched all the time.

Years have passed and I've thought about Jiggs many times. There was a great lesson to learn from him: he didn't start fires; *he put them out.*

Too bad some people in church, in business, in school, and in every other circle don't act like Jiggs. They generate sparks and build fires in our society. Anyone can cause trouble, but it takes a righteous talent to prevent it (if that's possible) and to maintain peace.

HANDLING DISCOURAGEMENT

· ·

Rejoicing in hope; patient in tribulation.

ROMANS 12:12

$\mathcal{T}$he name of Thomas Edison is greatly cherished because of his inventions, among them the incandescent light, the telephone, storage battery, microphone and talking movies. They have blessed the world.

On a freezing December night the alarm of "Fire! Fire!" was sounded. Thomas Edison's plant was on fire. Though fire equipment from eight surrounding towns came to fight the blaze, *everything* was destroyed.

But it was neither the building nor the records that worried the inventor's son. His father was missing. Had he been working (for he worked day and night) and died in the fire? If he survived, had it broken the spirit of the sixty-seven-year-old man?

To his relief, his father came running to him and said, "Where's Mom? Go get her! Tell her to hurry and bring her friends. They'll *never* see a fire like this again!"

The next day, with the fire barely under control, Edison summoned his employees and said, "We're rebuilding." He ordered one employee to rent all the machine shops in the area. Another was told to get a wrecking crane. Then, as if he'd almost forgotten, he asked, "Oh, by the way, does anybody know where we can get some money?"

He could handle disappointment. The genius tried again and again—many times—before his inventions worked. Now he was tried by fire. But hope never yields to disappointment. Hope always finds another chance and dreams another dream.

PRESENT-TENSE LIVING

. . . .

Today if you will hear His voice,
do not harden your hearts.

HEBREWS 4:7

Many people have mixed up their tenses. Some are living in the future. Others are living in the past. But happy and victorious living is in the present tense.

Yes, there *are* blessings to be gained from the past. A past mistake can be a warning so we don't stumble over the same rock twice. Inspiration from a past success can strengthen us. Hope of the future can also enrich and stimulate us.

But, as far as living is concerned, it's strictly present tense. We see this life principle in the Scriptures:

§ "Whoever hears these sayings of Mine, and does them, I will liken him unto a wise man" (Matthew 7:24). *Present* tense.

§ "Search me, O God, and know my heart: try me, and know my thoughts: And see if there be any wicked way in me, and lead me in the way everlasting" (Psalm 139:23-24). *Present* tense.

§ "Who comforts me in all our tribulation, that we may be able to comfort them who are in any trouble" (2 Corinthians 1:4). *Present* tense.

Duty is in the present tense. Not yesterday! Not tomorrow! If we think we can grasp our potentialities and ideals some uncertain tomorrow, it won't happen! Our tomorrow will be the result of our today. All of the possibilities of life are in the present tense.

PEOPLE WITH A PURPOSE

To every thing there is a season,
and a time to every purpose under heaven:...
a time to plant...a time to gather...a time to get.

ECCLESIASTES 3:1-6

*P*rosperous people have definitely intended to pull ahead. Singleness of purpose has kept them on the road to their goals. Success begins with a purpose.

In every success story there is a man or woman who is determined to rise above the ordinary. This force of will to be or to achieve is actually the first sign of greatness and the starting point in a successful career.

Singleness of purpose
is one of the chief essentials for success in life,
no matter what may be one's purpose in life.

JOHN D. ROCKEFELLER, JR.

Also, winners know that getting to the top is their own responsibility. Not the other fellow's. Not the community's. Not the government's. They know that with God's help, getting there is up to them. Knowing that their compensation must come from their own hands ("the recompense of a man's hands shall be rendered unto him," Proverbs 12:14), they climb their ladder rung by rung.

Furthermore, have you noticed that the people at the top have a habit of doing the things that experience has proved are most likely to work? And have you also observed that they make it a point *not* to do the things that have a record of failure?

Would You Sell the Parrot?

· ·

You shall not go about
as a talebearer among your people.

LEVITICUS 19:16

Five preachers met for a friendly gathering to exchange views and encourage one another. During the session one preacher said, "Our people come to us with open hearts, confess their sins, and express certain needs. Don't you think it would be good for us to do the same? We're frail, have weaknesses, make mistakes and have needs like everybody else. We are all made from the same clay."

After some discussion, it was agreed that they should do the same, that confession is good for the soul.

The first one confessed that he enjoyed going to nightclubs, and sometimes when away from home he would sneak in and visit but not participate. The second confessed to liking to play cards but that he would never play for more than a dime. The third confessed to enjoying cigars and to indulging in them on rare occasion. The fourth confessed that sometimes he drank a little in an effort to quiet his turbulent feelings. The fifth one didn't want to confess anything. But the others insisted, "We've confessed ours. Now it's your turn. What's your secret weakness or sin?"

Reluctantly he admitted, "It's gossiping, and I can hardly wait to get out of here and start talking!"

All of us need to learn that what Jesus said was "Go into all the world and preach the gospel," *not* "Go into all the world and preach the gossip."

Will Rogers has given us some timely advice: "So live that you wouldn't be ashamed to sell the family parrot to the town gossip."

THE ONE WHOSE PRESENCE IS MOST NEEDED

For where two or three are gathered together
in My name, there am I in the midst of them.
MATTHEW 18:20

The story has been told that one day the telephone rang in the minister's office of the Washington church that was attended by President Franklin Roosevelt. An inquisitive voice asked, "Do you expect President Roosevelt to be in church on Sunday?"

"That," answered the preacher, "I cannot promise. But we expect the Lord to be present, and we fancy that should be incentive enough for a reasonably large crowd."

❧ A government head errs, but the Lord does *not*. "Who did no sin, neither was guile found in His mouth" (1 Peter 2:22).

❧ A government leader is sometimes a respecter of man, but God is *not*. "Of a truth I perceive that God is no respecter of persons" (Acts 10:34).

❧ A president will die and leave us, but God will *not*. "Have you not known? have you not heard, that the everlasting God, the Lord, the Creator of the ends of the earth, fainteth not, neither is weary?" (Isaiah 40:28).

Therefore it is wiser for us to place the honor and the glory where it belongs—on the Lord, not on man.

SOMETHING SPECIAL

What is man, that You should magnify him,
that You should set Your heart upon him?

JOB 7:17

The brilliant Daniel Webster said:

If we work upon marble,
It will perish;
If we work upon brass,
Time will efface it;
If we rear temples,
They will crumble into dust;
But, if we work upon immortal souls,
If we imbue them with principles,
With the just fear of God
And the love of fellowman,
We engrave on those tablets
Something which will brighten all eternity.

Man is a creature of great potential for this world and a sure thing for everlasting existence in the ceaseless ages to come. This marks him as something special, Heaven's masterpiece.

Despite the laudatory remarks, man is weak and subject to temptation. Oh, how contemptible he is unless raised above the degradation of sin!

While man is weak like a reed, he is a thinking reed to be cultivated. Man—the object of God's love—is clay to be molded into a masterpiece of distinction. Man—an intellectual being—is born without manners and is a challenge to be shaped into a vessel of accomplishment and refinement. Man—an eternal being—is spirit housed in mortal body, and spirit does not die. So in contemplating man, we contemplate the immortal.

A PREPARED PLACE

. . . .

I go to prepare a place for you.

JOHN 14:2

There is an intriguing story about a preacher who decided to leave a church he had served for two years. With moist eyes, he stood up in the Sunday-morning service and bid goodbye to the sad congregation.

"Brothers and sisters," he said, clearing his throat and restraining his emotion, "I wish to say farewell. The Lord has called me to another place. I don't think He loves you very much, for none of you ever dies; He doesn't seem to want you. And you don't seem to love each other, for I haven't had wedding ceremonies for any of you. And you don't seem to love me, either, for you haven't paid me enough to live substantially.

"And so, brothers and sisters, I am resigning. I have accepted a chaplaincy at the state penitentiary. In closing, I am reminded of the Scripture verse, 'I go to prepare a place for you...that where I am, there you may be also.'"

I'd like to believe that the preacher was kindly and humorous and he was just teasing them. If so, it's proof he liked them, for we don't tease people we don't like.

However, the story does emphasize the need to be ready to enter a prepared place. Even if it is a penitentiary, one has to qualify to enter it—whether positively, as an employee or ministry volunteer; or negatively, in the position of an inmate.

There is a prepared job out there for you, but you have to be prepared to do it. The school is a prepared place, but the student must be prepared to appropriate it. The church is a prepared body, but a person must be prepared for its fellowship. Jesus said, "I go to prepare a place for you," but that place is a prepared place for prepared people.

GONE TO MEDDLING

. . . .

Preach the word; be instant in season,
out of season; reprove, rebuke, exhort
with all long-suffering and doctrine.

2 TIMOTHY 4:2

A mechanic went to hear an evangelist in a little town. That night the preacher preached on money, and he used three sermon points to cover the topic.

 First point, *"Make all you can."* The mechanic nudged his wife and said, "That man is the best I've ever heard. He's no nitwit. He knows what it's all about. He is smart."

 Second point, *"Save all you can."* This excited the mechanic, so he whispered again, "This beats anything I've ever heard. He's smart enough to be president. This town has never had a preacher that could hold a candle to him." When the preacher commended hard work and thrift, denouncing laziness and waste, the mechanic couldn't keep quiet. He whispered, "I've believed in this all my life. Salvation has finally come to us."

 Third point, *"Give all you can."* "What?" exclaimed the mechanic. "Now he's gone crazy! He's quit preaching and gone to meddling!"

Some people's conception of great preaching is a sermon that compliments them and rebukes someone else. We need to remember that our preachers haven't authored the Bible. They aren't responsible for writing a *single* word in it, but they are responsible for preaching *every* word in it. And when they preach from the Word of God, people judge themselves by His Word.

LEANING TREES

I call to remembrance the genuine faith that is in you,
which dwelled first in your grandmother Lois,
and your mother Eunice, and, I am persuaded
now lives in you also.

2 TIMOTHY 1:5

The grandmother inspired and molded her daughter, and the daughter influenced her son. His name was Timothy.

On my first visit along the California coast I observed that the trees leaned away from the ocean and toward the east. The relentless, never-ending wind that blew in from the Pacific had forced them to grow at a slant.

Then a little cloud blew up into a gale from the opposite direction. It forced those trees to bend the other way, but only temporarily. When the gale subsided, they went back to their original position. They were too old to depart from the direction they had grown. Bend? Yes, but not permanently. Reminded me of Solomon's assertion on rearing children: "Train up a child in the way he should go: and when he is old, he will not depart from it" (Proverbs 22:6).

At church I noticed a little girl who was carrying a copybook that her teacher had given her. I was struck with the idea that the parent's life is the child's most effective copybook. The parent creates impressions that are more indelible and far-reaching than all others—more than the minister's, the Sunday School teacher's, the public school teacher's or any other person's.

A PAGE OF EXAMPLE

· ·

You are our epistle written in our hearts,
known and read of all men.

2 CORINTHIANS 3:2

There are four Gospels in the New Testament—Matthew, Mark, Luke and John. But there's a fifth, too, and it's *you*. You are the gospel that is most read by your associates.

The Gospels of Matthew, Mark, Luke and John
Are read by more than a few,
But the one that is most read and commented on
Is the gospel according to You.

You are writing a gospel, a chapter each day,
By things that you do and words that you say.
Men read what you write, whether faithless or true.
Say, what is the gospel according to You?

Is the gospel according to you one of love? Forgiveness? Helpfulness? Fairness? Truthfulness? Ethics? Kindness? Maybe it's courtesy. Tolerance. Clean speech. Unselfishness.

These qualities will make you an effective living letter from the Savior, admired and loved by those who read you. One thing is for sure: *they will read you!*

A page of example is sometimes worth far more than a whole book of preaching.

GO AND DO

. . . .

Then Jesus said to him,
"Go and do likewise."
LUKE 10:37

While a little girl was playing with some lettered blocks, she made a delightful discovery. Her mother had shown her how to spell the word *good* and explained how important it was to be good. The little girl ran into the kitchen and exclaimed, "Mommy, come see two words I found in the word *good*. They were *go* and *do*.

From a child's play we have a powerful lesson on successful pursuit—that it demands more than play.

  ❧ We can't just play neighbor; we must *go* and *do*.

  ❧ We can't just play business; we must *go* and *do*.

  ❧ We can't just play government; we must *go* and *do*.

  ❧ We can't just play education; we must *go* and *do*.

  ❧ We can't just play church; we must *go* and *do*.

  ❧ We can't just play good; we must *be* good.

THEY DON'T KNOW MY SON

Who stands before you, he shall go in there.
Encourage him, for he shall cause Israel to inherit.
DEUTERONOMY 1:38

School lasted only six or seven months a year in our little village. I grew up believing that the most important factor in education was not the length of the school term but the depth of the student's mind.

We had all the grades except the last year. When I reached that level I moved into town, lived with my grandmother and went to school there. On registration day I was kindly but firmly told that no one from a small school with such short terms could possibly finish in one year, that it was much harder than a country school, that it always took two years for students with my background to graduate.

I replied, "If you don't mind, please see that I have all the required courses and enough credits so that if I do pass, I'll finish in one year"

"All right, but you may be disappointed."

I didn't believe it, but the thought of it cast gloom over me. Later, still feeling the despondency, I told my mother what the school official had said. I shall never forget her sweet, assuring words, "They don't know my son."

The nine months soon became history and graduation night arrived. Not only did I pass, but I received a college scholarship. The point I'm trying to make here is not that I did well enough to win a scholarship, but that my mother encouraged me. It made all the difference in the way I felt about myself. At times everybody needs encouragement. It's oxygen to the heart. Giving it can save a person from fainting.

CAUSE-AND-EFFECT

· ·

And David said, "What have I now done?
Is there not a cause?"

1 SAMUEL 17:29

*E*very effect must have a cause. In a Sunday-morning worship service, a lay person was leading the congregation in prayer. Once again he prayed the prayer he always prayed in public, and once again he used the same words. Nearly everyone there had heard the prayer so often that they could go three words ahead of him. He prayed, "O Lord, since we last called upon Thee, the cobwebs have come between us and Thee. We pray that Thou wilt remove the cobwebs that we may look upon Thy face once again."

At this very point in his prayer, someone interjected, "O Lord, kill the spider!"

That's right. It's good to get the cobwebs cleaned out, but it's better to kill the spider. If we remove the cause, the results will go too.

Many wish to deal with effects instead of causes, which is a short-sighted view. But the Bible makes a powerful statement about cause-and-effect: "Whatever a man sows, that shall he also reap" (Galatians 6:7).

No one succeeds or fails, gains or loses, is well or ill, is happy or miserable, by chance. All of life is regulated by the inflexible rule of cause-and-effect.

EYES CAN PLAY TRICKS

. . . .

Do not receive an accusation against an elder
except from two or three witnesses.

1 TIMOTHY 5:19

A man came into my office, and he was terribly distraught. His voice trembled with emotion. He thought he had nearly set himself up to violate one of the Ten Commandments: "Thou shalt not bear false witness."

He said, "I drove by a tavern, and I thought I saw one of the church elders sitting there, drinking beer. There was no question in my mind. I was absolutely certain. And he wasn't taking a little for 'his stomach's sake.' Fortunately, I decided to drive by more slowly and take another look. When I did, I realized that I was wrong. He wasn't the man I'd thought. He certainly looked like him, but he wasn't.

"If I hadn't gone back and looked again, the chances are I would have told someone that he was hitting the bottle. It scares me to think of the injury I might have done to him."

Due to the imperfection of man, a single witness is no witness at all. People don't always see what they think they see. The varying testimonies of witnesses to wrecks prove this. Be doubly, *doubly* sure before accusing a person of wrongdoing.

It's easy to understand why God commanded that an accusation be substantiated by at least two or three witnesses. Though one is honest, he still might be mistaken in what he thought he saw or heard.

RETREAT TO FIGHT AGAIN

. . . .

When Pharaoh heard of this matter, he sought to kill Moses.
But Moses fled from the face of Pharaoh.

EXODUS 2:15

*M*oses fled from Pharaoh, but he returned to attack again. He made havoc of Pharaoh's kingdom by delivering the children of God from their bondage.

There are times to advance and times to retreat. We can make an honorable retreat, and an honorable retreat is in itself a victory.

> *He that fights and runs away*
> *May live to fight another day.*
>
> BUTLER

In Texas' War of Independence, General Santa Anna, Mexico's president, attacked the Alamo and slaughtered its defenders to the last man. Then he and his large, well-equipped army went on to attack Sam Houston and the ragged group of Texas volunteers. He hoped to smash the revolution once and for all. But Houston retreated and retreated and retreated until the moment he was waiting for finally came. Just when the Mexicans were enjoying siesta and least expecting an attack, the Texans turned and captured the entire Mexican army, including President Santa Anna himself. Knowing when to retreat and when to attack gave birth to a new nation, the Republic of Texas, which ten years later voluntarily became a part of the United States.

Today the knowledge of when to retreat and when to attack still wins victories. It can build a business, affect sales, shape the thinking of social and political groups, and introduce people to Jesus Christ. When you have gone far enough for the moment, pull back and wait for another day.

PUTTING TOGETHER A SUCCESSFUL LIFE

I have put my life in my hand.

1 SAMUEL 28:21

For a triumphant and happy life one must:

❧ *Think*; it is the source of human power. "For as he thinks in his heart, so is he" (Proverbs 23:7).

❧ *Work*; it is the source of production. "Let him labor...that he may have" (Ephesians 4:28).

❧ *Be thrifty*; it is the means of preservation. "Gather up the fragments that remain, that nothing be lost" (John 6:12).

❧ *Play*; it is the secret of perennial youth. There are several references in the Bible to games and contests which show that they were acceptable pastimes (2 Timothy 2:5).

❧ *Be sensitive*; it is the heart that beats with the joys and sorrows of others. "Rejoice with those who do rejoice, and weep with those who weep" (Romans 12:15).

❧ *Be friendly*; it is the road that leads to friends. "A man who has friends must show himself friendly" (Proverbs 18:24).

❧ *Think of others*; it is the way to enlarge your own heart, view of life and fruitfulness. "Look not every man on his own things, but every man also on the things of others" (Philippians 2:4).

❧ *Honor God*; this is the conclusion of the whole effort. "Let us hear the conclusion of the whole matter: Fear God and keep His commandments: for this is the whole duty of man" (Ecclesiastes 12:13).

THE RAINBOW SPEAKS

I set My rainbow in the cloud,
and it shall be for the sign of the covenant
between Me and the earth.

GENESIS 9:13

A little city boy went with his father on his first vacation. They went to the mountains, where they camped, hiked and enjoyed the wonders of nature. On one of their hikes, standing on a high mountain peak, his father pointed out a colorful rainbow.

The television-oriented youngster, who had seen many a commercial, commented, "It's pretty, Daddy. What's it advertising?"

I don't know how his father answered him, but he might have said, "It's advertising the grace of God and a special promise. After the Flood back in Old Testament times, God promised Noah that He would never again destroy the earth with water, and He set a beautiful rainbow in the sky as the sign of His promise."

Furthermore, all of nature is one big signboard after another declaring the glory of God and His handiwork. Many of nature's sights are so enchanting that we first gaze on them in breathless silence, and then when breath is restored we exclaim, "O Lord, our Lord, how excellent is Your name in all the earth! You have set Your glory above the heavens" (Psalm 8:1).

RELIGION WITHOUT ICE

Greet Priscilla and Aquilla,
my helpers in Christ Jesus.

ROMANS 16:3

One true helper in the Lord's work was a little lady who lived in a small town. When she moved there she found no congregation of the denomination of which she was a member. She immediately made an inquiry and located two other members, a man and his wife. Through her insistence they decided to plant a church.

The lady located a hall they could rent for their assembly. It was a second floor, reached only by climbing a stairway. The same hall was used for Saturday-night dances. She and the couple would get up early on Sunday morning to clean up the rubbish and disarray of the night before. This hall wasn't her choice, but it did put them in operation for the Lord.

Wanting an evangelistic meeting, she wrote to a preacher she knew, explained the circumstances, and invited him to do the preaching. She told him they could provide him with board and room and pay for his bus fare. The self-sacrificing preacher came.

But he was not the only one to sacrifice. This widow did without ice the entire summer (had no electric refrigerators then) to save enough money to pay the bus fare.

The church prospered. Hard struggle, but it grew. Today it stands as a reminder of what one dedicated woman can do in the Master's vineyard. Strong people just naturally find a way to make an impact. Light shines wherever it is. Salt seasons whatever it touches.

AND TOUCHED THEM

· ·

And Jesus came and touched them,
and said, "Arise and do not be afraid."

MATTHEW 17:7

Touch has a tongue that says what a lonely and burdened world wants to hear. It is the natural touch, energized by a friendly heart. When we don't know what to say to someone, a warm touch on the shoulder might be the best expression of our concern.

In a Friendly Sort o' Way

When a man ain't got a cent,
and he's feeling kind o' blue,
An' the clouds hang dark and heavy,
an' won't let the sunshine through,
It's a Great Thing, O my brethren,
for a feller just to lay
His hand upon your shoulder in
a friendly sort o' way!

Oh, the world's a curious compound,
with its honey and its gall,
With its cares and bitter crosses,
but a good world, after all.
An' a good God must have made it—
leastways, that is what I say,
When a hand is on my shoulder
in a friendly sort o' way.

JAMES WHITCOMB RILEY

Oh, for the touch of a loving hand!

A PRICELESS MOTHER

. . . .

Her price is far above rubies.

PROVERBS 31:10

Solomon the wise man has paid a lofty compliment to the worthy mother: "Her price is far above rubies." No quantity of precious stones can equal her worth. It is utterly impossible to appraise her true value.

She is good to both her husband and children. "She will do him good and not evil all the days of her life" (Proverbs 31:12). It is no problem for her to be good, because she *is* good. For her, goodness is as natural as breathing. I have observed that good people are good to all; and evil people, when circumstances are trying, are evil to all.

Another one of her invaluable attributes is that *she works willingly* (Proverbs 31:13). She finds joy in unselfish service to her loved ones. Moreover, her attendance to the family's needs is rendered cheerfully, and we know why; her heart is in it. Willing work contributes to a pleasant and happy home life.

"She rises also while it is yet night, and gives meat to her household" (Proverbs 31:15). Her diligence enables the members of the family to enter their labors without delay, interruption and tension. This has a major influence in giving the cheerful and unconquerable spirit to the entire family as they face their day.

No wonder her husband praises her (Proverbs 31:28). She has the approbation of her husband and children because she has earned it.

My Mother

. . . .

And Adam called his wife's name Eve;
because she was the mother of all living.

GENESIS 3:20

*A*t this season of the year, it is comforting to read this classic tribute that has touched the heart of countless numbers.

My Mother

Who fed me from her gentle breast
And hushed me in her arms to rest,
And on my cheek sweet kisses prest?
My mother.
When sleep forsook my open eye,
Who was it sung sweet lullaby
And rocked me that I should not cry?
My mother.
When pain and sickness made me cry,
Who gazed upon my heavy eye
And wept, for fear that I should die?
My mother.
Who ran to help me when I fell
And would some pretty story tell,
Or kiss the part to make it well?
My mother.
Who taught my infant lips to pray,
To love God's holy word and day,
And walk in wisdom's pleasant way?
My mother.
When thou art feeble, old and gray,
My healthy arm shall be thy stay,
And I will soothe thy pains away,
My mother.
And when I see thee hang thy head,
'Twill be my turn to watch thy bed,
And tears of sweet affection shed—
My mother.

JANE TAYLOR

MOTHER, THE HEROINE

Now there stood by the cross of Jesus
His mother.

JOHN 19:25

Influential and forceful mothers have one character trait in common: *courage.* It's a quality of the heart, not the result of circumstances. It depends on what's *in* a mother, not on what is around her. Courage is a dynamic, internal power that controls her behavior in the face of difficulties, trials and dangers.

Physical courage is seen when someone risks life for someone else or for a cause. The soldier who sacrifices his life for his country is honored among the nation's heroes, but too often we forget the heroism of mothers who live and serve and die a little every day at home.

It takes the bravest kind of courage to face the everyday affairs of life. On this battlefield mothers display a heroic nature that is unexcelled. They unflinchingly triumph amid all the opposition and friction, strain and heartbreak of life.

Brave is the woman who knows how to handle the anxieties, cares, disappointments and sorrows of life. As she daily demonstrates this bravery, she inspires, builds and molds this same quality in her children.

The universal need for all the services a mother renders compels her to become a creature of bravery. Too much is at stake for her to be otherwise. And every victory won fits her to win another.

ROCK ME TO SLEEP

My son, keep your father's command,
and do not forsake the law of your mother.

PROVERBS 6:20

The most wonderful world is the child's world, for it is the realest world—no shams, no baseness. It is to our good that a child's world exists. One of our blessings is the ability to retain much of it in memory.

Backward, turn backward, O Time, in your flight,
Make me a child again just for tonight!
Mother, come back from the echoless shore,
Take me again to your heart as of yore;
Kiss from my forehead the furrows of care,
Smooth the few silver threads out of my hair;
Over my slumbers your loving watch keep;
Rock me to sleep, Mother—rock me to sleep!

Tired of the hollow, the base, the untrue,
Mother, O Mother, my heart calls for you!
Many a summer the grass has grown green,
Blossomed and faded, our faces between:
Yet, with strong yearning and passionate pain,
Long I tonight for your presence again.
Come from the silence so long and so deep;
Rock me to sleep, Mother—rock me to sleep.

ELIZABETH AKERS ALLEN

Our Second Chance

. . . .

Let the little children come to Me,
and do not forbid them;
for of such is the kingdom of heaven.

MATTHEW 19:14

A childless neighbor said, "Your children will be such a comfort to you in your old age."

"Yes, I'm sure they will be, and they'll help me reach it faster, too," replied the fatigued, nerve-tattered mother.

But a child is our second chance. Moreover, a child teaches the parent many important lessons—including patience. He also teaches us that he is an individual and that we can abandon all cut-and-dried theories on rearing children. John Wilmont (1647-1680) said, "I had six theories about bringing up children; now I have six children and no theories."

Jesus put a child in the midst. What He did is an apt example for parents; keep them in your midst as much as you can. Give them plenty of love. And the chances are the only bad luck you will ever have with them is *they will grow up.*

Send Them to Bed With a Kiss

O mothers, so fatigued, discouraged,
Worn out with the cares of the day,
You often grow tired and impatient,
Weary of the noise and the play;
For the day brings so many vexations,
So many things going amiss,
But mothers, whatever may vex you,
Send the children to bed with a kiss.

ALL THE WAY TO THE MOON

. . . .

But his mother kept
all these sayings in her heart.

LUKE 2:51

A little boy's mother has just made a new observation. A startling one. Her precious ten-year-old son has started coming to the table with washed face and hands. No prompting on her part. It's brought tears to her eyes.

The little boy, sparked with wonder and excitement and with a frog in his pocket, will soon outgrow his careless and sometimes vexing childhood. Time passes fast. He will soon need many pockets, briefcases and filing cabinets to carry the weighty responsibilities of manhood. Before long he will be running fast—not to catch butterflies, but to endless appointments.

Perchance there will be pressures to serve on committees. None will be like his present committee to dig the worms for the fishing trips, but he will have to dig into human events. Now he has a dog to protect him. Later he must learn to protect himself from the wolves of society.

Another tear is shed when his mother recalls the times when she deemed it necessary to spank him for some infraction and he would say, "Mama, I love you all the way to the moon." That put her into orbit and into a sweeter world.

It is understandable why she wipes a tear. She is watching her boy grow into a man. One day he may reach the stars, but more importantly, she prays that he may never lose sight of the God who created those stars.

A PRAYER FOR MOTHERS

· ·

Give ear, O Lord, to my prayer;
and attend to the voice of my supplications.

PSALM 86:6

Our Father in Heaven, the One in whom we live and move and have our being, we thank You for mothers—the makers of humanity, the torchbearers of life and the foundation of civilization. We are grateful for our own dear mothers who bore us in travail and loved us all the more for the pain we brought; who suffered for us in body, mind and soul; who gave us a confident security by their tireless sacrifices and undying devotion; for the agony with which they watched over us in sickness and nursed us back to health; for the sorrow that pierced their hearts when we were foolish; for the smiles of appreciation and joy that played across their faces when we achieved some little accomplishment; for the thousand little tasks they performed daily to make life better for us.

O God of our being, we implore You to grant support, patience and courage to deserving mothers that they may not break under their heavy burdens in life's most strenuous tasks. As each new day dawns, may faith undimmed and optimism unclouded shine anew in their deserving hearts.

And for us we pray, our Father, that the hallowed memories of such illustrious mothers may inspire us to nobler living and lift us to higher ground. May we live the praises due them. In Christ's name. Amen.

STANDARD OF ETHICS

. . . .

And if I have taken anything from any man
by false accusation, I restore him fourfold.

LUKE 19:8

This is exceedingly ethical. A man explained to his son, "Ethics is vital to a workable and confident society. For instance, today a friend paid back a hundred dollars I'd loaned him. He handed me a new hundred-dollar bill. Later I discovered there were *two* hundred-dollar bills stuck together. Now it's a question of ethics. Should I tell your mother?"

But ethics can't be confined to family relationships and interest, with everybody else free to be ripped off.

Here is a five-way test of ethics:

1) *Is it free from deception?*
2) *Is it honest?*
3) *Is it the truth?*
4) *Is it fair?*
5) *Is it in keeping with the Golden Rule?*

Ethics is concerned with what is *right,* not with mere legalism that considers only what is within the law. Our world is full of legal loopholes whereby a person can legally cheat and steal from others. But the people of God are above this; they live by a higher standard.

ROOM AT THE TOP

The desire accomplished is sweet to the soul.

PROVERBS 13:19

Every year thousands of people visit the White House. It is a popular tour for students. Teachers hope that it will do more than satisfy their curiosity, that it will light within the heart the fires of ambition and patriotism.

After one teacher had taken her high school students on this tour, she asked them to write their impressions of the visit. Many interesting replies were given, but the one that most affected the teacher stated, "I was glad to get to visit my future home." Lightning won't strike for every child to become the President of the United States, but every person *can* soar high when ambition gives him eagle's wings.

There are two reasons why there is room at the top: First, so few get there. Second, of those who do, some go to sleep and fall off.

If you would rise, get on ambition's ladder and round by round, *climb*. Climb, and keep climbing. Don't look down; you might get dizzy. And when you have once attained the utmost round, turn not your back to the ladder and look in the clouds and scorn the lowly base from which you did ascend.

THIS MIGHT HAPPEN TO YOU

Therefore let him who thinks he stands
take heed lest he fall.

1 CORINTHIANS 10:12

The residents of a little village were distressed because motorists raced through their village at murderous speeds, paying no attention to the large warning sign, "Drive Slowly," erected at a visible place right at the entrance. In their desperation, they finally dragged a badly wrecked car to the spot and placed over it the sign, "This Might Happen to You!" That sign did make a difference.

Perhaps we should put up signs concerning all the end results we don't want and add this warning in red paint: "This Might Happen to You!" Then let's take heed that it doesn't happen to us.

This shall happen to us:

  ❧ *poverty,* if we deal with a slack hand (Proverbs 10:4).

  ❧ *want,* if we waste our substance (Luke 15:13).

  ❧ *strife,* if we are contentious (Proverbs 26:21).

  ❧ *cynicism,* if we see only the faults of others (Matthew 7:3).

  ❧ *misery,* if we think only of self (Philippians 2:4).

  ❧ *poor health,* if we live without the medicine of merriment (Proverbs 17:22).

  ❧ *family disruption,* if we do not work for peace (Romans 14:19).

We have to remember that the worst wreck is a human wreck. Let's watch our driving and where we're headed.

MY FAITH LOOKS UP TO THEE

Let us draw near with a true heart in full assurance of faith.

HEBREWS 10:22

This immortal hymn was written by Ray Palmer, an American minister, when he was only twenty-two years old. One day in 1830, sitting in his little room, he was engrossed in his personal problems. Discouraged and almost overwhelmed, he then and there took paper and pen and wrote this hymn, and put it away without showing it to anybody.

Years later, he met Dr. Lowell Mason in Boston. Dr. Mason asked him to write a hymn for a new hymnal he planned to publish. Palmer thought of the one he had written years before. He made a copy and gave it to Mason.

A little time passed and the two again met on the street. Hardly taking time to greet him, Dr. Mason said, "Mr. Palmer, you may do many things; you may live many years and accomplish much, but you will be known to posterity as the man who wrote, 'My Faith Looks Up to Thee.'"

My faith looks up to Thee,
Thou Lamb of Calvary,
Savior Divine!
Now hear me while I pray;
Take all my guilt away;
O let me from this day
Be wholly Thine.

When ends life's transient dream,
When death's cold, sullen stream
Shall o'er me roll,
Blest Savior, then, in love,
Fear and distrust remove;
O bear me safe above,
A ransomed soul!

DISTRACTIONS ON EVERY HAND

I am doing a great work, so that I cannot come down:
why should the work cease, while I leave it,
and come down to you?

NEHEMIAH 6:3

Years ago, a very insistent man came to visit me. He explained that some people were buying a camp for boys and girls. In these threatening times for young people, it would provide uplifting associations, clean recreation and even Bible study, supervised by honorable personnel. Different groups could go there for periods of two weeks. Then he asked me, "What do you think of it?"

"I think it's an excellent project," was my reply.

"Then you'll get out there and call on the church members and raise money to help pay for it?"

"No, I can't do that."

He continued, "If you think it's excellent, why can't you do it?"

I responded, "I do believe that it can be a good and fruitful endeavor. But just look up and down these streets. I have more work now than I can do. I can announce it. I can pray for it. And I personally can give a little money toward it, *but I can't do your job.* I must stick to mine."

Since we can't do everything, we must decide what has priority and then do it. If I had permitted these extra requests to come ahead of my own work, I never would have been able to manage the responsibilities God has given me.

AND THIS IS SUCCESS

This book of the law shall not depart from your mouth; but you shall meditate in it day and night, that you may observe to do according to all that is written in it. For then you will make your way prosperous, and then you will have good success.

JOSHUA 1:8

The word *success* appears only once in the Bible, in the above verse. In a further consideration, we offer some specifics.

And *this* is success:

> A good name is rather to be chosen than great riches, and loving favor rather than silver and gold.

PROVERBS 22:1

And *this* is success:

> A wise son makes a glad father.

PROVERBS 10:1

And *this* is success:

> Her children rise up, and call her blessed; her husband also, and he praises her.

PROVERBS 31:28

And *this* is success:

> Because I delivered the poor that cried, and the fatherless, and him that had none to help him.

JOB 29:12

And *this* is success:

> In all these things we are more than conquerors through Him who loved us.

ROMANS 8:37

And *this* is success:

> I have fought a good fight, I have finished my course, I have kept the faith: Henceforth there is laid up for me a crown of righteousness.

LOST-AND-FOUND COLUMN

He who finds his life will lose it,
and he who loses his life for My sake will find it.

MATTHEW 10:39

Jesus, the author of the above words, ran His own lost-and-found column; and there is more to it than watches and diamonds, dogs and cats. Man's happiness is there. He who finds his life within himself loses it, but he who loses his life outside of himself finds it.

The world's greatest book on psychology is the Bible. The highest cause in which we can lose ourselves is *God's* religion, for it includes all the principles that can take us out of our selfish selves and extend us to God and to others.

Those who live in the shell of self habitually focus their attention inwardly until outside interests have little appeal. The result is discontent and boredom, and even worse—one becomes the prison for his soul.

> *Oh, doom beyond the saddest guess,*
> *As the long years of God unroll,*
> *To make thy dreary selfishness*
> *The prison of a soul.*

JOHN GREENLEAF WHITTIER

On the other hand, we can find a new life of delight in simply losing ourselves in another interest. Getting out of the hull of self will take the emptiness out of life and fill it with rapture. As the little flower seed never becomes beautiful and fragrant until it breaks out of itself and grows up and blossoms, so it is with us.

REACHING FOR THE BETTER LIFE

. . . .

Therefore leaving the principles of the doctrine of Christ, let us go on unto perfection.

HEBREWS 6:1

*H*ere are some noble principles that, if we follow them, will assure us of a meaningful and illustrious life:

❧ *Walk with God.* The direction is right. The journey is joyful. And it gives no room to go astray.

❧ *Be a friend to man.* Let's help those in need. It is bread cast on the waters. It always returns.

❧ *Behave ourselves like adults.* We can't whimper like a baby, fuss like a child or quit like an adolescent.

❧ *Be a watchman on duty.* We must guard our speech, guard our faith, guard our honor.

❧ *Treat everybody with respect and courtesy,* for each is in the image of God.

❧ *Honor every commitment to God and man.* It is better not to vow than to vow and then break it.

❧ *Be an example.* People follow better than they take orders.

❧ *Keep a cool head.* Hot heads don't solve problems. Operating with a short fuse makes for a quick explosion.

❧ *Keep a warm heart.* We need to be tender, sympathetic, kind. A heart that feels with others is always welcome.

❧ *"Let all that you do be done in love"* (1 Corinthians 16:13). When motivated by love, any mistake we may make will be only one of judgment.

DEALING WITH DISAPPOINTMENT

. . . .

That night they caught nothing.

JOHN 21:3

Disappointment! Disappointment! It comes in many ways and in many forms. But the letdown is always the same. How low we sink is determined by the the height of our hopes and the value we've placed on them.

On the Take

She took my hand without a blush,
She took my candy with a rush,
She took the costly wrap of fur,
She took the diamonds I bought her,
She took my flowers and did ware,
She took my time I could spare,
She took my ring with loving smile,
She took my rides mile after mile,
She took my kisses, happy girl,
She took my plans for our new world,
She took everything I could buy,
And then—she took the other guy.

Life has its disappointments: Courtship without marriage. Clouds without rain. Trees without fruit. Crops without harvest. Business without profit. Education without practicality. Work without promotion. Home without love. Manuscript without publisher.

But it is better to hope, plan, pursue and be disappointed than to expect nothing. That kind of living is not living, only a disappointing existence.

OUR PERSONAL WAR

Beloved, I beg you as sojourners and pilgrims,
abstain from fleshly lusts which war against the soul.

1 PETER 2:11

Concerning the war that rages, we further read: "For the flesh lusts against the Spirit, and the Spirit against the flesh; so that you cannot do the things that you would" (Galatians 5:17).

There is a conflict between two powers, and man is caught in the middle. If he wills to do good, he is opposed by the flesh; if he wills to do evil, he is countered by the Spirit. The Christian life is one long conflict between the opposing forces of the flesh and the Spirit. The inclinations and desires of the flesh are contrary to those formed in us by the renewing of the Spirit. They can never be harmonized. One set of principles must win over the other.

It is a war for the soul on the battlefield of life. How may the better nature win?

❦ First, we must *resolve to triumph.* There is power in resolution.

❦ Second, we must *fortify ourselves with prayer.* "Watch and pray that you enter not into temptation."

❦ Third, we must *strengthen ourselves with the Word of God.* The Psalmist did this: "Your word have I hid in my heart, that I might not sin against You" (Psalm 119:11).

❦ Fourth, we must *fight off evil by staying busy doing good.* Idleness makes one vulnerable to attack.

❦ Fifth, let's *trust God as if all depends on Him,* and strive with all our might as if everything depends on us. This double power will suffice.

Every victory won strengthens us to win another.

LIGHTS FOR A DARK WORLD

That you may become blameless
and harmless, children of God without fault
in the midst of a crooked and perverse generation,
among whom you shine as lights in the world.

PHILIPPIANS 2:15

Centuries ago Christ launched His movement to enlighten a benighted world. He selected twelve Apostles to whom He handed the torch. You know the inspiring story of their heroic devotion to the history-making cause. After His crucifixion those Twelve in just a few years had faithfully and tirelessly spread Christianity throughout the world.

Today the fainthearted say, "I am only one among billions. What can little *me* do?"

Alone we are all weak, but shining together we are powerful.

It has been reported that an unusual request was made in a religious service in which 90,000 had assembled. The lights were turned out and darkness settled over the crowd of people who sat there in curious silence. A voice over the loudspeaker cut through the blackness: "Look this way. I'm going to light a match." Immediately there was the small gleam of the tiny flame. Again the voice was heard: "Now I want each of you to light a match, please." Here and there flames appeared, more and more, until the stadium was aglow with brightness.

It all started with one match. If each will shine, it will light our nation and our world.

A Psalm of Life

. . . .

Blessed are the dead which die in the Lord from henceforth:
Yes, says the Spirit, that they may rest from their labors;
and their works do follow them.

REVELATION 14:13

There are two sublime thoughts that are exceedingly encouraging. One, when a man's body dies his spirit continues to live. The second, man's works continue to live and follow after him.

Life is real! Life is earnest!
and the grave is not its goal;
"Dust thou art, to dust returnest,"
Was not spoken of the soul.

In the world's broad field of battle,
In the bivouac of life,
Be not dumb driven cattle!
Be a hero in the strife.

Lives of great men all remind us
We can make our lives sublime,
And, departing, leave behind us
Footprints on the sands of time.

Footprints, that perhaps another,
Sailing o'er life's solemn main,
A forlorn and shipwrecked brother,
Seeing, shall take heart again.

Let us, then, be up and doing,
With a heart for any fate;
Still achieving, still pursuing,
Learn to labor and to wait.

HENRY WADSWORTH LONGFELLOW

WHAT MAKES ME

. . . .

For as he thinks in his heart,
so is he.

PROVERBS 23:7

Said in few words, what we *think,* we *are.*

 ❖ A person consists of what he thinks.

 ❖ The tranquil, peaceful life comes from thinking; so does the troubled one.

 ❖ The most necessary task for man is to think wisely.

 ❖ Thinking is the hardest work in the world; it is easier to stay in the rut.

 ❖ Thoughts are mightier than the hand.

 ❖ A moment's thinking is worth an hour's work.

 ❖ When one thinks, he does more than "hitch his wagon to a star"; he becomes a star, and shine he does.

 ❖ If people would think for themselves, they would avoid much exploitation.

 ❖ Thinking without acting takes one nowhere.

 ❖ The person who says just what he thinks should stop and think before he says it.

 ❖ If we think, there is a good chance we will go aright. It is the thoughtless who go astray.

THINK WITH WINGS

. . . .

But they that wait upon the Lord shall renew their strength;
they shall mount up with wings as eagles; they shall run,
and not be weary; and they shall walk, and not faint.

ISAIAH 40:31

Are you weary? Do you feel defeated? Are you about to faint? Then put wings on your thoughts. Think positively. Think constructively. The measure of a person is in his thoughts. "For as he thinks in his heart, so is he" (Proverbs 23:7). This was Solomon's summation of a person: his strength or weakness, his courage or cowardice, his peace or confusion, and his happiness or gloom. Indeed, *we are what we think.*

Each of us needs to recognize that he can change his life by changing his attitude.

Most assuredly there is power in believing. What we believe, in keeping with reality, has a way of happening. If we believe that life is a wonderful, glorious, thrilling experience, our belief will go far toward making it so. Anybody who starts thinking he is strong *will* find strength. If he thinks he can bear what is placed upon him, he *will* hold up. If he thinks he can overcome, he *will* triumph. He is giving his thoughts wings.

But the opposite is just as true. If we think negatively, our lives will be shrouded with gloom and despair. One negatively sick man said, "I always expect the worst and I have never been disappointed!"

Positive, optimistic, unshaken thinking has the power to open new worlds to us. If you are dissatisfied with the little world your thoughts have created and pulled in around you, then change your thinking and a new world will open up.

THE HARDEST THING TO KEEP

. . . .

Whoever guards his mouth and tongue
keeps his soul from troubles.

PROVERBS 21:23

The hardest thing for any person to keep is his tongue. He can keep his house, his car, his job, his health, his payments, his credit up, and his weight down, easier than he can keep his tongue.

The Tongue

"The boneless tongue so small and weak
Can crush and kill," declared the Greek;
"The tongue destroys a greater horde,"
The Turk asserts, "than does the sword."

The Persian proverb wisely saith,
"A lengthy tongue—an early death,"
Or sometimes takes this form instead,
"Don't let your tongue cut off your head."

"The tongue can speak a word, whose speed,"
Says the Chinese, "outstrips the steed,"
While Arab sages this impart:
"The tongue's great storehouse is the heart."

From Hebrew with the maxim sprung:
"Though feet may slip, ne'er let the tongue";
The sacred writer crowns the whole:
"Who keeps his tongue, doth keep his soul."

Knowing it is difficult for us to keep the tongue, God has given us this admonition in the sacred writings: "Let every man be swift to hear, slow to speak" (James 1:19).

OUR HERITAGE

. . . .

One generation passes away,
and another generation comes;
but the earth abides for ever.

ECCLESIASTES 1:4

Hugh Black has said, "All things we cherish, our order of life, our institutions, all that we call our civilization, have come to us as a heritage from the past.

"They are the labors of countless generations of men and women who have lived and died. Craven must we be, if we lay down the load and put an end to the dream.

"It is a long way we have come, a long and toilsome climb, and there are blood marks on every flinty track. The checkered human career has in its deeds of high emprise, acts of sacrifice, tales of heroism that glorify the race. Lives have been lived with patience and courage and selfless love that create in us reverence for man.

"They make it easy for us to believe great things of the race to which they and we belong. We are unworthy of our past heritage and our present privilege if we forget the great society of the noble living and the noble dead."

When we take all this into consideration we see there is hope for the human race. In every infant born—regardless of parentage and circumstances—the hope of mankind is born anew. That child is born with a spark of divinity that lends itself to knowledge, refinement, virtue, brotherhood and the power to make this old earth turn a little easier. It makes us very glad that Noah and his family didn't miss the boat.

HARD ON RELIGION

. . . .

Watch and pray, lest you enter into temptation.
The spirit indeed is willing, but the flesh is weak.

MATTHEW 26:41

One of my jobs when I was a boy was to milk at least one or two cows twice daily. An old, contrary cow can really try one's nerves...and one's religion. I know. I've had my vexing episodes. I have been in the milk shed bright and early, when the temperature hovered just a little above zero. The cow's tail was loaded with cockleburs she had picked up in the pasture. Without any provocation on my part, she kicked, knocked over the milk pail, came down with her foot on my frozen foot, and simultaneously whisked and raked that cocklebur tail across my cold face. Now that was hard on religion.

I wondered how any living thing could get that mean. I never hurt her, but I must admit I did threaten her. I would tell her, "You do that just one more time and we're going to have steak for dinner instead of milk!"

Now looking back to yesteryear, I'm grateful for the experiences. Wouldn't take anything for them. I learned a little more about self-control and a lot more about the value of a glass of milk. *We have to live to be prepared for living.* In every problem we overcome, God gives us a little more determination and power for the next one.

BOBBY AND THE CONCRETE
· ·
Verily, verily...
JOHN 3 :3

"Verily." It's a little word, but it's concrete. On Sunday morning the preacher spoke tenderly and eloquently on "The Compassionate Jesus." One of his points was that Jesus loved little children, gathered them to Him and blessed them. It was a moving sermon of great substance.

The following week the preacher was in a different role; he was the director of the church's Vacation Bible School. The children were fresh out of school, possessed with the vacation spirit, and ready to free their pent-up feelings.

After a few days the preacher's nerves became edgy. An added pressure was the contractor's pouring of concrete on the parking lot. The breaking point came when the minister spotted Bobby stepping in the concrete. He thundered, "Bobby! Bobby! *Bobby!*" (getting louder each time). "Get out of there! Don't you know better than that?"

Bobby (his mother's little, never-rebuked darling) went home crying. Immediately the irate mother called the nerve-tattered preacher and reminded him of last Sunday's sermon. "It was excellent rhetoric," she said, "but what about putting it into practice yourself? If you love Bobby, why did you speak so harshly to him?"

"Listen, lady," replied the minister, "I do love Bobby, but I must admit that I'm being tempted to love him in the abstract, not in the concrete."

Really, Christianity is a concrete religion. It pertains to the practical and particular as opposed to the general. It centers our thoughts on that which is real and involves us in the living of actual events.

GROW UNTIL YOU OUTGROW YOUR SHELL
. . . .

The righteous shall flourish like the palm tree:
he shall grow like a cedar in Lebanon.

PSALM 92:12

A man once said, "If you think I'm awful now, be glad you didn't know me when I was worse. I am improving." Ounce-by-ounce improvement shall in time make a ton of difference.

It is incumbent upon us to grow. The status quo is not good enough. The challenge is for improvement. It is difficult to remain stationary; one either progresses or regresses. There are two major lessons to learn in growing: to control oneself and to be under God's control.

It is wonderful and exhilarating that we can grow into a larger and more beautiful person. Growth is a lifetime activity. We need to grow, grow, grow, until we outgrow your shell and move into a more stately mansion. Oliver Wendell Holmes put it this way:

> *Build thee more stately mansions, oh, my soul,*
> *As the swift seasons roll!*
> *Leave thy low-vaulted past!*
> *Let each new temple, nobler than the last,*
> *Shut thee from heaven with a dome more vast,*
> *Till thou at length are free,*
> *Leaving thine outgrown shell by life's unresting sea!*

THE GOOD MAN'S TRIUMPH

· ·

They that seek the Lord
shall not want any good thing.

PSALM 34:10

This Psalm has been called "The Good Man's Triumph." There are many present and eternal advantages in seeking and serving the Lord. Here are some of His assurances:

❧ *We shall not want for salvation.* "For You, Lord, are good, and ready to forgive" (Psalm 86:5).

❧ *We shall not want for rest.* "Come unto me, all you who labor and are heavy laden, and I will give you rest" (Matthew 11:28).

❧ *We shall not want for direction.* "leaving us an example, that you should follow in His steps" (1 Peter 2:21).

❧ *We shall not want for companionship.* "Lo, I am with you always, even unto the end of the world" (Matthew 28:20).

❧ *We shall not want for light.* "He who follows Me shall not walk in darkness" (John 8:12).

❧ *We shall not want for peace.* "When a man's ways please the Lord, He makes even his enemies to be at peace with him" (Proverbs 16:7).

❧ *We shall not want for help in time of trouble.* "In the day of my trouble I will call upon You: for You will answer me" (Psalm 86:7).

❧ *We shall not want for confidence in death.* "Though I walk through the valley of the shadow of death, I will fear no evil" (Psalm 23:4).

ACCORDING TO YOUR FAITH

. . . .

According to your faith let it be to you.

MATTHEW 9:29

The man took a little Bible from his pocket and said, "I owe all my success to this book. I wouldn't have made the grade without it. I was a good clerk in a store and had ambitions to have my own store, but I was shackled with inferiority. Ambition pulled me one way, and misgivings pulled me another. The result was tattered nerves. In my desperation, I went through the Bible and underscored the verses I thought would help me the most in overcoming my problem of doubt and defeatism. Then I memorized certain ones. I said them every day. At first they seemed like empty words, but they gradually took on meaning and became an integral part of me. They changed my whole outlook on life and brought optimism and happiness to my troubled spirit."

In addition to the above Scripture, two others he marked were:

He staggered not at the promise of God through unbelief.

ROMANS 4:20

For we walk by faith, not by sight.

2 CORINTHIANS 5:7

God gave each person a mind which is his "thought factory"; there his thoughts are turned out. As to whether the thoughts are positive or negative depends on what he believes or does not believe. This is how simple it is: have *doubt,* fail and be unhappy; *believe,* succeed and be happy.

A TIGHT PLACE

· ·

He went away sorrowful,
for he had great possessions.

MATTHEW 19:22

Several years ago, a rich but miserly old man was asked to contribute money toward a statue of George Washington that would be erected in New York.

"Of Washington? Washington! How useless!" the rich man exclaimed. "Washington does not need a statue. I keep him enshrined in my heart."

The solicitor gave point after point as to why it was a worthy cause, but to no avail. Naturally he became a little perturbed at the millionaire's closeness. He quietly remarked as he rose to leave, "All I can say is, if the 'Father of our Country' is in your heart, he's in a very tight place."

Even the most greedy, however, will give in death that which he cannot take with him.

There is a fable about a pig which lamented its lack of popularity. In speaking to a cow the pig admitted that cows give milk and cream, but insisted that pigs give more. The pig said, "We pigs give bacon, ham and porkchops. People even pickle our feet. I don't see why you cows are so highly esteemed."

The cow thought for a moment and replied, "Maybe it's because we give while we're still living."

Living and giving go together for an enrichment and happiness that cannot be obtained in death's gift.

THE GREATEST GIFT

. . . .

And this they did, not as we hoped,
but first gave themselves to the Lord,
and then to us by the will of God.

2 CORINTHIANS 8:5

The charming story has come to me concerning some Christian natives in a foreign land. The missionary who introduced them to Christ them later taught them sacrifice, which is the basis of Christianity. God sacrificed His Son. The Son sacrificed His life. And the early Christians sacrificed their lives; if not in one final act, they did in daily activities.

To simplify and facilitate the lesson giving, the missionary drew a large circle on the ground and had them place their gifts within it. Different gifts were offered: corn, watermelons, shells, beads, a puppy, whatever one had. One poor native walked into the ring and said, "I give myself."

And that was the greatest gift of all: *self.* Self is a rarer gift than gold. All gifts fade into nothingness when the giver holds back himself. One thing that can impede the growth of Christianity today is the gift without the giver—a gift from the hand but not the heart. The same imbalance—a gift without the giver—can be injurious to the rearing of children, the sustaining of the husband-wife relationship, and the continuance of employee-employer connection. If the heart isn't there, it's only routine service. When self is no part of rich gifts, how paltry they are!

Not what we give,
But what we share—
For the gift without
The giver is bare.

JAMES RUSSELL LOWELL

A FRIEND

. . . .

To him who is afflicted,
pity should be shown by his friend.

JOB 6:14

There is no higher calling than to be a friend to mankind. Neither is there a better way to help self. For in doing for others we actually do for ourselves. Every act of kindness shown to fellow pilgrims makes us a little stronger and happier ourselves.

Back in 700 B.C. Homer said of an ideal man, "He was a friend to man, and he lived in a house by the side of the road." Centuries later Sam Walter Foss gave us a very meaningful poem based on the same thought:

The House by the Side of the Road

Let me live in a house by the side of the road,
Where the race of men go by—
The men who are good and the men who are bad,
As good and as bad as I.
I would not sit in the scorner's seat,
Or hurl the cynic's ban—
Let me live in a house by the side of the road
And be a friend to man.

I see from my house by the side of the road,
By the side of the highway of life,
The men who press with the ardor of hope,
The men who are faint with the strife.
But I turn not away from their smiles nor their tears,
Both parts of an infinite plan—
Let me live in a house by the side of the road
And be a friend to man.

WHEN WE ARE WRONG

Zaccheus...said...
if I have taken anything from anyone
by false accusation, I restore fourfold.

LUKE 19:8

A man sold my father a cow soon after she had been bitten by a mad dog. My father, unaware of this, put the cow out on the range. Within a few days she developed hydrophobia (rabies), and this crazed, charging animal almost killed my father. Later the seller apologized: "I was wrong to sell you that cow. I'm sorry."

Nobody is perfect. Everybody commits wrong. "For all have sinned." As great as the Apostle Peter was, he was not above wrong. The Apostle Paul said, "But when Peter had come to Antioch, I withstood him to the face, because he was to be blamed" (Galatians 2:11). And concerning himself, Paul said, "I do not consider myself yet to have taken hold of it" (Philippians 3:13). He was still imperfect.

But one area in which we *can* be perfect is the correction of wrongs. We can change, apologize, restore, make amends, make restitution. We can right our wrongs. Repentance, which is demanded of all of us, requires restitution.

If wrong has been done, refusing to admit it will not blot it out. This only adds wrong to wrong. When we've done wrong, we can't make it right by committing another wrong to try to cover it up or by persecuting the person we have wronged.

The only right and honorable action to take when we have done something wrong is to say so. When we can correct a wrong, it is our responsibility to do so. To err is human; to correct is to be a better human.

WHO BUILT THE HOUSE?

For every house is built by someone,
but He who built all things is God.
HEBREWS 3:4

This verse from the Scriptures is an appeal to logic. The house didn't just happen. It had to have a builder. The world didn't just happen, either. It had to have a Creator.

Logic is the mother of all arts and the safeguard of society's sanity. If we disregard it, we will pay the price. Unsound thinking has an extremely high price tag.

Many of the wise sayings are nothing but worded logic. And the art of being wise is the art of perceiving the logical. It's plain common sense.

Note these maxims of common sense:

- *Don't expect a full barn unless you fill it.*
- *Don't run with the hare and hold with the hound.*
- *An ounce of prevention is worth a pound of cure.*
- *As the twig is bent so grows the tree.*
- *If you want eggs, be willing to put up with the hen's cackle.*

The Bible is filled with logic. Here are some examples:

*Does a spring send forth fresh water and bitter
from the same opening?*
JAMES 3:11

Neither do they light a candle, and put it under a bushel.
MATTHEW 5:15

For whatever a man sows, that he will also reap.
GALATIANS 6:7

Let's shape our lives by logic. The best place to get it is the Bible. Let's read it to be wise.

MAKE ME SOMEBODY

. . . .

Make me walk in the path of Your commandments,
for I delight in it.

PSALM 119:35

The highest and most ideal life is one consecrated to God and dedicated to helping and serving man, expressed by the Psalmist in the prayer which says, "O Lord...make me." It is elevating for a person to have the noble ambition to be somebody and for his life to be useful and helpful. It is uplifting that we, too, have such consummate aims.

§ *Make me a channel of blessing* that flows into the lives of others.

§ *Make me a vessel of salvation* to those who stand in need of pardon.

§ *Make me a light* that shines in a world darkened by wrong, exploitation and sin.

§ *Make me a soldier* who defends the true and the right.

§ *Make me an ambassador of peace* in a world torn by strife and war.

§ *Make me a tree* planted by the rivers of water that produces good fruit for a morally and spiritually famished society.

§ *Make me a healing balm* for the hearts that mourn and break.

God is ready to help. Are we ready to ask?

THE CLOUDS PASS

Weeping may endure for a night,
but joy comes in the morning.

PSALM 30:5

Every life must have some clouds, some more and worse
than others. But the clouds pass. As William Cowper said,

> *God moves in a mysterious way*
> *His wonders to perform,*
> *And plants His footsteps in the sea*
> *And rides upon the storm.*

> *Ye fearful saints, fresh courage take,*
> *The clouds ye so much dread*
> *Are big with mercy and shall break*
> *With blessings on your head.*

Pain passes. All of us have some pain, ranging from mild
to severe. But our bodies have been made to adjust to circumstances. Time is needed for pain to pass. If the pain does
not pass, however, God can give us the strength to bear it.
He did that for Paul who had a thorn in his flesh, whatever
that thorn might have been. Paul's pain remained but so did
the God who strengthened him.

Sorrow and grief pass. The black cloud hangs low at
times. Not being able to see through it, we just walk through
it by faith. At first it seems the hurt will never lessen, but it
gradually eases as we adjust to the loss and revise our living.
It is comforting to know that the clouds can break with
blessings on our head. "Our light affliction, which is but for
a moment, is working for us a far more exceeding and eternal weight of glory" (2 Corinthians 4:17).

I'M STILL STANDING UP INSIDE

. . . .

My son, do not despise the chastening of the Lord,
nor be discouraged when you are rebuked by Him;
for whom the Lord loves He chastens,
and scourges every son whom He receives.

HEBREWS 12:5-6

A teacher said to a child who had been misbehaving, "Richard, this is the fifth time this week I have had to punish you. What do you have to say?"

Richard replied, "I'm glad it's Friday."

The end of the school week would not end the problem. It was deeper than that.

An even smaller child has illustrated this fact. Oh, how we learn from children! Two-year-old Jimmy kept standing up in his highchair, although his mother kept reseating him and admonishing him to stay seated. After the fourth time Jimmy stayed down, but he protested, "Mommy, I'm still standing up inside."

The mother disciplined Jimmy because she loved him. God also chastens us for the same reason—He loves us. I don't always know the form or manner in which the chastening will come. But I know the God who will administer it. This means it is for my good. And whatever is for my good, though unpleasant at the time, should be endured patiently, looking forward to the end result of a better person and happier days.

I SHALL NOT PASS AGAIN THIS WAY

· ·

When a few years are finished,
I shall go the way of no return.

JOB 16:22

The bread that bringeth strength I want to give,
The water pure that bids the thirsty live;
I want to help the fainting day by day;
I'm sure I shall not pass again this way.

I want to give goodness and joy for tears,
The faith to conquer crowding doubts and fears;
Beauty for ashes may I give always;
I'm sure I shall not pass again this way.

I want to give to others hope and faith,
I want to do all that the Master saith;
I want to live aright from day to day;
I'm sure I shall not pass again this way.

The certainty of the proposition "I shall not pass again this way" dictates to us that whatever we intend to do we need to do now. Too much time has already been lost and therefore it is incumbent upon us to make the best use of the fleeting moments that remain.

Our little day passes so quickly. The shadow we cast quickly lengthens until it fades into night. "I go to the place from which I shall not return, even to the land of darkness and the shadow of death" (Job 10:21). The day is passing. We must race with the sun to accomplish our purposes.

THE POWER OF LITTLE THINGS

. . . .

See how great a forest a little fire kindles!

JAMES 3:5

In the same vein and logic we can say:

- *how great a strife* a little word ignites.
- *how great a liar* a little fib commences.
- *how great a murderer* a little hate kindles.
- *how great a wrath* a little temper foments.
- *how great a fool* a little riches can manifest.
- *how great a drunkard* a little wine produces.
- *how great an apostasy* a little error starts.
- *how great a destruction* a little neglect effects.

But also:

- *how great a church* a little beginning starts.
- *how great a movement* a little vision awakens.
- *how great a person* a little child becomes.
- *how great a lump* a little leaven changes.
- *how great a friendship* a little effort produces.
- *how great a joy* a little smile gives.
- *how great an encouragement* a little word provides.
- *how great an appreciation* a little gift stirs.
- *how great a beam* a little candle throws.
- *how great an oak* a little acorn becomes.

Greatness is inherent in people, qualities, things and circumstances, just as it is in an oak. I am little and I know it, but with God's help I can be a powerful force.

HONORING FATHERS

. . . .

Honor your father and mother.

EPHESIANS 6:2

One of the ancient duties enjoined upon mankind is to honor parents. It is old in origin but just as new in its essentiality and practicality as ever. It is an urgent need of each new generation. A person can no more outgrow this need than one can outgrow the need of basic character.

A flagrant disregard of this divine law to honor our fathers has in it the seeds of frustration, violence and degradation. Violation of it will produce in children a mischievous self-assertion and bitter resentment of all authority and superiority. So one of the preventions of juvenile delinquency is to honor the father and accept his headship in the family.

Disrespect, ingratitude and neglect of the father destroy individual character, which in turn tears at the whole social structure; for the family is the cornerstone of society. Affection and respect for our fathers are cardinal virtues, and a society divested of them cannot long survive.

Now for a little confession. Our fathers deserved more honor than we could appreciate or give when we were young. Young people have to grow up, and time is an effective teacher. The years are fraught with strong opposition and staggering blows from a world that young people often think is easy to conquer. Sons and daughters may not learn this until their fathers are either old or dead, but there is one thing sure: *they will learn.*

FATHER, AN IDEAL

. . . .

We have a father, an old man.

GENESIS 44:20

The demands upon a father are great. God knew that our world would require courageous minds, watchful eyes, ready hands and true faith (actually, many strong, enduring qualities), so He created *fathers*.

An Ideal

I wish I were as big a man,
As big a man,
As bright a man,
I wish I were as right a man in all this earthly show,
As broad and high and long a man,
As strong a man,
As fine a man,
As pretty near divine a man as one I used to know.

I wish I were as grave a man,
As brave a man,
As keen a man,
As learned and serene a man, as fair to friend and foe;
I wish I owned sagaciousness
And graciousness,
As should a man
Who hopes to be as good a man as one I used to know.

I'd be a creature glorious,
Victorious,
A wonder-man,
Not just-as-now-a blunder man whose ways
And thoughts are slow.
If I could only be the man,
One-half of one degree the man,
I used to think my father was, when I was ten or so.

BENTON BRALEY

THE HEROIC FATHER

. . . .

O my son Absalom! my son, my son Absalom! if only
I had died in your place! O Absalom, my son, my son!

2 SAMUEL 18:33

We esteem our fathers because of their heroism. Their sweat and tears and blood, shed for us, testify to their heroic nature. He who struggles for others when the easy way is to run *is a hero*, call him what you will. You know the brave story of your father's sacrifices—his rigorous toil and long hours, maybe two jobs, his unremitting thrift, the slow accumulation of savings, at times his bitter discouragement, but also the outpouring of happiness as he realized his hopes for you.

Too often we forget the price that our fathers have paid. We enjoy the fruits of their labors but fail to see the sacrifices behind those blessings. The world sees the glitter of the gold and not the sweat of the man who wielded the pick in yonder mountainside.

Perhaps we have been woefully negligent in honoring the heroic father who takes the wounds of the everyday struggles of life. We are protected because he courageously dared. The highest and noblest spirit is "that a man lay down his life for another." Our fathers did this not in one supreme gift but in the giving of themselves little by little, day by day. The daily conflicts of earning a living and heading a household bring out the slumbering qualities of the hero.

Not at the battle front merited in story,
Not in the blazing wreck, steering to glory;
Not while in martyr-pangs soul and flesh sever,
Lives he—this hero now; hero forever.

JAMES BRAIDWOOD

A Father Refuses to Weaken

. . . .

My father fought for you and adventured his life.

JUDGES 9:17

A father knows he cannot weaken, because his children believe in him; he cannot falter, because they trust him.

Years ago a father and a son were following a dangerous mountain trail. They came to a place where a huge rock jutted out over the precipice, leaving only a hanging portion as the pathway. With much difficulty and danger the father traversed the perilous spot. Then holding to the rock with one big hand, he reached the other out over the cliff and told the boy to step on his hand and thus pass around the rock to safety: "Don't be afraid to step on my hand. It's strong; it won't give way." The boy did and the hand held.

Thousands of less dramatic examples could be cited. It is a common practice in the everyday struggles of life. A father extends his hand over countless precipices and chasms and says, "Step on it; it will not give way." There is too much faith in a father for his big, manly hand to weaken, and by more trust in it and more usage it becomes as iron.

This is a father's prayer:

However humble the place I may hold
On the lowly trails I have trod,
There's a child who bases his faith in me;
There's a dog who thinks I'm a god.

Lord, keep me worthy—Lord, keep me clean
And fearless and undefiled,
Lest I lose caste in the sight of a dog,
And the wide clear eyes of a child!

C. T. DAVIS

A Father's Tribute to His Son

· ·

A wise son makes a glad father.

PROVERBS 10:1

One of the grandest tributes a father ever gave to a deceased son was given by Charles G. Dawes. The son, Rufus Fearing Dawes, had drowned. The father had been comptroller of the currency under President Cleveland and had held other high positions. The father's tribute was read by the minister at the young man's funeral. Among other things, the father said:

"I have taken him with me among the greatest in the nation, and looked in vain for any evidence in him of awe or even curiosity. He has taken me, asking me to help them, among the poor and lowly of earth.... He did not smoke, nor swear, nor drink. He was absolutely clean. I never saw him angry. In twenty-one years he never gave me just cause for serious reproach. He was extremely ambitious. He was extremely proud. Upon one occasion, years ago, when I mistakenly reproached him, he patiently explained my error, and then peremptorily demanded and received an apology from me.... My boy lived long enough to 'win out.' Whatever the years would have added would be only material. In a man's character is his real career."

This tribute came from memories. The son was taken, but the father was left a world of precious memories which meant more than the world itself. Our memories are companions and he who has them is not alone. Beautiful memories are helpful friends, inspiring us to reach upward to the higher and nobler life. To our dead who have fallen asleep in the Lord, we say: *Though you have moved on, a lot of you remains here. To live in hearts that love you is not to die.*

MAKE ME A CHILD
. . . .

Little children...
of such is the kingdom of heaven.
MATTHEW 19:14

Last night my little boy confessed to me
Some childish wrong;
And kneeling at my knee
He prayed with tears—
"Dear God, make me a man
Like Daddy—wise and strong.
I know You can."

Then while he slept
I knelt beside his bed,
Confessed my sins,
And prayed with low-bowed head,
"O God, make me a child
Like my child here—
Pure, guileless,
Trusting Thee with faith sincere."

Nothing is as thirsty as a child who has just gone to bed. The parent who desires the purity of a child is also thirsty— for the living water of which the Lord spoke.

The child is very believing—believes every word he or she is told. So do the godly parents, *if* that word has come from the Lord. Faith and faithfulness are linked together. The Bible says, "Be not faithless, but believing" (John 20:27).

No human is as forgiving as a little child. Adults must be forgiving to be childlike and to find forgiveness for themselves.

So this is my prayer: *Lord, make me a child.*

ONLY SIX BUT HE COULD READ

. . . .

Till I come, give attendance to reading,
to exhortation, to doctrine.

1 TIMOTHY 4:13

My little grandson had just finished the first grade. He could read unusually well, and I was very proud of him. Feeling the need of his comradeship, one day I took him with me to the hospital, where he was to wait in the reception room while I went up to encourage a patient. In the waiting room we happened to meet friends who were reading the newspaper. This presented an opportunity for the six-year-old to read the newspaper aloud for them. They marveled at his reading skill.

Reading is an accomplishment God intends for all of us to attain and use often. I know He does, because our God is the God of literature. He wrote the Ten Commandments on tablets of stone. He commanded Jeremiah, "Write all the words that I have spoken to you in a book" (Jeremiah 30:2). Jesus said, "But these are written, that you might believe" (John 20:31). Why did He write if He did not intend for us to read?

The person who does not read simply because he doesn't care to has no advantage over the person who cannot read. Reading gets us out of the rut of our own thinking and allows us to look into the minds others. Reading increases our knowledge, boosts our spirits, augments our thinking, enhances our self-confidence and makes us more useful on the job. Even if we read only a little, it will make a big difference in a year.

KEEP ON KEEPING ON

· ·

Indeed we count them blessed who endure.

JAMES 5:11

The teacher thought her lecture on perseverance was making a positive impression on her audience. In describing the gritty, never-turn-back person, she said, "He drove straight down the road to his goal. He never looked to the left or right, but pushed forward, moved by the drive to get there. His purpose was definite and inflexible. Neither friend nor stranger could have turned him from his course. All who crossed his path should have known that he was coming head-on. What would you call such a man?"

One student spoke up: "A truck driver."

Perseverance! Endurance! Stickability! No amount of talent, education, finesse or looks will serve as a substitute for the old bulldog spirit of hanging in there. Without it we are doomed to failure or, at best, to mediocrity.

"Faint heart never won a fair lady," nor outran one either.

And we won't need to make a "comeback" if we keep going. So if we're chugging along on the right road, let's not quit.

Don't Quit

When things go wrong, as they sometimes will,
When the road you're trudging seems all uphill,
When the funds are low and the debts are high,
And you want to smile, but you have to sigh,
When care is pressing you down a bit,
Rest, if you must; but don't you quit.

I HAVE THE EDGE

. . . .

But for him who is joined to all the living there is hope,
for a living dog is better than a dead lion.

ECCLESIASTES 9:4

I have the edge, for I have life. Here is an outline of Life:
Tender Teens, Teachable Twenties, Tireless Thirties,
Fiery Forties, Forceful Fifties, Serious Sixties, Sacred
Seventies, Aching Eighties, Nappy Nineties, and Shortening
Breath...Death.

As long as I'm breathing, there is hope for me. For where
there's life there's hope. And for this reason a living dog is
better than a dead lion.

Life is an opportunity to improve. Every today is another
chance.

Life lets me *think*. May my thoughts be constructive, elevating and uplifting. Life lets me *talk*. May my speech be
true, pure and helpful. Life lets me *do*. May my efforts center on the things that count the most and last the longest.

For a greater edge and more fruitful living, let's look to
God, who is the giver of life. He holds the key.

Indeed, life is a story in volumes three:

The Past
The Present
The Yet-to-Be
The first is finished and laid away,
The second we're reading day by day,
The third and last of volume three
Is locked from sight;
God holds the key.

TACT, THE BEST TACTIC

. . . .

I think myself happy, King Agrippa,
because today I shall answer for myself...,
especially because you are an expert in all customs
and questions which have to do with the Jews.

ACTS 26:2-3

The above passage, which is the Apostle Paul's introduction to his speech in his own defense, is a classic in diplomacy. Inasmuch as the Apostle saw the need of tact, surely all of us should as well.

Abraham Lincoln was asked to define diplomacy. After musing for a moment, he said: "I guess you might say that it's the knack of letting the other fellow have your way." In another definition of tact, Lincoln said, "It is the ability to describe others as they see themselves."

It is the flair to make a point without sticking the person. Diplomacy is the art of telling a person where to get off when he thinks he's getting on. Tact is a virtue that adapts to circumstances. It is remembering a woman's birthday without remembering her age. It is the genius to deal with a man as though he has an open mind when he has a hole in his head. It is the art of saying "Nice doggie" at the sound of growls.

Lest we be misled, tact based on double talk is not tact but hypocrisy and should be shunned. Furthermore, no matter how good diplomacy may be, in some instances it won't work. I had a wolf pup when I was a boy; and, as he grew up, I learned that pitching steaks to him wouldn't make him a vegetarian. Nevertheless, tact is the best tactic. We need to use it freely.

I CARRIED YOU

. . . .

In His love and in His pity He redeemed them;
and He bore them and carried them all the days of old.

ISAIAH 63:9

*P*erhaps we have all read and loved the anonymous but beautiful "Footprints":

"One night a man had a dream. It was plain to him that he was walking along the beach with the Lord. Across the sky flashed scenes from his life. For each scene, he noticed two sets of footprints in the sand; one belonging to him, and the other to the Lord.

"When the last scene of his life flashed before him, he looked back at the footprints in the sand. He noticed that many times along the path of his life there was only one set of footprints. He also noticed that it happened at the very lowest and saddest times in his life.

"This really bothered him and he questioned the Lord about it. 'Lord, You said that once I decided to follow, You'd walk with me all the way. But I have noticed that during the most troublesome times in my life, there is only one set of footprints. I don't understand why when I needed You most You would leave me.'

"The Lord replied, 'My precious, precious child, I love you and I would never leave you. During your times of trial and suffering, when you see only one set of footprints, it was then that I carried you.'"

Surely He hath carried our griefs and borne our sorrows.

ISAIAH 53:4

THE BASIS OF ALL IMPROVEMENT

. . . .

Examine yourselves.

2 CORINTHIANS 13:5

*L*et's examine ourselves, not the other poor soul! Did you ever notice that when we point a finger at someone else, three of our fingers are pointing back at us? This is significant, for there are at least three times as many reasons to look at self as at the other fellow.

§ First, *I can live only one life*—mine, not the other person's.

§ Second, *I am responsible for what I do,* not for what someone else does.

§ Third, *I am the master of my fate*; no one else is.

Indeed, much is gained by earnest self-examination. It is the foundation of all progress. Self-knowledge is a prerequisite for self-improvement. The most successful people are those who know themselves. See yourself as you are and go from there. Never be satisfied with your faults and weaknesses. The desire to improve shows what we are made of.

It is highly incumbent upon each of us to pull back the drapery of our own life and ask a few questions. There is no greater accomplishment than a consciousness of sincerity as the examination proceeds.

SOME MORE CHALK

· ·

Blessed is he whose transgression is forgiven,
whose sin is covered.

PSALM 32:1

At a preachers' luncheon a preacher stated in his speech that he dreamed he had gone to heaven and looked, and Grandpa was not there.

They laughed.

When his turn to speak came, Grandpa said, "That's funny, Jim, because *I* had a dream about *you* last night. I dreamed I went to heaven and the Lord gave me a piece of chalk and said, 'Go over there and write down all your sins.' And just at that moment I saw you leaving. I said, 'Jim, what are you doing? Why are you going that way?' And you said, 'I'm going to get some more chalk.'"

And the preachers roared with laughter.

One thing sure, *sin is not what it's cracked up to be.* "The way of transgressors is hard" (Proverbs 13:15). Another thing sure, *"All have sinned and come short of the glory of God"* (Romans 3:23). Moreover, *unless sin is checked it feeds on itself and multiplies,* "for our transgressions are multiplied before You, and our sins testify against us" (Isaiah 59:12).

And another thing sure, *God loves us though we are sinners*; "God commended His love toward us, in that, while we were yet sinners, Christ died for us" (Romans 5:8). And still another thing sure, *God is anxious to forgive.* "Though your sins be as scarlet, they shall be as white as snow; though they be red like crimson, they shall be as wool" (Isaiah 1:18).

MAKE HASTE SLOWLY

. . . .

You shall not go out with haste.

ISAIAH 52:12

We are told that the idea for the steam engine was born in the daydreaming of James Watt as he watched a teapot bubble. Such original ideas spring from wonder and imagination.

Ideas refuse to be rushed. They come in their own way and in their own time.

However, the motto today is, "Don't just stand there. Do something. *Do anything!*" This is because we tend to confuse mere bustle with actual achievement. But years of observation and personal experience have taught us that these maxims are not vain rhetoric:

§ Do in haste and repent in leisure.

§ Good and haste seldom meet.

§ He who is hasty fishes in an empty pond.

§ Hasty people have never hastened the sun.

§ Make haste slowly.

§ Haste is ever the parent of failure.

§ Haste makes waste...and frustration and ulcers.

Wouldn't all of us in this fast, restless, nervous world get more out of our years—and have *more* years—if we spent more time in helpful thinking? It would free us to think out answers to some of our problems and help us develop into the kind of people we would like to be.

YOU WILL BE MISSED

. . . .

Then Jonathan said to David,
"Tomorrow is the new moon; and you will be missed,
because your seat will be empty."

1 SAMUEL 20:18

It should be the ambition of all of us to live so that when we are gone, whether because of death or a move to another community, we are sure to be missed. I can't think of anything more tragic than for a departed person not to be missed.

It is possible for you to be missed for many reasons:

❧ *Your seat will be empty.* Empty chair in family circle. Empty chair in office. Empty chair in civic club. Empty seat at church.

❧ *Your tongue will be silenced.* We have been blessed many times by a wise, considerate, helpful tongue. It gave direction. It gave encouragement. "A word fitly spoken is like apples of gold in pictures of silver" (Proverbs 25:11).

❧ *Your ears will be deaf.* We shall miss those ears into which we have poured our troubles. All of us need someone in whom we can confide. It means much just to have someone to listen to us.

❧ *Your hands will be stilled.* Your hands have *worked* so that others could *have.* When Dorcas was gone, those left behind wept and looked at the garments she had made. Her hands had contributed to her good works and almsdeeds.

PUFF OF WIND

Make no friendship with an angry man,
and with a furious man do not go;
lest you learn his ways, and set a snare for your soul.

PROVERBS 22:24-25

I recall very vividly the first time I ever drove across the Great Divide in Colorado. I was struck with the awesome thought of influence and responsibility. I was at the very dividing line at which a raindrop might go toward the Atlantic Ocean or the opposite way, toward the Pacific Ocean. Then I thought on the momentous power of a little puff of wind in determining the destiny of a raindrop, how the wind it can send it on its way to one ocean or the other. I realized more fully that a little human sway at a critical point in another's life could mark the fate of that person.

Blow winds of influence, *blow!* If you're going the way I want to go, fine. If not, I will grab a limb and hold on right where I am. Our friends and associates write their names in our guest books, but they do more; they make imprints on our hearts. Many a tearful parent has said to me, "Oh, if my son (or daughter) had not gone with the wrong crowd!"

For our present and future good, we must select our associates carefully because:

⚘ a person is known by the *company* he or she keeps.

⚘ *good company* is a good coach.

⚘ *bad company* teams us with a losing coach.

JUDGE NOT

. . . .

Judge not, that you be not judged.
For with what judgment you judge, you will be judged;
and with the same measure you use,
it will be measured back to you.

MATTHEW 7:1-2

Our limited knowledge of the facts, of the hidden chain of circumstances, of all the provocative causes, keeps us from being infallible judges.

Upbringing, bias, likes and dislikes, beliefs and disbeliefs, loves and hates influence our judgment of others. This disqualifies every human from being a perfect judge.

Unquestionably, a woman's love for a man can make her a very poor judge of character; and vice versa, a man's love for a woman can cloud his judgment as well. Furthermore, we are inclined to judge people by what they have instead of what they are. This superficial assessment too prevents flawless judgment.

Another thing: our judging the inefficiencies and mistakes of others may be an indirect way of trying to call attention to our superiority and to lift ourselves by stepping on them. Judging can be an effort to compliment self by pointing out another's fault. It can be a sneaky way of saying, "See how bad that fellow is, but see how good I am."

In light of the above facts, isn't it better to leave judging to the Perfect One?

PASSING THE BUCK

. . . .

And I said to the king, "If it pleases the king,
and if your servant has found favor in your sight,
I ask that you send me to Judah, to the city
of my fathers' tombs, that I may rebuild it."

NEHEMIAH 2:5

The reason Jerusalem was in decay and disarray was that the buck had been passed too long. Now Nehemiah was willing to accept the buck and rebuild the city.

Will Rogers, one of America's favorite humorists, stated that there have been three periods in American history: "Passing of the Indian," "Passing of the Buffalo" and "Passing of the Buck."

Why "Passing of the Buck"? Maybe because of a prevailing attitude: I won't have to assume the responsibility. I won't have to be a target for criticism. If it fails, I won't be blamed; I can blame the other fellow instead. If it fails, I can be a postmortem expert.

Let's give the buck-passer his due; he is especially talented and quick in the utterance of two sets of four words: "Let George do it," and if it fails, "It is George's fault." When the buck is passed to George, of course he sometimes fails. But George gets the recognition, the honor, the role of leadership, the thrill that comes from challenge, the victory over boredom and the joy of the struggle.

We must live up to our calling, which demands responsibility and performance. We cannot live like a cow or horse that is content to whisk away the flies and eat the grass around its hoofs.

DOING GOOD

. . . .

Who went about doing good.

ACTS 10:38

This passage has reference to Christ. Every footprint He left on the sands of time points toward doing good. If we would walk in those prints, we *must* do good. Christianity demands more than confession; it requires that good be done.

Trying to get to heaven in a vessel of selfishness (helping *me* only) is about like trying to sail the Atlantic Ocean in a paper sack.

It was easy for Jesus to do good because *He was good*, and that's the secret of doing good. Flowing wells don't have to be pumped. Unless good comes out of us to help others, there is not much good in us. Understandably, the better we are, the more good we do. Doing good is one argument the atheist can't knock. So the words of John Wesley are very pertinent:

> *Do all the good you can,*
> *By all the means you can,*
> *In all the ways you can,*
> *In all the places you can,*
> *At all the times you can,*
> *To all the people you can,*
> *As long as ever you can.*

By doing good we give this old earth a little semblance of heaven. The good we do never dies. It lives on and on after we are gone. "They may rest from their labors; and their works do follow them" (Revelation 14:13).

OF FISH AND FAILURE

Master, we have toiled all night and caught nothing;
nevertheless at Your word I will let down the net.

LUKE 5:5

No doubt it was the same old story: the fish were not running, or the wind was in the wrong direction, or the water was too muddy. Anyway, Jesus' Disciples had caught nothing. *Failure.* But when they took His advice, "Launch out into the deep, and let down your nets for a catch," they caught more than the net would hold. *Success.*

At first Peter was a little reluctant to follow instruction, because he was an experienced fisherman and his opinion ruled it out; but when he threw the responsibility of success entirely upon the shoulders of the Lord, he found true success. In failure he learned to put more trust in the Lord and less trust in self. He had to fail before he could succeed.

Failure always has a victorious effect upon us when it leads us to do what Jesus commands, regardless of apparent reasons to the contrary. When we pursue this course and depend upon it, there will never be real failure.

Of course Peter still had to do what he could for himself. Christ's plan called for Peter to launch out, cast the net and pull it in. Some people fail because they expect the Lord to do everything, while others fail because they expect Him to do nothing. God gives us directions, but we have to follow them; figuratively He tells us where the fish are, but *we* have to cast the net.

SEEDS OF WISDOM

· ·

Hear instruction, and be wise,
and refuse it not.

PROVERBS 8:33

Little statements of facts have big messages. Here are enough to reshape any person's life:

❧ No one's vision is ever so keen as when he sees an opportunity to do good.

❧ No one ever stands so tall as when he stoops to lift another who has fallen.

❧ No one can walk both sides of the street at the same time.

❧ No one can climb the mountain with one step.

❧ No one can be great without serving.

❧ No one can shine and not be seen.

❧ No one can build a lasting house on the sand.

❧ No one can find ease in walking the transgressor's way.

❧ No one is stronger than he thinks he is.

❧ No one can be braver than his conscience.

❧ No one is better than his word.

❧ No one is right just because he thinks he is right.

❧ No one can find the truth who will not consider and weigh the opposite of what he believes.

❧ No one can go forward while stepping back, or walk straight while going in circles.

❧ No one can serve God in Satan's kingdom.

THE LORDLY DISH

. . . .

He asked for water, and she gave him milk;
she brought forth butter in a lordly dish.

JUDGES 5:25

Why the lordly dish? It was used only when the most distinguished and notable people were entertained in the most grandiose style. It was a gesture of the best for the best. Jael made the guest Sisera feel very important, greatly honored, and highly extolled, which allayed any suspicions that he was in any danger. However, he was in grave peril...just didn't know it. He was caught in the trap of flattery. His susceptibility to honeyed treatment literally cost him his head; he was beheaded.

Flattery has caused many a person to lose his head—if not physically, at least spiritually. People get caught up in the intoxication of flattery and fall for tricks and schemes that otherwise could not entrap them. They like to eat out of the lordly dish.

There is an expressive and spicy chapter in Solomon's Proverbs that gives an account of a man's capture by a flattering woman who wished to entice him. This is not fanciful; it is real. Solomon said: "With her enticing speech she caused him to yield, with her flattering lips she seduced him. Immediately he went after her, as an ox goes to the slaughter, or as a fool to the correction of the stocks, till an arrow struck his liver. As a bird hastens to the snare, he did not know it would take his life" (Proverbs 7:21-23).

Then why are we duped by flattery when we know it's not true? First, we like to hear it, though we know it's false. Second, even though we see through the blarney, it shows that the flatterer sees in us something worth courting. This necessitates that we be cautious of the lordly dish and beware of poison within it. Let's just look at it, not swallow it.

THE FIGHTER

. . . .

But recall the former days in which,
after you were illuminated, you endured
a great struggle with sufferings.

HEBREWS 10:32

My father used to say, "It's not the size of the dog in the fight but the size of the fight in the dog that counts."

Fighting for a noble cause ennobles the fighter, but to refuse to fight labels one as complacent or cowardly. All defeat has to do to prevail is for good people to refuse to fight.

I must forever be on guard
Against the doubts that skulk along;
I get ahead by fighting hard,
But fighting keeps my spirit strong.

My victories are small and few,
It matters not how hard I strive;
Each day the fight begins anew,
But fighting keeps my hopes alive.

My progress has been slow and hard,
I've had to climb and crawl and swim,
Fighting for every stubborn yard,
But I have kept in fighting trim.

My dearest plans keep going wrong,
Events combine to thwart my will,
But fighting keeps my spirit strong,
And I am undefeated still.

SAMUEL E. KISER

A Little Rest and Re-Creation

And they found rich, good pasture,
and the land was broad, quiet, and peaceful.

1 Chronicles 4:40

If we can't live in a place that is free, untouchable and unbothered all the time, at least we should find such a refuge part of the time.

A couple sent a playpen to some out-of-state friends who had been blessed with the arrival of their fourth child. Two weeks later the mother responded with this note: "Thanks, many thanks, and thanks again for the playpen. It comes in so handy. I sit in it every afternoon and read and think. In it the children can't get near me."

Her whimsical note emphasizes everyone's need of a quiet place. Our crowded minds and tired bodies cry out for relaxation, preferably for a place where we can lie down in green pastures and walk beside still waters—a place where nature will communicate with our spirit and whisper, "Tempest, be still."

To re-*create* body, we need to play and rest. To re-*create* mind, remove the worries and stress and then repose. To re-*create* cheerfulness, put trust in God and think of how many more things succeed than fail.

Recreation is not wasted time. It is creating, once again, that which is wanting. Life is too sacred and time is too short not to follow a course that prolongs our health and enjoyment.

A LITTLE LOWER THAN ANGELS

What is man that You are mindful of him,
and the son of man that You visit him?
For You have made him a little lower than the angels,
And You have crowned him with glory and honor.
You have made him to have dominion over the works
of Your hands; You have put all things under his feet,
all sheep and oxen even the beasts of the field,
the birds of the air, and the fish of the sea
that pass through the paths of the seas.

PSALM 8:4-8

Now this is man: a being, in God's divine order, "a little lower than the angels." He is adorned with the crown of reason, is internally endowed with a conscience, and in understanding and action is closer to the angels.

"You have made him to have dominion over the works of Your hands." God has given him the honor of being in charge of His creation. This distinction belongs to man alone.

The earth and the universe are for man. The sun in the heavens is his lamp. Night is the shade for his window. His furnace is the energies stored up in the earth, and if they should become depleted he has the sun. The vegetation and the flocks and the herds are for his sustenance and clothing. The seas can float him around the world. Space permits him to travel faster. The breathtaking spectacle of sky and sea and earth are for his good and happiness. God has given such to man, saying, "All this is for you. Have dominion over it. Be faithful to your stewardship."

LITTLE BOYS AND GIRLS
. . . .
Children's children are the crown of old men;
and the glory of children is their father.
PROVERBS 17:6

*R*eflecting on childhood gives zest to life. It renews the spark of life for older ones who are now running the last laps of their race.

I like the way Alan Beck has put it:

"*Boys* come in assorted sizes, weights and colors. They are found everywhere—on top of, underneath, inside of, climbing on, swinging from, running around or jumping to. A boy is Truth with dirt on its face, Wisdom with bubble gum in its hair and the Hope of the future with a frog in its pocket. A boy is a magical creature—you can lock him out of your workshop, but you can't lock him out of your heart.

"*Little girls*...the nicest things that happen to people. They are born with a little bit of angel-shine about them and though it wears thin sometimes, there is always enough left to lasso your heart—even when they are sitting in the mud or crying temperamental tears, or parading up the street in Mother's best clothes. A girl is Innocence playing in the mud, Beauty standing on its head, and Motherhood dragging a doll by its foot. A little girl...can muss up your home, your hair, and your dignity—spend your money, your time, and your temper—then just when your patience is ready to crack, her sunshine peeks through and you've lost again."

Truly, children are a gift from God.

THE EGG

. . . .

Watch therefore, for you do not know
what hour your Lord is coming.

MATTHEW 24:42

The egg—yes, *the egg,* because this egg was different.

Years ago, when I was holding a revival meeting in a little town, a strange thing happened. In the late afternoon as the children were gathering *eggs,* they found one that had this message indented in its shell: "Beware twelve o'clock tonight." News of this strange omen soon spread through the town and pandemonium broke loose. As the night wore on, anxiety increased. Some who had not been to church in years attended that night. Little groups sat up in prayerful vigilance, waiting for the fateful hour to come. But when the clock struck twelve, nothing unusual occurred—just a sigh of relief.

You ask, "What's the explanation?" One of the young men in that little town had gone away to college and gotten very bright. He learned that the shell of an egg could be softened by putting it in a certain solution and that words could be inscribed on it, and then by putting it in another solution it would harden, leaving the indentations. This he did and slipped it into a neighbor's hen house.

What I had not been able to do with the help of the Bible that old hen easily did with the help of a prankster. She made the townspeople think on several important matters: their ways, the brevity of life, the uncertainty of time and the end of the world.

Only God knows if the message of the mysterious egg was long-lasting.

THE ART OF IMAGINATION

Eyes have they, but they do not see;
they have ears but they do not hear.

PSALM 115:5-6

The Psalmist was describing an idol made of silver or gold. But the verses he's written also describe a person devoid of imagination, with eyes that see not and ears that hear not.

Grandmother saw Billy running around the house slapping himself and she wondered why. "Well," said Billy, "I just got so tired of doing nothing that I thought I'd ride my horse for awhile." Little Billy's imagination came to his aid. If he keeps it going, his possibilities shall become unlimited.

Einstein said, "Imagination is more powerful than knowledge." Without it, thought comes to a halt.

Imagination gives fresh eyes to look at everything, as though we had just emerged from the darkness of night into the light of day. It lifts eyes to unknown lands and charts new paths to higher goals.

This great human power of imagination, in the words of Shakespeare, "gives to airy nothing a local habitation and a name." Man, woman, boy or girl reaches into the heavens to grasp an idea and then brings it down to earth, clothes it in practicality and makes it work.

Wander among the clouds. Then come down to earth. This is the art of imagination!

WHAT CAN I DO?

. . . .

I can do all things through Christ
who strengthens me.

PHILIPPIANS 4:13

*E*ach of us has to watch the "can'ts" and "cans." We can't get off dead center if we think we can't. We can't aim low and rise high. We can't succeed if we don't try. We need to learn that we as individuals *can* do much more than we've ever thought possible. It is a known fact that nearly everybody lives below his or her potential for achievement.

It is stimulating, therefore, to think on what Horace Traubel has said:

What can I do? I can speak out when others are silent. I can say man when others say money. I can stay up when others are asleep. I can keep on working when others have stopped to play.

I can give life big meanings when others give life little meanings. I can say love when others say hate. I can say every man when others say one man. I can try events by a hard test when others try them by an easy test.

What can I do? I can give myself to life when others may refuse themselves to life.

What can you and I do as individuals? We can be tiny lights in a world of darkness. Soldiers in the army of God. Sowers who scatter good seed. A little leaven that affects the whole lump. True, life has its bitterness, but it has also has a sweetness for those who pour in the sugar.

PASS ON THE PRAISE

. . . .

If there be any virtue, and if there be any praise,
think on these things.

PHILIPPIANS 4:8

One of the moving characteristics of human nature is the desire to be appreciated. The hunger for recognition and praise leads to the highest excellence, for it spurs people to do their best.

Praise, however, should be limited to those who are worthy; for praise makes good people better but bad people worse. To acclaim those who don't deserve it is only satire in disguise.

ᔥ *Husband,* praise your wife even though it may shock her. It will put a song on her lips as she works.

ᔥ *Wife,* praise your husband even if it does cause him to think you want something. He'll get over it. Compliment him. This will encourage him to do even better.

ᔥ *Parents,* if your child is good, tell him about it. Of course there are times to censure, but don't forget the deeds and occasions deserving applause.

ᔥ *Teacher,* if a student deserves honor, grant it to him. This will inspire him to be a greater achiever. For the art of praising is the art of pleasing, and the art of pleasing can be the art of shaping.

ᔥ *Employer,* if your employee does a good job, tell him so. He will appreciate this, for a conscientious, dedicated employee does not work for salary alone.

ᔥ *Neighbor,* if your neighbors are an asset to the neighborhood and give you a secure feeling, tell them how fortunate you are to have them.

THE ANCHOR HOLDS

· ·

This hope we have as an anchor of the soul,
both sure and steadfast.

HEBREWS 6:19

In carrying out the symbol given in this Scripture we can say that life is a voyage. Even the most successful people find the voyage of life tumultuous at times. The anchor is very essential to a safe journey.

There are at least two sources of peril:

❧ *The danger of drifting.* It is much easier to float with the tide than to go against it. This is the peril that carries many people into the worst conditions of life. They permit themselves to drift.

❧ *The storms that strike.* There are the pressures of temptation. Secular anxieties. Physical infirmities. Family afflictions. Spiritual conflicts. All beat down upon us with a mighty wrath and they can wreck us unless we have an anchor that holds.

The only anchor that will not snap or budge in the tempest is hope in God. He is sure and steadfast. Anchoring hope in Him steadies the soul so that we can face the tides and storms of this world with confidence. Let's remember that having this anchor does not *preclude* storms, but rather *protects* in storms.

Every strain fixes the anchor deeper, to hold even in the hour of death. This was exemplified by a dying sailor. Near the end a friend said, "Well, mate, how is it with you now?" The dying man with poise and assurance replied, "The anchor holds." May all of us be able to say in both life and death, "The anchor holds."

Some Things I Have Learned Since Leaving College

For I have learned by experience.

GENESIS 30:27

৬ *It pays to do much preventive work.* Then one doesn't have to do so much corrective work. The best way to cure trouble is not to let it happen.

৬ *The bad that is reported in most cases is not as bad as it is pictured.* The evil, threat or despair that gets reported is often highly exaggerated.

৬ *The good that is aired in most instances is not as good as it is portrayed.* It is easy for people and things to get pictured better than they really are.

৬ *People's appraisal of a man is determined by whether or not he agrees with them.* If he does, he is applauded for his brilliance. If he doesn't, he is scorned for his inferior thinking.

৬ *Some people are against everything.* This keeps them from having to assume the responsibility of launching out. Their negative views have defeated them.

৬ *Some are too proud to ever change when once they are wrong.* When they say that two plus two equals five, to them it will always be five.

৬ *It is a mistake to let people tell you too much about their sins.* Later they may be embarrassed in your presence and hate you, not because of what you have done but because of what you know about them.

THINGS WORK OUT

. . . .

I have been young, and now I am old;
yet I have not seen the righteous forsaken,
nor his seed begging bread.

PSALM 37:25

The Psalmist is a witness to the comforting thought that things work out. He had never seen the righteous forsaken.

We know that setbacks occur, but they are not failures unless we make them such. Let us recall that the roads we have taken had their bridges; and occasionally if one was out, the detour was not long.

Because it rains when we wish it wouldn't,
Because men do what they often shouldn't,
Because crops fail and plans go wrong,
Some of us grumble the whole day long.
But somehow in spite of the care and doubt,
It seems at last that things work out.

Because we lose what we hoped to gain,
Because we suffer a little pain,
Because we must work when we'd like to play,
Some of us whimper along life's way.
But, somehow, as day will follow night,
Most of our troubles work out all right.

So bend to your trouble and meet your care,
For the clouds must break, and the sky grow fair.
Let the rain come down, as it must and will,
But keep on working and hoping still,
For in spite of the grumblers who stand about,
Somehow, it seems, all things work out.

REARING CHILDREN

. . . .

And, you fathers, do not provoke
your children to wrath, but bring them up
in the training and admonition of the Lord.

EPHESIANS 6:4

A minister asked a six-year-old girl how many children there were in her family.

"Seven," she replied.

The preacher remarked that so many children must cost a lot.

"Oh, no, we don't buy 'em, we raise 'em," replied the child.

We *don't* buy them. It's the *upkeep,* the *upbringing,* that's costly. And I'm not talking about money. I'm talking about bringing children up in the way they should go. It costs time, guidance, example, patience, work, play, study and thought.

Training is everything. Candied yams are country sweet potatoes that went to a cooking school. Oh for a thousand pens and tongues to declare the urgency of rearing children properly! The future of the world depends on it.

Ably rearing children requires us to:

  § *love them* and not to spoil them.

  § *discipline them* and not to domineer them.

  § *lead them* and not to master them.

  § *protect them* and not to smother them.

  § *help them* and not to hinder them.

  § *hold them* and not to possess them.

  § *treasure them* and not to hoard them.

IS YOUR MAINSPRING BROKEN?

. . . .

Faith working through love.

GALATIANS 5:6

*Y*ears ago my watch quit running, which prompted me to take it to the jeweler. After examining it, he said, "The mainspring is broken." This was the source of energy that kept it ticking. With the mainspring broken, time had gone off and left my old timepiece behind.

Now from a spiritual viewpoint, each of us needs to ask himself, *What about my mainspring, my faith?* For faith is the energetic power to move man. It moved Noah, of whom we read, "By faith Noah...moved" (Hebrews 11:7). Paul recognized this mainspring of life, because he said, "Faith which works." Faith works. It moves. It ticks.

Some people's mainsprings are wound tight—that is, they have more faith than others. Some have very little faith ("O you of little faith"). Others have much more and are described as having "great faith."

Many things will test your faith, but never let it break and it shall sustain and comfort you when the night is dark.

Lead, Kindly Light, amid the encircling gloom,
Lead thou me on!
The night is dark, and I am far from home—
Lead thou me on!
Keep thou my feet. I do not ask to see
The distant scene—one step is enough for me.

JOHN HENRY NEWMAN

BE A WINNER

. . . .

Do you not know that those who run
in a race all run, but one receives the prize?
Run in such a way that you may obtain it.

1 CORINTHIANS 9:24

No matter what the contest is, *be a winner*.

Winston Churchill, that grand old statesman of World War II, had the spirit to win. Drive, determination, courage and eloquence were his trademarks. I can still hear his bolstering words spoken in deep, resonant tones. His forceful speeches sounding the note of victory kept the British people from despair when the threat of defeat was upon them. In one of his speeches he said, "Victory at all costs, victory in spite of all terror, victory however long and hard the road may be."

Before Churchill's day it was Napoleon who said, "Victory belongs to the most persevering."

Very definitely, *a winner doesn't quit*. He may have been knocked down, he may been in the process of being counted out; but he still *doesn't quit*.

It is not enough to try, to work, to run, to fight. It's the spirit we bring to the effort that decides the outcome. Healthy morale wins the victory. We can lose some battles and still win the war. So we fight on and on. Then when the time comes for us to lay aside our armor and go home to be with the Lord, we can say in the heroic language of the Apostle Paul, "I have fought a good fight, I have finished my course" (2 Timothy 4:7).

And that makes us winners.

TANNING HIDES

. . . .

Reprove, rebuke, exhort with all longsuffering.

II TIMOTHY 4:2

A few years ago a preacher called on one of the members who lived in the backwoods a few miles from town. The backwoodsman was out at the barn tanning hides of animals he had trapped. He was so engrossed in his work that he was unaware of the minister's presence until he tapped him on the shoulder. In startled confusion, the hunter apologized, "I'm ashamed that you found me in this condition. I'm so poorly groomed for company."

The preacher replied, "Oh, that's all right. There is not much difference between us. Our works are very similar. You tan dead hides, and I tan live ones."

Human beings are so constituted that there are times when they need to be complimented and other times when they need to be censured. All of one and none of the other makes for imbalance.

One of the specific guidelines for a preacher calls for rebuke—a little tanning: "Rebuke them sharply, that they may be sound in the faith" (Titus 1:13). You don't straighten out people by silently watching them get more twisted. There is no true course but to speak out. And those who listen will judge themselves to be wise or foolish by their own reactions to what is said:

Reprove not a scorner, lest he hate thee: rebuke a wise man, and he shall love thee.

PROVERBS 9:8

Give instruction to a wise man, and he will be yet wiser.

PROVERBS 9:9

TESTED BY DISAPPOINTMENT

After they were come to Mysia, they assayed to go into
Bithynia: but the Spirit suffered them not.

ACTS 16:7

*P*aul and his company wanted to go to Bithynia, but God had bigger plans for them. Disappointed! But appointed—to bigger works.

One of the hardest blows for any person to bear is disappointment. It comes in every form: broken love, broken home, job stalemate, friend's betrayal, surgery that fails to cure, loss of fortune, defeat in athletics, defeat in politics, church plans that fizzle, cancelled trip, and children who come back from college with unusual philosophies and different morals.

When I was a boy I watched my mother sift flour through a sieve. The fine flour went through easily, but the larger bits of grain were not affected by the shaking and remained on top. Life is like that. We go through testing periods, but if we are big enough—have big enough faith, hope, love and courage—we can endure the shaking and remain on top.

Sometimes we have to suffer disappointment and bafflement in order to reach higher levels. If Hawthorne had been permitted to keep working at the custom house, he never would have become famous as a writer. If Harry Truman had not failed at selling men's furnishings, he never would have become President. It was A. B. Alcott who said, "We mount to heaven mostly on the ruins of our cherished schemes, finding our failures were successes." And William Penn said, "No pain, no palm; no thorns, no throne; no gall, no glory; no cross, no crown."

YOU TELL ON YOURSELF

. . . .

For every tree is known by its own fruit.

LUKE 6:44

You can't fool very many people for very long. Eventually you'll tell on yourself. Living on false pretense is a vain and pitiful gesture. Avoid it. Sooner or later your true self will come through and be recognized.

A person—whether wise or foolish—tells on himself by his words. "The tongue of the wise uses knowledge rightly, but the mouth of fools pours forth foolishness" (Proverbs 15:2).

Also, a person makes himself known by his deeds. "Even a child is known by his doings, whether his work be pure, and whether it be right" (Proverbs 20:11).

> *You tell on yourself by the friends you seek,*
> *By the very manner in which you speak,*
> *By the way you employ your leisure time,*
> *By the use you make of dollar and dime.*
>
> *You tell what you are by the way you walk,*
> *By the things of which you delight to talk,*
> *By the manner in which you bear defeat,*
> *By so simple a thing as how you eat.*
>
> *By the books you choose from the well-filled shelf;*
> *By these ways and more, you tell on yourself;*
> *So there's really no particle of sense*
> *In an effort to keep up false pretense.*

And all because a tree is known by its fruit. Present yourself to others honestly. If that's not good enough, ask God to help you improve yourself.

EXAMPLE WORKED WHEN PRECEPT FAILED

Likewise you wives, be submissive to your own husbands,
that if some do not obey the word, they, without a word,
may be won by the conduct of their wives.

1 PETER 3:1

When words fail, example may win.

Years ago a farmer became very ill. Worse than suffering any physical ailment, he was highly biased against Christianity. His getting sick was poorly timed (of course, there is never a good time). It happened in the spring and his crops desperately needed working. Weeds and grass were about to get ahead of the corn and cotton.

A neighbor, who was an outstanding Christian, took his boys and hired help and went over to the helpless man's farm and weeded his crops, free of charge. One day when this "Good Samaritan" and his crew were working in the fields, in the burning sun, the sick man's hardness began to soften. Looking through a window at the workers' toiling outside, he said to his wife, "When they have their gospel meeting this summer, we're going to go."

The man recovered. The meeting was held. He and his wife became Christians. Spiritually he grew fast and was soon leading prayers and making talks. He had natural leadership ability that came to the front in a hurry.

Later, in another city, he planted a church and did the preaching. The church grew and became a great candlestick.

When people won't hear your sermon, try living one.

AN AMAZING AND AGELESS PRODUCTION
· ·

Holy men of God spoke
as they were moved by the Holy Spirit.

2 PETER 1:21

The Bible—*what a sublime product!*

How amazing and marvelous is its authorship! It was written over a span of about sixteen hundred years by about forty different writers with a cross section of abilities, accomplishments and occupations.

Moses, for instance, was educated in the wisdom of the Egyptians and was a shepherd and a leader. Joshua was a soldier and a spy. Ezra was a famous scribe and a pious priest. Nehemiah was cupbearer to the king. David was a shepherd, musician, war hero and king. Solomon was the wisest man on earth and a powerful king. Isaiah was a prophet. Ezekiel was a Jewish exile. Daniel was a statesman. Amos was a shepherd and peasant. Matthew was a tax collector. Peter and John, both fishermen, were "unlearned and ignorant men." Luke was a physician. And Paul was a tentmaker and a scholar taught at the feet of Gamaliel.

How could men so different in abilities, customs and occupations have written a book that is the lamp that outshines all other lights, the book of all splendors, the gesture of heaven to kiss the earth with its glories? There is no human explanation. The only conclusion is, "The Spirit gave them utterance" (Acts 2:4), or expression. Men furnished the tongue or the hand. The Holy Spirit furnished the power behind it. Thus "all Scripture is given by the inspiration of God" (2 Timothy 3:16).

LOVE IS THE STRONGEST SUPPORT

Jacob served seven years for Rachel;
and they seemed to him but a few days,
for the love he had for her.

GENESIS 29:20

Perhaps no man who occupied the White House has ever received as much praise and malediction as Andrew Jackson. When he retired to the Hermitage on the outskirts of Nashville, he had the supporting memories of his notable victory over Wellington's troops at New Orleans and his two presidential terms.

Yet, those were not the things on which his thoughts lingered as life's sun was sinking lower every day. They paled to insignificance in comparison with other things far more precious. It has been said that visitors saw the old man sitting before the fire, and nearby were his Bible and a miniature of his beloved wife, Rachel.

Inscribed on her tomb in the Hermitage grounds is the beautiful tribute Jackson made to his companion of thirty-five years: "Here lie the remains of Mrs. Rachel Jackson, wife of President Jackson, who died the twenty-second of December, 1828. Age sixty-one years. Her face was fair, her person pleasing, her temper amiable, her heart kind. A being so gentle and so virtuous, slander might wound but could not dishonor. Even death, when he bore her from the arms of her husband, could but transport her to the bosom of her God."

What gave the greatest satisfaction and sweetest comfort to the old warrior were not the plaudits for his grand victory at New Orleans nor his eight years as head of state, but rather the cherished memories of the affections and devotions of his loving Rachel.

I'll Make a Man Out of Myself Yet

. . . .

Put on the new man
which was created according to God,
in righteousness and true holiness.

EPHESIANS 4:24

It has been reported that a university student was expelled for participating in a shameful prank in which another student lost his life. Before leaving the campus, the dismissed student went to one of the professors and thanked him for what he had tried to do for him. One thing he said was, "I'll make a man out of myself yet."

Let the past lie in the realm of what cannot be changed. Let's be more concerned with the future, for it is there that we shall spend the rest of our lives. And the best way to meet it is to start with the present.

Life is a story in volumes three,
The Past,
The Present,
The Yet-to-Be—
That's up to me.

The only good in thinking about the past is to use it as an anvil on which a better person may be hammered out. This was the usage the Apostle Paul made of it. In speaking of his past he said, "Many of the saints did I shut up in prison...and when they were put to death, I gave my voice against them" (Acts 26:10). We know the change he made.

Starting anew is the constant challenge of life. When we speak of a faulty past, a cleansed present and a helpful future, this is what life is really all about. It is saying, "I'll make a man or a woman out of myself yet."

DOING GOOD

. . . .

[Jesus] went about doing good.

ACTS 10:38

This is what all of us are aim and strive to do: *do good.* The world needs it and we need to do it. What are some of the main elements that make up such a fruitful life?

❧ *Sympathy is the starter.* First we must have a heart that goes out to others. If this feeling is lacking, all is lacking. Sympathy can be cultivated. Let's cultivate it.

❧ *The cheerful, hopeful attitude is essential.* People who are unhappy and despondent repel rather than help. This broadens the distance between them and others and leaves them too far away to be of any service. They aren't close enough to help. We need a live, optimistic, enchanting view of life. Let's look up and then we shall live up. Let's live up and then we shall lift up.

❧ *Purity is required.* No thirsty traveler can be blessed when drinking from an impure river. We are made better by being in the company of good people. A pure life exerts an influence.

❧ *Open eyes that see needs are necessary.* The needs are there in one form or another. But we can't see them unless we take our eyes off ourselves. We are commanded to work in the vineyard—to do good, not just sit there and eat grapes.

No matter what our calling in life may be, remember that our greatest calling is to *do good.* This makes a better world!

I, MYSELF AND ME

· ·

Love...does not seek its own.

1 CORINTHIANS 13:5

A ten-year-old was enjoying an all-day sucker. His play-mate who had none looked with craving eyes. Finally the playmate said, "When you're through, will you let me have the stick for a lick?"

"When I'm through licking there won't be a stick left," was the reply.

There are adults who, figuratively speaking, will lick a stick to nothing before they will let anyone else have any. The selfish live on the basis that everything should come only to themselves, as the water of a river flows to the sea.

A person perverts the life God has given him and hurts himself when he is interested in only three persons—*Me, Myself* and *I.*

A Tea Party

I had a little tea party
This afternoon at three.
'Twas very small—
Three guests in all—
Just I, Myself and Me.

Myself ate all the sandwiches,
While I drank up the tea;
'Twas also I who ate the pie
And passed the cake to Me.

We hear it said, "Every man for himself." How much bet-ter it would be to say, "Every man for God, for others and for self."

THE HIGH PRICE OF SPITE

. . . .

But You [O God] have seen it,
for You observe trouble and grief.

PSALM 10:14

A few years ago I visited in Natchez, Mississippi, and took the Natchez Pilgrimage Tour. It was fascinating to go through the elegant houses of yesteryear. One thing I found especially interesting was a picture hanging in Governor Holmes' house, which was built in 1794. It was not the picture itself that I found so engaging but rather the story behind it.

Keene Richard was married to a very young lady. They lived together for awhile and she died. Nine years later Mr. Richard married again. The story is that the family of his first and deceased wife had a large picture (perhaps five feet square) painted of the deceased woman. She was depicted with a sad, forlorn look; a white rose pinned to the bosom of her dress; and seated on a coffin. The family gave this painting to his new bride as a wedding gift.

What was in the heart of the givers we don't know for sure. But their gift surely bears the interpretation of spite, for it would be a tool of annoyance and irritation.

Spite comes in every ugly form from embittered and hateful hearts. It is the spirit of getting even though the offense may be only imaginary. It seeks to get even although the cost is high. They are willing to give up one of their eyes if it will knock out both eyes of the one they wish to hurt.

Oh, how much sweeter life is when one is motivated by the spirit of love that is kind, thinks no evil and bears all things!

LIFE GETS BETTER DAY BY DAY
. . . .
Therefore we do not lose heart.
Even though our outward man is perishing,
yet the inward man is being renewed day by day.
2 CORINTHIANS 4:16

In reply to congratulations on his eighty-sixth birthday,
Sir William Mulock stated:

*I am still at work, with my hand to the plow, and my face
to the future. The shadows of evening lengthen about me,
but morning is in my heart.... I have had varied fields of labor
and full contact with men and things, and have warmed
both hands before the fire of life.*

*The best of life is always further on. Its real lure is hidden
from our eyes somewhere beyond the Hills of Time.*

The Bible pays a beautiful tribute to age: "The beauty of
old men is the gray head" (Proverbs 20:29). "Days should
speak, and multitude of years should teach wisdom" (Job
32:7). This is due to the lessons learned from rest and labor,
health and illness, achievement and disappointment, ease
and struggle, peace and war, sowing and reaping. They have
experienced life in every form. They have seen the best of
days and the worst of days.

The most adorable and lovely people in the world are
those who have been mellowed and softened by the passing
of many years. They radiate kindness and consideration,
calmness and tranquility, knowledge and wisdom. And now,
seasoned and matured by years of experience, they are living
in their Golden Years. Look the world over for beauty, and
you will find none greater than this.

THE GOAT ATE HIS SPEECH

I was mute with silence, I held my peace,
even from good; and my sorrow was stirred up.

PSALM 39:2

At a Vacation Bible School a special program was planned for the last day. All classes would meet in the auditorium. Parents were invited to this special event. Children who had shown outstanding talent were invited to recite. However, the morning of the program the minister received this note from a distraught mother: "Dear Preacher, I'm sorry, but Henry will not be able to be on the program. The goat ate his speech. Since the speech was very religious, my only consolation is we may have a better goat."

The goat got his speech. What is it that gets the speech of many adults and silences their tongue? Not the goat.

❧ *Could it be a lack of faith?* The Apostle Paul gave faith as the motivation, the compelling power, in his speaking. Deep convictions are anxious to speak out. When the fire of faith burns, then one speaks.

❧ *Could a lack of knowledge tie the tongue of some?* Feeling they are unknowledgeable, they decide not to say anything or only very little. They fear they might get in over their head. But any person with average ability can overcome this deficiency. Study will do it.

❧ *Could discouragement keep us silent?* We needn't be dismayed. God's Word will not return unto Him void, but will accomplish what He pleases and prosper in the thing whereto He sends it. If your words are His words, they will accomplish good, some way, somehow, somewhere, sometime. So take heart!

No Fear of Night

. . . .

You shall not be afraid of the terror by night.

PSALM 91:5

Night is feared because of crime. More crimes are committed under cover of darkness than in broad daylight. But it is not night itself that is dangerous, but the criminals who use it to hide their misdeeds.

Some fear the coming of night because of pain. A night of pain can be an eternity. But when the tired body calls for sleep, night is never long enough.

Others dread night because they are more restlessness then. They spend the night tumbling, tossing and growing gray.

For some people night is haunted by conscience. In the stillness of the night it bites deeply.

Many find night frightening because, even when awake, they can see so little in the darkness; and if asleep, they have no awareness of approaching danger. There is so much fear in night that Edward Young said, "By night an atheist half believes a God."

But night was meant to bless us. It even kisses the grass with a fresh, sparkling dew. Think how much more it does for man. It is a time to rest, relax, sleep and gain strength for the challenges of another day. Even the cattle lie down for a night's repose. Night is a time to gather home. Thomas Gray said:

The curfew tolls the knell of parting day,
The lowing herd winds slowly o'er the lea,
The plowman homeward plods his weary way,
And leaves the world to darkness and to me.

THE CHILD WITHIN LIVES AGAIN
....

When I was a child, I spoke as a child.
I understood as a child, I thought as a child:
but when I became a man,
I put away childish things.

1 CORINTHIANS 13:11

A slender, wrinkled, gray-haired woman in her fifties looked worn down. On that rain-chilled morning she was on the bus going to her job at the laundry. She looked terribly tired and in need of a little encouragement. No doubt life had been hard for her.

Then suddenly, out of the clouds and dampness of the day, something happened. A station wagon stopped in the halted lane next to the woman's window. A little girl, probably three, very cute and beautifully dressed, looked up from that station wagon into that lonely woman's face. The little girl smiled and waved. The woman smiled and with a hand of honest toil waved back. The child was delighted and so was the woman. The face of each radiated with gladness. The smiling and waving continued until traffic started up again.

Later, when the woman got off the bus, there had been a renewal of spirit and rekindling of energy within her. Her burden was lighter and her eyes twinkled with a new gladness.

This sort of thing happens all the time between children and adults. There are those unspoken acts of sharing a little of each other, which enriches both. Even people who are usually bored and glum come alive when they communicate with a child. In such a moment we find renewal of spirit, because the child within us lives again.

SOME THINGS THAT HELP US TO LIVE BETTER
. . . .
The righteous shall flourish like the palm tree,
he shall grow like a cedar in Lebanon.
PSALM 92:12

❧ *Reading the Bible has a cleansing effect.* "Now you are clean through the word which I have spoken unto you" (John 15:3). It is the mirror of the soul that lets us see ourselves as we are, which is the first condition of improvement.

❧ *Prayer is a bulwark against evil.* "Watch and pray, that you do not enter into temptation" (Matthew 26:41). More things have been wrought by prayer than the world knows.

❧ *Helping others lifts us higher.* The doer is actually blessed more than the recipient. "It is more blessed to give than to receive" (Acts 20:35). Lending a helping hand gives a feeling of usefulness and importance. It will enhance our self-image, which will encourage us to be better persons. Some people are too down on themselves ever to lift themselves up.

❧ *Wholesome associates bring out our better side.* "Do you not know that a little leaven leavens the whole lump?" (1 Corinthians 5:6). May that leaven be beneficial. In the presence of some people it's easy to be good because they are good.

❧ *Reflecting on the brevity of life is sobering.* "You do not know what will happen tomorrow" (James 4:14). Whatever stature you wish to attain, start working on it now, for hours and flowers soon fade away.

WHAT MONEY WILL AND WILL NOT BUY

For wisdom is a defense, and money is a defense:
but the excellency of knowledge is, that wisdom
gives life to those who have it.

ECCLESIASTES 7:12

Money will buy:

❦ an education, but *not wisdom.*

❦ tuition, but *not knowledge.*

❦ books, but *not brains.*

❦ a house, but *not a home.*

❦ a bed, but *not sleep.*

❦ food, but *not an appetite.*

❦ clothes, but *not a godly person* to wear them.

❦ medicine, but *not health.*

❦ finery, but *not beauty.*

❦ amusement, but *not happiness.*

❦ gifts, but *not love.*

❦ employees, but *not loyalty.*

❦ electricity, but *not spark* for a personality.

❦ attention, but *not respect.*

❦ communication, but *not character.*

❦ a fine funeral, but *not eternal life.*

❦ some people, but *not God.*

❦ a lot of earth, but *none of heaven.*

While money has its values (and the possibility of liabilities), it will not buy the most valuable needs of man. Such benefits must be obtained otherwise and by other means.

LIKE A PARACHUTE
. . . .
And he said, "How can I, unless someone guides me?"
And he asked Philip come up and sit with him.
ACTS 8:31

Acts 8:31 concerns the Ethiopian Treasurer. It's very evident that the man had an open mind.

The justice of the peace in a little town made preparations to go on vacation. Just before he left, he hung a sign on his office door: "Closed: But My Mind Is Still Open."

That shows the kind of thinking that gets a man re-elected. Not only should the judge have an open mind, but that should be true of all of us. We're the jurors. In the everyday affairs of life we hand down the decisions on ourselves. How tragic if the mind is closed, denying fulfillment of the wonderful possibilities within us.

Many people boast of an open mind when it's only a vacant space. Others think they have an open mind when it's only an elastic conscience. The easiest way to build an undeserved reputation for having an open mind is not to think at all; instead, nod approval to everything other people suggest. Obviously this is not having an open mind, just *no* mind. If such is the case, a different sign ought to be hung out: "Closed for Repairs." The open mind examines and weighs a matter, free of prejudice and bias, and then decides what is true and right.

We must keep our minds open. If we do, a piece of knowledge might enter. The mind is like a parachute; it operates only when it's open.

CAN GOD FURNISH A TABLE?
· ·
They spoke against God.
They said, "Can God prepare a table
in the wilderness?"

PSALM 78:19

Pessimists, the lot of them! They took a *gloomy* view!

A visiting minister was looking at the farmer's hogs. The preacher remarked, "Those are the finest hogs I've ever seen. Why, you have enough meat standing there to feed your family two or three years!"

"Oh, I know," replied the pessimistic farmer, "but only the Lord knows what's going to happen to us after that."

> *'Twixt optimist and pessimist*
> *The difference is droll.*
> *The optimist sees the doughnut,*
> *While the pessimist sees the hole.*

The optimist gladdens; the pessimist saddens. The optimist sees a tiny, flickering flame of light; but the pessimist, when he hears of it, runs and throws water on it. Driving in city traffic, an optimist thinks he'll find a parking space in the next block, but a pessimist thinks he'll have a wreck before he ever finds one. An optimist makes the best of it when he gets the worst of it, but the pessimist makes the worst of it when he gets the best of it. The optimist enjoys his journey on the sea of life, but the pessimist is seasick the entire trip.

I like what W. L. Phelps said: "I am an optimist because I believe in God. Those who have no faith are quite naturally pessimistic, and I do not blame them."

UNDERNEATH THE STONE

. . . .

There is one who makes himself rich, yet has nothing;
and one who makes himself poor, yet has great riches.

PROVERBS 13:7

There is an age-old story about a very rich man (rich materially *and* spiritually), who lived in a big house on a hill overlooking a village. He had become rich through diligent labor and thrift. In contrast, many other people with the same opportunities were poor.

In spite of the fact that they had failed where he had succeeded, he tried to help them. He planted trees, set up a park, did much for the children at Christmas, gave handouts, loaned money and created jobs.

One day he got up early in the morning and placed a boulder in the middle of the road near his house. Then he hid behind the hedge to see what would happen. Along came a poor man leading a horse. He raged, walked around the stone and went on his way. A farmer came next. He ranted, drove around the boulder, and went about his business. The day passed. Many had come by, but not one had pushed the boulder out of the way.

Then at nightfall an old man came along, and thought to himself, "Somebody might fall over this boulder in the dark and get hurt. I'd better move it to the side." Being thin and weak, he had to tug and tug, push and pull. Finally he got the boulder to roll over, and there to his surprise lay a bag of gold with this note: "This gold belongs to the one who moves this stone."

While gold is valuable, our greatest enrichment is in what we do for others—rolling stones out of their way, lifting them up, pointing them to a better life.

THE BIBLE LIVES

· ·

Heaven and earth shall pass away,
but My words shall not pass away.

MATTHEW 24:35

The Bible lives. Century follows century, *yet it lives.* Empires rise and fall and are forgotten, *yet it lives.* Kings, dictators, presidents, come and go, *yet it lives.* Hated, despised, cursed, *yet it lives.* Scorned, *yet it lives.* Despised and torn to pieces, *yet it lives.* Misunderstood and misrepresented, *yet it lives.* Abandoned in unbelief, *yet it lives.* Railed at by atheists, *yet it lives.* The Bible is the anvil that has withstood the constant blows of unbelievers.

The Anvil

Last eve I passed the blacksmith's door,
And heard the anvil ring the vesper chime;
Then looking on, I saw upon the floor
Old hammers worn with use in former time.
"How many anvils have you had?" said I,
"To wear and batter all those hammers so?"
"Just one," said he; then said, with twinkling eyes,
"The anvil wears the hammers out, you know."
And so, I thought, the anvil of God's Word
For ages skeptic blows have beat upon;
Yet though the noise of falling blows was heard,
The anvil is unharmed, the hammers gone.

SHORT BUT POTENT

. . . .

They think that they will be heard for their many words.

MATTHEW 6:7

The richest treasures come in small amounts. Now let us see if we can get some powerful lessons from some short statements.

- A smile has face value in every land.
- The way to get rid of a past is to get a future out of it.
- Blessed is he whose calendar has the Lord's Day on it.
- Every ending can be a new beginning.
- Money can feed you but not make you.
- The church is not a convention; don't send a delegate.
- Every day brings a clean page.
- A hungry soul may abide in a well-fed body.
- There's a difference between a home and a filling station.
- Some so-called open minds are open to everything.
- Don't argue; discuss.
- Redeeming the past enriches the future.
- One of the most useless things on earth is an excuse.
- A purchased friend never lasts.
- A diamond is a chunk of coal that stuck to its job.
- Grumblers, like Satan, take no vacation.
- Sapwood character makes poor building material.
- Tarry before you marry.
- Opportunity to do good is an opportunity to be good.
- Before passing judgment on the sermon, try it out in practice.
- The war that will end war will not be fought with guns.
- The world at its best is man at his best.
- Almighty God cannot be exhausted.

BE COURTEOUS

. . . .

Finally, all of you be of one mind,
having compassion for one another;
love as brothers, be tenderhearted, be courteous.

1 PETER 3:8

My father taught me many valuable lessons as I grew up, working in a general merchandise store. One was: "Son, if others are rude, you don't have to stoop to their level. Be courteous. In the first place, it's right; in the second place, it keeps us in business."

Identify Me

I come only from the well-bred.
I am found in hovel and palace.
I make faces smile and hearts warm.
I unlock doors that rudeness has closed.
I ease tensions and smooth relationships.
I disarm enemies and make friends.
I overcome prejudice.
I am praised by many and condemned by none.
I am little but produce big results.
I cost nothing.
I am Courtesy.

So even common sense says, "Be not savage, cruel and rude." The impolite make life hard for themselves. They go out and butt heads when courtesy would often spare them the head-knocking ordeal. After all, we're not goats.

Rudeness is no hinge on which doors open. Neither is it a bridge that spans the difference between people. It is acid from which people pull back. However, courtesy is the universal language appreciated on every shore and in every clime. Speak it! Speak it! And you'll be heard.

CORN ON THE COB

· ·

God said, "See, I have given you
every herb...and every tree."

GENESIS 1:29

My wife and I and our five-year-old son, Paul, were enjoying a very delicious meal. One of the dishes was corn on the cob, tender, sweet and juicy. After Paul's corn disappeared like a train going through a tunnel, he passed his plate and said, "Will you put some more corn on my cob, please?"

This kind of talk is natural for a child. But what about us adults? Have we really forgotten who put the corn on the cob? And a thousand other things God has done for us?

In this age of expanding development, it's easy (if we are not thoughtful) to forget how much the Creator has done for us and how wholly dependent we are on Him.

Man plants but God gives the increase.

We can do much in appropriating and changing the created, but there our work ends. We can't start with nothing. We can't create. We are still human, and God is still God. As long as we can make this distinction there is hope for us.

We have come a long way. But from where? Name it and it will be a place God has given. And where are we going? Wherever it is, God is there. "Where shall I go from Your Spirit? or where shall I flee from Your presence?" (Psalm 139:7). His handiwork is stamped on everything we behold.

LET US BE GLAD

. . . .

The Lord has done great things for us;
wherefof we are glad.

PSALM 126:3

A friend suggested that we go to a gospel meeting in a neighboring city, and I was glad. "I was glad when they said to me, Let us go to the house of the Lord" (Psalm 122:1).

❧ *Belief in the God of Forgiveness fills the heart with joy.* To Him we say, "Forgive us our debts." We need the slate wiped clean. We need to start again. It makes for gladness.

❧ *Thanksgiving produces gladness.* You can find delight in counting your blessings. Most people in the world would be very happy to have what you have.

❧ *Commitment to a great and meaningful cause gives rise to gladness.* "I will very gladly spend and be spent," stated the Apostle Paul. Some people have nothing that really holds their interest and challenges them. Get involved.

❧ *Seeing a friend makes the heart glad.* "And when he sees you, he will be glad in his heart" (Exodus 4:14). The fellowship of kindred spirits is a delightful experience.

❧ Additionally, *gladness comes from confident living.* You can't be unhappy while you believe everything will turn out all right. Trust the Power greater than you. Learn to say, "I know whom I have believed."

ROCK OF AGES

Lead me to the rock that is higher than I.
For You have been a shelter for me.

PSALM 61:2-3

"Rock of Ages," the hymn written by A. M. Toplady, was first published in 1775. One day when Toplady was walking in rocky terrain, he was caught in a severe thunderstorm. Seeking refuge, all he could find was a big split in a granite rock. He climbed into the narrow cleft and was sheltered from the storm. As lightning flashed and thunder roared, he composed the words of this hymn. When he got home he wrote down the verses. He died at the early age of thirty-eight, but the hymn he wrote will live forever.

Rock of Ages, cleft for me,
Let me hide myself in Thee;
Let the water and the blood,
From Thy riven side which flowed,
Be of sin the double cure,
Cleanse me from its guilt and power.

Not the labors of my hands
Can fulfill Thy law's demands;
Could my zeal no respite know,
Could my tears forever flow,
All for sin could not atone,
Thou must save, and Thou alone.

While I draw this fleeting breath,
When mine eyelids close in death,
When I rise to worlds unknown,
See Thee on Thy judgment throne,
Rock of Ages, cleft for me,
Let me hide myself in Thee.

SELF-LOVE IS ESSENTIAL

. . . .

You shall love your neighbor as yourself.

MATTHEW 22:39

For us to love others properly, we must love ourselves. Of course the correct balance must be kept. It's unfortunate that love of self has been attacked, because it is actually a virtue essential to self-preservation. It's only the perversion of loving oneself that is wrong.

As seen in Matthew 22:39 ("You shall love your neighbor as yourself"), the second commandment of the Law is based on the kind of self-love that is linked with love for others.

A principal reason some people are so bitter toward humanity is that they don't like themselves. It stands to reason that no one can love another when he does not like himself. Hence, it is fitting that we point out some of the fundamentals in learning to love self. We need to:

- ᕦ see ourselves as the objects of God's love, as people who are worth loving.
- ᕦ expect of ourselves only that which is reasonable.
- ᕦ refuse to compare ourselves with other people.
- ᕦ accept ourselves as we are.
- ᕦ keep a clear conscience.
- ᕦ have the gratification of doing the best we can.
- ᕦ be the kind of persons we can be proud of.

All of this encourages self-respect and self-love, and then we are ready to love humanity.

JOINING HANDS

. . . .

We then, as workers together with Him.

2 CORINTHIANS 6:1

An intriguing little story about a painting project emphasizes the absolute necessity of working together. A can of paint, already mixed and waiting in the garage, said, "*I'm* going to paint the house." The paintbrush bristled with displeasure and stormed, "No you won't. *I'm* going to paint it." "Oh, you think you are?" snorted the ladder, which stood against the wall. "How far would either of you get without *me*?" Just then the painter who overheard these self-centered remarks put in a word: "Perhaps *I'd* better go on vacation. I wonder if the house would be painted by the time I got back."

Let's remember that even the most efficient one of us is only a tool in the hands of the Infinite Worker. God does many things in which people have no part. He lifts the clouds, reddens the sunsets, keeps the stars in their orbits, sends the showers and the sunshine, sprouts the seeds, gives the seasons, paints the roses and lilies and perfumes them with their fragrance.

But there are other things just as beautiful and great in which He permits us to be His co-workers. By working with Him we have a part in putting attractive tints on human souls. What a distinct honor to be co-workers with God in transforming lives...in dispelling darkness and despair...in bringing light, purpose and happiness to human souls...in making known the cure for misery and sin! It is not our accumulation of wealth or attainment in society but our service to others that is the real test of greatness.

HELPERS OR HONKERS?

. . . .

If you have come peaceably to me to help me,
my heart will be united with you.

1 CHRONICLES 12:17

A woman driver had the misfortune of having her car stall in heavy traffic. If that weren't bad enough, she couldn't get it started, either. The man in the car behind her blew his horn every few seconds. Finally the perturbed and shaken lady got out of the car, walked to the honker's car and said, "I'm having difficulty starting my car. I'll make you this proposition: if you'll try to start my car for me, I'll honk your horn for you.'"

There are a lot more honkers than helpers, for the simple reason that it's easier to honk than to help. It's easier to talk than to work. It's easier to criticize than to assist.

If we really want to help others, we can lift a hand, even if it's *off* the horn.

When we are stalled on life's highway, we can be thankful that God doesn't blow a horn at us. He *helps* us. In recognition of His help, the Psalmist said, "My help comes from the Lord, who made heaven and earth. He will not allow your foot to be moved; He who keeps you will not slumber" (Psalm 121:2-3).

With deep appreciation we sing:

When other helpers fail, and comforts flee,
Help of the helpless, O abide with me.

WE RECEIVE IN KIND

· ·

Judge not, and you shall not be judged.
Condemn not, and you shall not be condemned.
Forgive, and you will be forgiven.
Give, and it will be given to you.

LUKE 6:37-38

An attorney, an accountant and I appeared before the Securities and Exchange Commission in Washington in behalf of a company in which we were interested. We met with three government attorneys who represented the Commission. At first they were the coldest, most unresponsive trio I had ever seen. Icicles formed from their breath. Nevertheless, we talked, suggested, reasoned and probed. And all the time we kept cool, considerate, kind and courteous. After about three hours of our warmth and their coldness, they opened up and turned out to be the kindest, most helpful group you could ever want to work with.

The next day, when our business was completed (and we did get everything we asked) and as we were getting ready to leave, I said, "If you don't mind, I'd like to ask you a question."

"Go ahead."

"The first three hours you were so cold, and then you became warm and helpful. What made the difference?"

"I'll tell you," one of the men replied. "We were in a meeting in Houston last week, and some of those Texans lost their temper, cursed us out and told us to get back to Washington. We didn't know what to expect of you."

That's the way life is. Kindness begets kindness, and kindness has won more triumphs than logic. This being true, you can be good to yourself by being good to others.

Bring on the Refreshments

. . . .

The Lord grant mercy to the house
of Onesiphorus; for he often refreshed me,
and was not ashamed of my chain.

2 Timothy 1:16

After Paul became a prisoner in Rome, there was a special friend who sought him and refreshed him. His name was Onesiphorus. One thing that was especially refreshing about this friend was the fact that he wasn't ashamed of Paul now that he was in jail. Paul, being only human, must have wearied in soul. What is so refreshing as the presence of a kind and sympathetic friend? We can imagine the words of cheer and hopefulness spoken by the free man to the prisoner.

How refreshing to one in trouble is a sympathetic and caring friend. Just the presence of some people is rejuvenating. They don't have to say or do much.

Hundreds of years ago the Moors occupied Granada in Spain. Their empire has been gone for a long time. Their palaces have crumbled into dust. But the irrigation streams that they built still remain.

Let's cut channels through barriers so that refreshment may flow into the world's prisons—the prisons of iron bars as well of those of loneliness, disappointment, illness, bereavement, failure, sin and guilt. After we are gone those channels will keep on flowing. For good never dies. And those who drink will be refreshed.

TOGETHER IN MARRIAGE

. . . .

Therefore shall a man leave his father and his mother,
and shall cleave unto his wife: and they shall be one flesh.

GENESIS 2:24

This passage in Genesis is in reference to our early parents, Adam and Eve. Centuries have passed, but it still constitutes the sweetest and most helpful human relationship in all the world. The togetherness of it makes each stronger. Solomon has aptly stated, "Two are better than one" (Ecclesiastes 4:9). Let today bring what it will, a couple standing together, hand in hand, can handle it.

Fifty years since we launched our craft
To sail life's sea with each other;
We have kept the faith, we have held to the vow
As sweethearts—as father and mother.

There have been bonnie breezes most of the way,
We have had more sunshine than sorrow;
And if sometimes dark clouds have covered the sky,
They were followed by sunlit tomorrows.

Then more happy years to us, husband and wife,
Companions so tender and true;
Through fair and foul weather may we both sail together
To the Heavenly Harbor whose waters are blue.

Marriage is the end of a quest. Not the beginning of a conquest. Nor an inquest.

"Marriage is honorable in all" (Hebrews 13:4). Hence, marriage was designed to be an honorable estate—and even more, an entrance into a holy of holies.

Our Candle Is Burning

· ·

Do this now, my son.

PROVERBS 6:3

A young man in training for the ministry was asked, "What are you doing to make the world better?"

He replied, "I'm a student getting ready to enter God's work."

"Well," continued the questioner, "when you light a candle, do you light it to make the candle more comfortable, or so that it will give light?"

"To give light," was the answer.

The inquirer then asked, "Do you expect it to give light after it is half burned or right away, the very moment you light it?"

He replied, "The moment I light it."

"Very well," was the reply. "Go and do likewise. Begin at once."

Your life is a burning candle. Don't let it burn up in vain. Start shining now. Start living now. Start enjoying life now. Start reaching for your goals now.

Procrastination is the art of letting today vainly become yesterday. It is not one of the finer arts. We can waste a lifetime just waiting for a better day.

Every day is the best day of the year. More people fail because of doing nothing than because of doing wrong. Go ahead and delay if you wish, but time will not tarry.

COPING WITH PROBLEMS

. . . .

My soul is weary of my life.

JOB 10:1

Guidelines from the immortal Twenty-third Psalm:

§ *Approach our problems with the positive attitude* that we and the Good Shepherd have the power and efficiency to handle it. Underrating ourselves will only harm us. We cannot afford to give way to the defeating negative "I can't." The Lord will help us. When faced with what appears to be an insurmountable problem, let's say, "I shall not want" (Psalm 23:1).

§ *Believe that our waning strength can be restored.* Everyone becomes tired and weary at times, and in this condition it is easy to feel that we are no match for problems. But let's take courage. Our vigor can be restored. If we give ourselves a little time, our energy will build up again. "He restores my soul" (Psalm 23:3).

§ *Be fearless in facing our difficulty.* Fear itself is a danger. Jesus said to the Disciples, "Arise, and be not afraid." Times and circumstances have changed, but He has not. "I will fear no evil" (Psalm 23:4).

§ *Find fortitude in the fact that we do not have to walk alone.* Even if we have to make new friends or reconcile differences with family members and old friends, we *can* be with others. Above all, the Lord will walk with us. "You are with me" (Psalm 23:4).

§ *Believe that goodness shall accompany us.* There is much more good than bad for us. Moreover, benefits can evolve from what we think at the time is dreadful. We can rely on the assurance that, with God, "Surely goodness and mercy shall follow me all the days of my life" (Psalm 23:6).

SHE INSISTED WE GO TO CHURCH

Not forsaking the assembling of ourselves together,
as is the manner of some, but exhorting one another,
and so much the more, as you see the day approaching.

HEBREWS 10:25

*B*ack in my college days, I made a special trip to be with my mother when she was to have serious surgery in a town thirty miles from home. As you perhaps know, any surgery back in the early 1900's was much more dangerous than it is now. Even now the prevailing view seems to be, "Any surgery *I* have is serious, but any *you* have is minor."

The doctors set the time for her operation at ten-thirty Sunday morning. That was church time in that town. My father, sister and brother-in-law were also at the hospital. We wondered, should we go to church or skip it this time? We didn't have to answer the question. Mother answered it. She insisted that we leave her there alone and go to church. She said, "I'll be all right; if not, there's nothing you could do anyway. And if you honor God by worshiping Him, your prayers in my behalf might have a better chance of getting through."

We honored her *and God* by going to church. When we returned to the hospital, the surgery was still in progress and everything was going well. After a few days Mother was able to go home. No other trouble has ever resulted from that operation.

I'm not saying there are never times when we should miss church, but I am saying that God's command to assemble and worship is often taken too lightly. I hold my mother's insistence that day in great esteem.

TAKE NO CHANCES

· ·

The devil walks about like a roaring lion,
seeking whom he may devour.

1 PETER 5:8

"Don't be afraid," said a mother to her little boy at a museum. "The lion is stuffed."

"Maybe so," responded the lad, "but he still might find enough room for a little boy like me."

He was taking no chances.

The boy's caution is actually good Bible doctrine *and good sense,* for the Bible says, "Resist the devil, and he will flee from you. Draw near to God, and He will draw near to you."

A man who decided to whip his alcohol problem quit parking his car in front of the liquor store. Instead, he began parking it down the street. He was taking no chances.

Years ago, a wealthy man wanted to hire a driver for his carriage, and he wasn't about to take any chances. He asked each of the two job applicants to drive over a narrow mountain road with a sheer cliff on the side. To show his skill, the first driver took the carriage as close to the edge as he could. The second driver hugged the bank, staying as far away from the edge as possible. Which one got the job? It was the driver who took no chances.

Practicing safety is good sense. It's not wise to see how close you can get to evil without partaking of it.

Abstain from all appearance of evil.

1 THESSALONIANS 5:22

SINGING IN THE RAIN

. . . .

Behold the fowls of the air.

MATTHEW 6:26

A sweet and smart woman who had suffered several long months of painful illness said to her minister, "A robin sings outside my window. As I lie here in the early morning, he serenades me." As her face brightened, she continued, "I love him because *he sings in the rain.*"

The robin is an example of attractive and winning behavior. And distinctive as well. When storms silence nearly all other songbirds, the robin sings on...even in the rain. Anybody can sing in the sunshine. But we need to sing in the midnight hour or when the clouds are pouring rain.

Because a company was folding, a veteran employee lost his job. His comment was, "Best thing that ever happened to me. This will force me to get out and get a better job." *Singing in the rain.*

A tornado destroyed a farmer's house. He reacted with this expression of gratitude and assurance: "Thank God no one was hurt. Now we will build a bigger and better house." *Singing in the rain.*

As a mother's baby lay cold in death, she said, "I don't understand why this happened. But God knows and I trust Him." *Singing in the rain.*

HUMAN AND DIVINE RULES

. . . .

Let us walk by the same rule,
let us mind the same thing.

PHILIPPIANS 3:16

There are many rules in life—some human, some divine. We have no qualms in altering human rules if it's for the better. For example, some of the old rules of English grammar are giving way to change. In mockery of the sometimes clumsy rule of not ending a sentence with a preposition, Berton Braley has written:

> *The grammar has a rule absurd*
> *Which I call an outworn myth:*
> *"A preposition is a word*
> *You mustn't end a sentence with!"*

But the divine rules remain as fresh, as relevant and as needed as ever. They are as up-to-date as tomorrow, for they were given for our good. For instances, look at these rules:

§ *Golden.* "Therefore, whatever you want men to do to you, do to them" (Matthew 7:12).

§ *Bible study.* "You shall not add to the word which I command you, nor take anything from it" (Deuteronomy 4:2).

§ *Sovereignty.* "You shall worship the Lord your God, and Him only you shall serve" (Matthew 4:10).

§ *Priorities.* "But seek first the kingdom of God, and His righteousness" (Matthew 6:33).

TEMPORARY TOGETHERNESS
. . . .

Let both grow together until the harvest,
and at the time of harvest I will say to the reapers,
"First gather together the tares, and bind them in bundles
to burn them, but gather the wheat into my barn."

MATTHEW 13:30

A responsible, hardworking farmer sowed good seed in his field. But while he slept, his enemy slipped in and sowed weeds among the wheat. This presented a challenging problem. For the weeds threatened the wheat. His workers asked permission to go into the field and gather up the weeds. But the wise farmer, willing to put up with the terrible weeds for the sake of the valuable crop, said, "No, lest while you gather up the weeds, you root up also the wheat with them. Let both grow together until harvest and then gather the weeds and burn them, but gather the wheat into my barn."

This is the greatest story ever told on the topic of tolerance. It was related by Jesus. It was one of His parables and was meant to illustrate how His people should behave in His kingdom. "Let both grow together until the harvest." This sums up the attitude of tolerance in a practical way.

Of all things, religion should not be a monstrous freak that breathes out of one lung the spirit of tolerance and out the other the spirit of persecution. We are not asked for toleration that throws God's Bible at the devil's feet. That's not toleration; that's compromise. Truth is not negotiable, but we can still behave in a civilized manner.

A FUNNYBONE

. . . .

Blind guides, who strain out a gnat,
and swallow a camel.

MATTHEW 23:24

*T*his little description from Matthew 23 is humor in its purest sense. It may shock some always-somber-never-smile people to learn that it came from Jesus Christ. Think what a cartoonist could do with the idea. Portray a person straining a gnat and then drinking down a camel. It's so ridiculous that it's funny.

In discussing Brother Sober Face, one man suggested that he was in dire need of surgery.

"How's that?"

"He needs a funnybone implanted up his sleeve."

Certainly there are times when we need to be somber, but just as certainly there are also times when we need to laugh. "A time to weep, and a time to laugh" comes from a better psychologist than any of us—Solomon (Ecclesiastes 3:4).

Humor relaxes us. It's an antidote for depression and a load-lightener for burdened hearts.

Abraham Lincoln, the great president of Civil War days, said, "With the fearful strain that is on me night and day, if I did not laugh I should die."

Thus it's obvious why the person of humor never wants for an audience. This vexed world is looking for something to dry a tear and spread a smile. Laugh and the world does more than laugh with you; it gathers around you.

A COMMON BUG

. . . .

Let no man deceive you with vain words.

EPHESIANS 5:6

Two college freshmen wanted to play a joke on their science professor. They caught a grasshopper, a beetle, a butterfly and a centipede, and from them they constructed a composite insect. They carefully glued together the centipede's body, the butterfly's wings, the beetle's head and the grasshopper's legs. Next, with their new bug in a box, they knocked at the professor's door.

"We caught this strange insect in a field," they said. "Can you tell us what kind it is?"

The scientist looked at the bug and then looked at the students with an amused expression on his face.

"Did it hum when you caught it?" he asked.

"Uh, yes it did," they answered, nudging each other.

"Then," said the professor, "it is a humbug."

One of the common bugs afflicting our society is *humbug*. Its bite is both painful and humiliating. Humbuggery is never good for anybody.

Here is some Biblical and ever-timely advice for all of us: "Take heed that you be not deceived." Never make spur-of-the-moment decisions. Investigate. Compare. Turn it over and take a look from the bottom side. Let's not be swayed by inconsequential matters. Let's seek the best counsel and remember, *not all's gold that glitters.*

LOVE OF HOME

. . . .

And they went to their own home.

1 SAMUEL 2:20

*B*e it ever so humble, there's no place like home, for at home the great are small and the small are great. Some of the world's most famous men and women have risen from the humblest origins. As Daniel Webster said:

"It is only shallow-minded pretenders who make...obscure origin a matter of personal reproach.

"It did not happen to me to be born in a log-cabin; but my elder brothers and sisters were born in a log-cabin, raised among the snowdrifts of New Hampshire. When the smoke first rose from its rude chimney, there was no similar evidence of a white man's habitation between it and the settlements on the rivers of Canada.

"Its remains still exist; I make it an annual visit. I carry my children to it, to teach them the hardships endured by the operations which have gone before them. I love to dwell on the tender recollections, the kindred ties, the early affections and the touching narratives and incidents which mingle with all I know of this primitive family abode.

"I weep to think that none of those who inhabited it are now among the living; and if ever I am ashamed of it, or if ever I fail in affectionate veneration for him who reared it and defended it against savage violence and destruction, cherished all the domestic virtues beneath its roof, and, through the fire and blood of seven years' revolutionary war, shrank from no danger, no toil, no sacrifice, to serve his country and to raise his children to a condition better than his own, may my name and the name of my posterity be blotted forever from the memory of mankind!"

BUILDING BRIDGES
. . . .
For the children ought not to lay up for the parents,
but the parents for the children.

2 CORINTHIANS 12:14

Each generation should lay up and do for the next. Whatever parents do for their children, those children should do for their own children. It makes for society's improvement. This constructive principle has been tenderly and graphically expressed in the popular poem "The Bridge Builder":

An old man going a lone highway
Came at evening, cold and gray,
To a chasm vast and wide and steep,
With waters rolling cold and deep.

The old man crossed in the twilight dim,
The sullen stream had no fears for him;
But he turned when safe on the other side,
And built a bridge to span the tide.

"Old man," said a fellow pilgrim near,
"You are wasting your strength with building here.
You've crossed the chasm, deep and wide,
Why build you this bridge at eventide?"

The builder lifted his old gray head.
"Good friend, in the path I have come," he said,
"There followeth after me today
A youth whose feet must pass this way.

"The chasm that was a naught to me,
To that fair-haired youth may a pitfall be;
He, too, must cross in the twilight dim—
Good friend, I am building this bridge for him."

If everyone were to follow this philosophy, the world could never get worse. It would always get better. Think about the bridges you can build. Even small ones help.

OUR BIRTHRIGHT

. . . .

Then God blessed them, and God said to them,
"Be fruitful and multiply; fill the earth and subdue it;
have dominion over the fish of the sea, over the birds of the
air, and over every living thing that moves on the earth."
And God said, "See, I have given you every herb
that yields seed which is on the face of all the earth,
and every tree whose fruit yields seed;
to you it shall be for food. Also, to every beast of the earth,
to every bird of the air, and to everything
that creeps on the earth, in which there is life,
I have given every green herb for food"; and it was so.
Then God saw everything that He had made,
and indeed it was very good.
So the evening and the morning were the sixth day.

GENESIS 1:28-31

This passage from the first chapter of Genesis makes known our birthright, bestowed upon mankind by our Creator. It's our charter for possession of the earth.

For our necessities, comfort and enjoyment, we are to utilize the immense resources of the earth—by agricultural productions, by mining operations, by scientific discoveries, by mechanical inventions and by manufacturing aids. The whole earth with all its boundless opportunities is our heritage. It is our right to use the earth and to be blessed by it.

What God commissions and calls *good* no man should call *bad*. Of course, any good thing can be perverted and misused, but this does not indict the constitutional goodness of it.

PROVIDING FOR OUR OWN

But if anyone does not provide for his own,
and especially for those of his own household,
he has denied the faith and is worse than an unbeliever.

1 TIMOTHY 5:8

That's God's brief on material duty. It's stern but right. So there is something worse than being an unbeliever. *Financial irresponsibility.* The God of all justice will not join hands with a freeloader. According to His Word, "If any would not work, neither should he eat" (2 Thessalonians 3:10). Of course this requirement does not apply to the elderly, the handicapped and the ill.

God meant for able-bodied people to work. For them His economic rule is *No work, no eat.* Application of this rule would reduce the unemployment figure in a hurry.

In the light of these two verses (1 Timothy 5:8 and 2 Thessalonians 3:10), it's obvious that a praying tongue and irresponsible hands would look ridiculous on the same body. A true view of God never blinds a person to his obligation to care for his family. Family responsibility is every man's divinely given duty.

Fulfilling this duty, however, is not the whole of life. There are also spiritual duties. Jesus stated, "Man shall not live by bread alone, but by every word that proceeds out of the mouth of God" (Matthew 4:4). We do live by bread but *not* by bread only. We have two needs—physical and spiritual—and neither takes the place of the other.

WORK TO HAVE

. . . .

Let him labor...that he may have.

EPHESIANS 4:28

Henry Ford said, "There will never be a system invented which will do away with the necessity of work."

God's plan *to get* is to *get with it*. Work. The text states God's uniform and immutable condition for man to obtain material benefits: "Let him labor."

Every handiwork of God bears the impress of the law of labor. The earth, the air and the water teem with laborious life. Life of every sort is busy working out the problem of its own existence. Nature never quits. She is doing her job. Now it is our turn.

The very tenor of the Bible is that of work and industry. It is a workaday world we see in the Bible, not an idlers' circus. Of all books, lazy people ought not to go to the Bible for comfort. To the contrary, the Bible strongly acclaims work and uncompromisingly holds idleness up to scorn.

This is the gospel of labor—ring it
ye bells of the kirk—
The Lord of love came down from above
to live with the men who work.
This is the rose that he planted, here in
the thorn-cursed soil;
Heaven is blest with perfect rest, but
the blessing of earth is toil.

HENRY VAN DYKE

HONORABLE, ESSENTIAL SWEAT

In the sweat of your face you shall eat bread.

GENESIS 3:19

A young man went into a business in Los Angeles and applied for a job. But what he really wanted was a *position*, a place to occupy. The owner said, "Sorry, but I wouldn't have enough work to keep you busy."

"But sir," said the applicant, "you don't realize how little work it takes to keep me busy."

And that was at least one reason why he didn't have a job in the first place.

The attitude toward work makes a difference in the potential for success or failure. I saw an poor but energetic man become affluent. A large lake had just been built and was attracting lots of fishermen. He went to the streams and seined minnows and sold them. The endeavor was so profitable that he eventually built his own minnow farm with many acres of ponds. His becoming well-to-do was no accident. It was the productivity of sound thinking and honorable sweat.

Life grants nothing to us except through hard work. All self-made people are hard workers. As Scripture proclaims, "The soul of the sluggard desires and has nothing; but the soul of the diligent shall be made rich" (Proverbs 13:4).

WORKING WITH GOD

"Be strong all you people of the land,"
says the Lord, "and work; for I am with you."
HAGGAI 2:4

The thought that lights up life's difficult days is that even the difficult days been appointed by God's wise providence. The discipline of drudgery can prepare us for greater and more responsible activities. This is seen in Joseph's going from the cruelties and deprivations of the prison to the glories of the palace. If he had evaded the galling prison life, he would not have come in contact with Pharaoh's servants who made it possible for him to become the second-highest official in the nation.

While living through the harshness of life, we cannot tell why God is exposing us to it. But the experience may be our schooling for better things ahead.

One thing sure, the faithful performance of unpleasant duties tends to form a nobler character. All that God wants of anyone is faithfulness. Not brilliance, not glamour, not publicity, but the careful and regular performance of common duties. To be "faithful in that which is least" will be rewarded as richly as to be "faithful in that which is much."

Furthermore, in every honest work no matter how laborious and commonplace, we are working with God. He will make the grain germinate and grow. But we must plant the seeds, thresh the grain, grind it into flour, make the loaves and distribute them. Only in this way can the people have their prayer answered when they cry, "Give us this day our daily bread."

THE DILIGENT HAND

. . . .

He who deals with a slack hand becomes poor,
but the hand of the diligent makes one rich.

PROVERBS 10:4

Financial prosperity is the fruit of a diligent hand, a courageous heart and a persevering backbone. It is attained in spite of the call of the shade tree, the lure of loafing and the temptation to take the easy road.

Like the kite, the person of self-made wealth has risen against the wind, not with it. As the kite is lifted by a little resistance, so is the gritty person. Yes, success is valiant, dauntless and at times almost lionhearted. It's *positive*—possesses a forward drive. It's *energetic*—knows the sweat of honest toil. It's *persevering*—refuses to quit.

The prosperous person picks the road that's lined with plenty instead of the one that's littered with penury.

He knows:

❧ *God gives the milk but not the bucket.*

❧ *Self do, self have.*

❧ *God helps those who help themselves.*

So he raises his hat to the past, takes off his coat to the present and rolls up his sleeves to the future.

Diligence and hard work are entitled to greater rewards. Here is a just standard of remuneration: "The laborer is worthy of his hire" (Luke 10:7). More labor, more compensation. Less labor, less compensation. No pains, no gains. This motive works well. And why shouldn't it? For it is Biblical.

DOES GODLINESS PAY?

. . . .

Godliness is profitable for all things,
having promise of the life that now is,
and of that which is to come.

1 TIMOTHY 4:8

The value and practice of godliness are matters of common sense. We can accept the discipline of godliness on the ground of self-interest, though it has other and higher grounds. Will godliness pay? Let's get our account books, study the prices, question the probabilities of profit and loss and decide whether or not it will pay us to invest in it.

❧ First, *is godliness profitable for the present?* Or does sin pay more? Unquestionably sin has turned some once-fine people into poor, wretched wrecks. It has cost them character, happiness, love, a father's sleepless hours, a mother's broken heart and their own broken dreams.

But how about godliness? It's well established that godliness pays from a business standpoint because it makes a person honest, industrious and earnest. And these are three of the highest qualities for temporal advancement. And as a general rule, godly homes are more pleasant and constructive than those that are not. Usually the children are better fed, better protected, better trained and even better loved.

Godliness also pays in joy and peace of mind. "That your joy may be full." "My peace give I unto you."

❧ Second, *is godliness profitable for the future?* There has to be another life to give sense to this one, or else the Creator's work would end in failure and nothing permanent would be gained. The Scripture says, "He shall reap life everlasting."

VEXATIONS

· ·

Therefore I hated life
because the work that was done
under the sun was grievous to me.

ECCLESIASTES 2:17

Grievous matters. Vexation of spirit. The story's told of campers in Louisiana who were besieged, tormented day and night, by colossal mosquitoes with electric drills and giant gnats with super wings. Finally one of the campers cried out, "*Lord, deliver us* from these buzzing mosquitoes and dreadful gnats! *We'll* take care of the alligators and wolves ourselves."

We often find that we need more help for the little, annoying trifles than for the knock-down problems. Life is filled with irritations that try our serenity. The washing machine failed to drain. The garbage disposal wouldn't work. The sewer stopped up. The vacuum cleaner spewed dust and trash all over the floor. You stumbled into a table and knocked off a lamp and it broke. Your cherished antique plate toppled over and cracked. Your car wouldn't start. The paperboy threw the paper into the flower bed. The boss changed your vacation time. You were overcharged on your groceries. Etcetera. Etcetera.

But you can live with it, for it's not the end of the world. Be determined to remain calm and unvexed. *Pray.* Many victories are won in prayer. *Read the Bible.* God brings peace to tattered nerves. *Realize it could have been worse.* Count how much more you're blessed than battered. *And smile.* Smiling people don't lose control.

BIBLE RULES OF BUSINESS SUCCESS

Beloved, I pray that you may prosper in all things
and be in health, just as your soul prospers.

3 JOHN 2

§ *Let's believe we can.* Say, "I can" (Philippians 4:13). Our ship won't come in unless we have the faith to send it out.

§ *Work.* "In the sweat of your face shall you eat bread, till you return to the ground" (Genesis 3:19). No amount of inspiration will succeed unless it's accompanied by perspiration.

§ *Be thrifty.* "Gather up the fragments that remain, that nothing be lost" (John 6:12). There is no way to have by wasting and destroying.

§ *Be visionary.* "Where there is no vision, the people perish" (Proverbs 29:18). This is essential to business survival and growth. Let's look for opportunities. Let's look harder and more closely than is customary.

§ *Use wisdom.* "Be therefore wise as serpents, and harmless as doves" (Matthew 10:16). To get ahead, we have to think, be analytical.

§ *Be enthusiastic.* "Whatever your hand finds to do, do it with your might" (Ecclesiastes 9:10). Enthusiasm will keep us charged.

§ *Count the cost.* "For which of you, intending to build a tower, does not sit down first and count the cost, whether he has sufficient to finish it" (Luke 14:28-30). Let's watch the figures.

WHEN SUCCESS TURNS TO FAILURE

. . . .

Command those who are rich not to be haughty,
nor to trust in uncertain riches but in the living God.

1 TIMOTHY 6:17

It has been reported that a group of the world's most successful financiers and industrialists met at a Chicago hotel in 1923. Those present were the president of the New York Stock Exchange, the president of the Bank of International Settlement, the president of the largest independent steel company, a member of the President's Cabinet, the greatest wheat speculator, and the head of the world's greatest monopoly.

Collectively these wizard magnates controlled more wealth than the United States Treasury contained. For years magazines and newspapers printed thrilling stories of their successes. They were held up as examples for young people to follow. But where were they twenty-five years later?

The president of the New York Stock Exchange, Richard Whitney, had been recently released from prison. The president of the Bank of International Settlement, Leon Fraser, had committed suicide. The president of the largest independent steel company, Charles Schwab, died penniless. The member of the President's Cabinet, Albert Fall, had been pardoned from prison so that he could die at home. The greatest wheat speculator, Arthur Cutten, died abroad in poverty. The head of the world's greatest monopoly, Ivar Kreuger, committed suicide.

These men were able to make money for a while, but they never learned how to live. So *success* turned to failure.

IF IT HADN'T HELPED

. . . .

And now, brethren, I commend you to God,
and to the word of His grace, which is able
to build you up, and give you an inheritance
among all those who are sanctified.

ACTS 20:32

An atheist who'd been in a shipwreck was washed ashore on an island of former cannibals. Stumbling inland, he came across a native reading the Bible. "Why are you reading that book?" snapped the atheist. "Missionaries must've deceived you. Get rid of it. The Bible never did anyone any good."

The native replied, "If it hadn't done me any good, you would be in my kettle right now."

The Bible's dynamic, revolutionary qualities make it a good influence. It is:

⚜ *a light that drives out darkness;* he who would fault the Bible would fault light.

⚜ *a word that cuts and pricks rebellious hearts;* this is a power for good.

⚜ *seed that produces a crop of good;* this cannot be called bad.

⚜ *a deterrent against sin, when hidden in the heart;* this must be appreciated.

⚜ *man's hope in what otherwise would be a dismal and meaningless world,* and that which gives hope must not be devalued.

Granted, our land is marred with dishonesty, irresponsibility, violence, crime, unhappiness and despair. However, this is not the fault of the Bible. Rather, it is due to insufficient study of it, and even more, failure to practice it.

PROVED

. . . .

By which have been given to us
exceedingly great and precious promises.

2 PETER 1:4

$\mathcal{T}$he story is told of an old man who was visited by his minister. His rheumatism was so bad he was unable to get out of his chair. His open Bible lay on his lap. The preacher picked up the Bible, turned a few pages, and noticed that the word "proved" was written in the margin alongside many Scriptures:

*The Lord...will be with you, He will not fail you,
neither forsake you.*

DEUTERONOMY 31:8

*The eternal God is your refuge, and underneath
are the everlasting arms.*

DEUTERONOMY 33:27

*Blessed be the Lord...there hath not failed one word
of all His good promise.*

1 KINGS 8:56

The Lord is my shepherd; I shall not want.

PSALM 23:1

*God is our refuge and strength,
a very present help in trouble.*

PSALM 46:1

*Cast your burden upon the Lord,
and He shall sustain you.*

PSALM 55:22

The dear old man had taken God's book and written his own experience in the margins: "Proved."

A neighbor who had walked in and observed said, "But what will you do if you get worse?"

The old man turned to Psalm 41:3 and said, "In that case I shall depend on this verse: 'The Lord will strengthen him upon the bed of languishing; You will make his bed in his sickness.'"

I Drew My Circle Again

. . . .

In whatever you judge another you condemn yourself.

ROMANS 2:1

This is the explanation of a man's loneliness:

"When I first became a member of the church, my circle was very large and I was delighted to be in the group; for it included all, like myself, who had accepted the faith. I rejoiced that there were so many excellent, believing people.

"But with my keen, observant mind I soon learned that I had been hasty in my conclusions. Many in my fellowship were erring. Being conscientious, I could not tolerate any people who were not right on all points of doctrine and practice. So there was nothing I could do but draw my circle again and leave them out.

"There in the small circle I was happy for awhile with those I presumed to be sound and righteous. Later I observed that many of them were not of the highest type. They were blind, stubborn, proud, unwilling to listen to me, even though they were not half as smart as I am. So there was no alternative but to draw my circle again and exclude them.

"We were fewer but happier and stronger. Those other publicans and sinners would defile any holy church. But once again my eagerness to accept people had gone too far. It was not long until I heard ugly rumors about the worldliness of some in my circle, that some were drinking coffee instead of tea, as I was drinking. So I had to draw my circle again.

"This shrank my circle to include only myself and my family. I had a good family, but to my shock they disagreed with me. I was always right. So in complete support of right, I drew my circle again, *leaving me all alone.*"

AIM AT YOUR GOAL

. . . .

One thing have I desired of the Lord, that will see:
that I may dwell in the house of the Lord all the days
of my life, to behold the beauty of the Lord.

PSALM 27:4

Having some aims in life is a vital prerequisite of success. An elderly man who had not gotten along very well in life explained his failure: "I aimed at nothing and hit it every time."

A national marksman while passing through a countryside saw evidences of expert shooting. There it was on barns, walls, trees and fences. Each showed a bullet hole in the exact center of the bull's eye. This was too much for his curiosity. "I've never seen shooting like this before!" said the astounded man. "How did you do it?"

"Not hard at all," replied the local marksman. "I shot first and drew the circle later."

This is the tragic mistake of many people who have a fast draw. They shoot before they aim, so they draw circle after circle, trying to make order out of their random shots.

Sometimes we sing, "I'm a pilgrim." A pilgrim is a lot different from a vagrant. The latter takes life at random, whereas the pilgrim has a fixed purpose and a compelling goal. Which are we? What are our aims? Are we drifters or pilgrims?

WHICH WAY DID THEY GO?

Let them alone. They are blind leaders of the blind.
And if the blind leads the blind, both will fall into the ditch.

MATTHEW 15:14

There is this original inscription on a tombstone:

Remember, friend, when passing by,
As you are now, so once was I.
As I am now, you soon will be;
Prepare for death and follow me.

Evidently some man thought about it, because he added these two lines:

To follow you I'm not content,
Until I know which way you went.

Jesus knew the value of such caution, for He warned against following unseeing leaders. He said, "If the blind leads the blind, both shall fall into the ditch."

All along humanity's highways, ditches are strewn with people who didn't heed this advice. The warning should be applied to all areas of life—to religion, business, finance, education, politics, government, and to our associates. Before we choose a highway, let's check the Bible to see which way the highway leads.

The leader who promises the most could be attempting to exploit us. In politics, he might be offering us in advance the fruits of our children's labors; we have to be wary of anyone who would mortgage our children to get our support. In religion, let's be cautious of those who offer special bargains and cut-rate prices in a competitive appeal to draw a crowd. It's better to take God's Word straight and pay the divinely stipulated price.

IF GOD LET US ALONE

. . . .

Humble yourselves therefore
under the mighty hand of God...
Casting all your care upon Him;
for He cares for you.
1 PETER 5:6-7

A little anecdote illustrates our blindness to God's care and providence. As the story goes, a farmer was showing his beautiful crop of oats to a cousin from the city.

The cousin remarked, "That's as fine a field of oats as I have ever seen." The farmer replied, "Yes, if God Almighty will only let it alone, it will make a fine harvest."

That very moment something happened. The crop stopped growing. God Almighty let it alone.

This is a parable to us. Many people are proposing that God leave us alone, that He stay out of our personal business and national affairs. They are suggesting that individuals and nations carry on without God, without thought of God, that if He withholds Himself we shall prosper.

But if God let us alone, we would perish. If He withheld the growing of crops, we would have no food. If He held back the rains, there would be no water to drink. Whether we like it or not, we are dependent upon a power outside of ourselves.

It is also true that the God of love and mercy sometimes disciplines us. This, too, is for our good.

THE CRITICIZED PREACHER

And He said unto them, "Go into all the world,
and preach the gospel to every creature."

MARK 16:15

§ If he's young, he "lacks experience"; if his hair is gray, he's "too old."

§ If he speaks from notes, he has "canned sermons"; if he is extemporaneous, he "wanders."

§ If he spends time in his study, he "neglects people"; if he visits, he's "a gadabout."

§ If he is attentive to the poor, he's "playing to the grandstand"; if to the wealthy, he's "trying to butter his bread."

§ If he suggests improvements, he's "a dictator"; if he doesn't, he's "short of vision."

§ If he condemns wrong, he's "cranky and intolerant"; if he doesn't, he's "a compromiser."

§ If he preaches thirty-five minutes, he's "windy"; if less, he's "lazy."

§ If he preaches the truth, he's "offensive"; if not, he's "a hypocrite."

§ If he fails to please everyone, he's "hurting the church"; if he does, he "has no convictions."

§ If he preaches on giving, he's "a money grabber"; if he doesn't, he's "not developing the people."

And some people think the preacher has an easy time.

AUTHOR UNKNOWN

THE MELTING POT

· ·

There is neither Jew nor Greek,
there is neither bond nor free,
there is neither male nor female;
for you are all one in Christ Jesus.

GALATIANS 3:28

Soon after my first arrival in New York city, I took a tour that included going to the Statue of Liberty. What it symbolizes should be held gratefully and uncompromisingly in American hearts. *Liberty*; its price has been too dear and its benefits are too large to let it slip away. As I stood there, reading this inscription, a tingling sensation ran down my spine:

Give me your tired, your poor,
Your huddled masses yearning to breathe free,
The wretched refuse of your teeming shore,
Send these, the homeless, tempest-tossed, to me:
I lift my lamp beside the golden door.

This grace has been the great equalizer—the "melting pot"—in our nation. It's been the true and kind, philosophical touch that has transported humanity from every corner of the earth to our shores.

Then I thought of a greater sanctuary for all races and classes of people in every station, condition and circumstances of life—Jesus Christ. He holds out a divine light and says, "Come unto Me, all you who labor and are heavy laden, and I will give you rest" (Matthew 11:28). *All!* The tired! The poor! The masses yearning to be free! The wretched! The homeless! The tempest-tossed! *All!* No condition or status excepted!

SHEEP OR GOATS?

. . . .

All the nations will be gathered before Him,
and He will separate them one from another,
as a shepherd divides his sheep from the goats.

MATTHEW 25:32

Well, in my judgment they have not accomplished anything! A group of scientists in Cambridge, England, have produced a cross between a sheep and a goat. You guessed it; they named the poor creature "Geep." It looks like a goat with long hair, cannot reproduce itself, and mingles and hobnobs with both sheep and goats. Being a cross, it doesn't know where it belongs.

What an unfortunate predicament!

Many people in the world, however, should be quite pleased with this animal, because it represents exactly their view of religion—not all-out for God and not all-out for Satan. A cross between the two. They want to be "Geeps," half goat and half sheep.

But Jesus made a clear distinction between goats and sheep. He said, "My sheep hear My voice, and I know them, and they follow Me" (John 10:27). Not the goats. This line of recognition and separation will become even more pronounced at the judgment. "And He shall set the sheep on His right hand, but the goats on the left" (Matthew 25:33).

The very nature of serving God does not permit a divided allegiance. "He that is not with Me is against Me." The words ring in our ears and put us in one camp or the other. God has no "Geeps."

STAY OUT OF THE WAY

. . . .

Alexander the coppersmith did me much harm.
May the Lord repay him according to his works.
2 TIMOTHY 4:14

Alexander not only refused to help in God's plan for the betterment of man, but he got in the way. Even worse, he opposed it intentionally.

A teacher asked her first-graders what they did to help at home. One by one, each gave the kind of answer she expected, such as "feed the dog," "feed the cat," "dry dishes," "get the paper" and "make my bed." But Fred hadn't said a word, so she called on him.

He hesitated a moment and then replied, "Mostly, I stay out of the way."

I wish all *adults* could say that.

If we're not willing to push the church, school, business, brotherhood of man, family, moral uplift, law enforcement and a stronger nation, at least we should get out of the way of those who would.

If we're not lifting a fallen person, we should stay out of his way as he struggles to get on his feet. If we're not helping to reclaim an alcoholic, we shouldn't offer him a drink as he strives to muster the will to leave it alone. Furthermore, if we don't want to go to church, the least we can do is stay out of the way of those who would, not make them have to climb over us to get there.

Just staying out of the way is not the biggest accomplishment, but it is some attainment.

NOW, SWIM!

· ·

Is not my help in me?
And is wisdom driven quite from me?

JOB 6:13

When I was eight or nine years old, I couldn't swim. As you would expect, my father and uncle thought I should learn how. I was all for it, not knowing just how the first lesson would be given. They took me to a pond and told me to undress. Standing there on a little bluff, my father took me by the hands and Uncle Roy took me by the feet. Then they began to swing me, and at the high point they let go and my father yelled, "Now, *swim!*"

That turned out to be about the nearest thing to perpetual motion any person ever saw. My arms and legs started flapping and kicking. I knocked and splashed water like a drunken whale, and I swallowed quite a lot of pond water, but I stayed afloat. I swam. I have been able to swim ever since, and with experience a little more gracefully.

My father was a strong believer in the School of Experience, the School of Hard Knocks and the School of Self-reliance. He believed that you learn to do by doing. To him there was no substitute for individual effort and struggle.

In the intervening years there have been times when threatening waters have risen around me, or the current was against me, or I was in over my head. Each time my father's words would ring in my memory, "Now, *swim!*" They have meant much to me; they have kept me from going under. A person must be self-reliant or he will sink.

THINKING PUTS YOU AHEAD

· ·

I thought on my ways,
and turned my feet to Your testimonies.

PSALM 119:59

"I thought...and turned." There was no turning until there was thinking. Indeed, each turns his own world by thinking.

A little girl was asked to define "drawing," and she did it with such accuracy and clarity that a philosopher could not have done better. She said, "Drawing is thinking and then marking around the think." Don't you like that?

Every achievement must begin with a thought.

God was surely smiling on man when He endowed him with the ability to think.

The greatest human power to make wealth is thinking. A Morse thinks of telegraphic communication, and the thought results in hundreds of millions of value in telegraph stock. A Stevenson thinks of locomotive traction, and the thought materializes in thousands of millions in railroads. A Bell thinks of speaking on wire, and from his thought springs billions in telephones.

Thinking does much more, however, than add wealth. It enables us to store up treasures in heaven daily by the thoughtful, conscious choices we make while on earth. The Psalmist thought and then chose to follow God. May we make the same divine choices every day.

THE SINGING HEART

· ·

Singing and making melody
in your heart to the Lord.

EPHESIANS 5:19

About seven in the morning a man walked into the lobby of a big hospital singing "What a Friend We Have in Jesus." Everybody stopped and listened. Then a man inquired, "Who's that?"

The answer: "He's one of the best surgeons in town." He was also my doctor and close friend.

Singing is one of the assets of mankind. It gives peace and joy. We are thrilled with its power. It is not necessary to have a trained voice to have a singing heart. In describing a beautiful and powerful inner life, Paul said, "Singing and making melody in your heart to the Lord."

Singing explains one of the reasons for the bravery and peace of early Christians who faced bitter and cruel persecution. It saved them from drooping spirits and lifted them to ecstasy when the going was rough. When Paul and Silas were wrongfully held in jail, they "sang praises to God: and the prisoners heard them" (Acts 16:25).

Life would be hard today if we did not have the singing heart which soothes us, summons us, strengthens us, day by day. Workers have it as they face their tasks. Parents feel it as they anxiously think about the welfare of their children. The sick lisp a melody in the night watches, and its music serves them as they launch onto the river of death. And over on the other side, the song of the heart becomes the song of the redeemed.

THE LAW OF COMPENSATION

. . . .

Give, and it shall be given unto you; good measure,
pressed down, and shaken together, and running over,
will be put into your bosom. For with the same measure
that you use, it will be measured back to you.

LUKE 6:38

Ours is a world of compensation. We reap what we sow; if not today, then later. Under a just God it cannot be any other way.

The world operates on the basis of paying each person in his own kind, and generally speaking it varies very little from this rule. If we smile, the world smiles back at us. If we frown, it frowns at us. If we sing, we will be invited to the chorus. If we think, our advice will be sought by the troubled. If we love mankind, we will be surrounded by loving friends. On the other hand, if we criticize, censure and hate, we will suffer the same from the people who know us. Every seed produces after its kind. *The law of compensation.*

Because of the rule of compensation, life has much more balance than we think. We obtain one thing at the price of giving up something else. The poor man cannot always have meat, and the rich man cannot always digest it.

Even our toil, suffering and sorrow can have compensations, depending upon our reaction to them. A man who had been hospitalized for several days later said that it had taught him to have a greater concern for the ill. His suffering had contributed to a finer person. *The law of compensation.*

OUTSIDE THE DOOR

· ·

For where your treasure is,
there will your heart be also.

MATTHEW 6:21

*Y*ears ago, Robert Southwell said, "Not where I breathe, but where I love, I live." No poised, successful person lives merely where his body occupies space. A person's family may be scattered, but if he loves them, that is where he lives.

Man—the exalted creature—is the only being or thing in all the world that can live outside himself or itself. We can become so absorbed in an outside interest that we live in it instead of ourselves.

We can find health-invigorating happiness and deep satisfaction outside of ourselves. The self-centered person tries to catch happiness, but it's always out of reach. The reason—he's looking for it within himself. If he would spring outside of himself, there, just outside the door, he could find happiness.

Who seeks within for happiness
Will find it not.
It stands a guest unheeded at thy very door today,
Open thine eyes to see,
Thine ears to hear,
Thy heart to feel,
The call for touch of human sympathy;
In answering this there is
And close outside thee sits
The guest thou soughtest in vain within.

ADAPTED, CAROLINE S. WOODRUFF

WHAT IS THE CAUSE?

Yes, I am he whom you seek:
what is the cause wherefore you are come?

ACTS 10:21

I once read the story of a man who experienced a little trembling in the night. Thinking he was taking a chill, he got up and took a cold tablet. Then he went back to bed and slept through the night. The next morning when he picked up the paper, the first thing he saw was this headline: "Earthquake Shakes City in Night."

He'd been mistaken. The world of reality calls upon us to deal with the matter of cause-and-effect. There is no escaping it. Thus when there is an effect, we need to know what the real cause is.

There is flagrant disregard for the rights of others. What is the cause? There is a dog-eat-dog spirit among us. What is the cause? There is crime in the land. What is the cause? There is a restlessness and nervousness among the people. What is the cause? There is far too much absenteeism at church. What is the cause?

It appears to me that the basic cause of our woes is a failure to live up to God's rock-bottom requirements of man. Here they are, stated simply and concretely:

He hath showed you, O man, what is good;
and what does the Lord require of you, but to do justly,
and to love mercy, and to walk humbly with your God?

MICAH 6:8

TIE A KNOT AND HANG ON

. . . .

Paul purposed...to go to Jerusalem, saying,
"After I have been there, I must also see Rome."

ACTS 19:21

*P*aul was determined to see Rome. And he did. Moreover, there he made saints in Caesar's household—the household of Nero, who was the brutal enemy of Christianity. This was the fruit of determination.

When I was a student in college, it was my privilege to know a student whose arms and legs were twisted and drawn, making it very difficult for him to walk. His head was bent to an angle, and his mouth was contorted. His irregular speech came laboriously and was hard to understand. He was a stumbling fellow physically, but he was tops in friendliness and mentality.

He was admired and loved by all who knew him. No one had dared to ask him what dealt him this fate until, one day, a special friend inquired. "Infantile paralysis," was the short reply.

His friend said, "With a blow like that, how can you face the world so confidently and lovingly, free from bitterness?" The young man answered in broken speech, "It never touched my head or heart."

He received a B.A. degree. Really, he could have been given a D.D. (Doctor of Determination). He proved that a person can submit to circumstances or master them. Sheer determination changed his life. So when we get to the end of our rope, there's still a chance. Let's tie a knot and *hang on.*

ANOTHER LIFE

. . . .

This mortal must put on immortality...
then...death is swallowed up in victory.

1 CORINTHIANS 15:53-54

In Philadelphia I went to the grave of the famous Benjamin Franklin, printer, writer, statesman and patriot. It was thought-provoking to stand there and read the epitaph that Franklin himself had written:

The Body of B. Franklin Printer

Like the cover of an old book
Its contents torn out
And stript of its lettering and gilding
Lies here food for worms.
But the work shall not be wholly lost
For it will, as he believes, appear once more
In a new and more perfect edition
Corrected and amended
By the author.

I was struck with this great American's intellect, wisdom and faith in immortality. He was walking in good company when he cherished another life and wrote of it. For the Apostle Paul pays recognition to those "who by patient continuance in well doing seek for glory and honor and immortality, eternal life" (Romans 2:7).

The chief hope of humanity has been and is another life in a fairer land. This one is too short and too burdened with problems to satisfy us mortals. The Indian dreamed of the Happy Hunting Ground; and the Christian, the Ivory Palaces.

Man is the only creature filled with such longings. Surely God would not have created him with this distinctive ability just to have it come to naught.

A STORY ABOUT A PRESIDENT
· ·
Not forsaking the assembling of ourselves together,
as is the manner of some.
HEBREWS 10:25

An interesting story is told of President Garfield's first
Sunday in Washington after his inauguration. A member of the cabinet requested that he call a Cabinet meeting
for ten o'clock the next morning (which was Sunday) to deal
with a matter that could lead to a national crisis. Garfield
refused on the ground that he had another appointment.
The perturbed Cabinet member insisted that the national
interest should take precedence over any other matter.

Garfield politely disagreed. Then the man remarked, "I
would like to know with whom you have an engagement so
important that it cannot be broken."

Garfield replied, "I will be as frank as you are. My
appointment is with the Lord to meet Him at His house at
ten-thirty tomorrow, and I shall be there."

He was there. The threatening crisis passed. The nation
survived. And President Garfield kept his appointment with
a greater ruler—the Prince of Peace—who had promised,
"For where two or three are gathered together in My name,
there am I in the midst of them" (Matthew 18:20). Garfield
had done considerable preaching. His reaction to the
Cabinet member's comments was as natural as breathing.

You will recall that President Garfield was assassinated
while in office. As family members and friends gathered
around the flower-decked casket to bid him good-bye, what
do you think gave them the most comfort? Not that he had
made it to the White House, but rather that he had made his
plans to dwell in a mansion made by the Lord.

HE IS NO PLAYFUL KITTEN

Be sober, be vigilant;
because your adversary the devil, as a roaring lion,
walks about, seeking whom he may devour.
1 PETER 5:8

Two little boys were walking home from Sunday Bible class. Their teacher had given them a stirring lesson on the devil. Worried about what he'd heard, one of the boys asked, "What do you think of the idea that there's a devil?"

"Aw, he's just like Santa Claus. He's really your daddy," replied the other one.

Most people believe in the existence of an all-powerful, all-good Spirit—God. By the same token, it's easy to believe in an all-sinister spirit that seeks to harm man. For the world that contains good also contains evil. With our physical eyes we cannot see either God or the devil, for both are spiritual beings and spirit is invisible. But we *can* see the works of both.

There is no way that we can drive to town and back and still not be convinced there is a devil. The outrageous, vile, dastardly things we see every day do not happen accidentally; they have some help from a wicked source. Evil has become so bold that kittens prey where only lions once dared to roar.

Satan is the great deceiver. He offers one thing and gives something else. If we take Satan into our boat, he will steer us right into the rapids and waterfalls. The most comforting thought is this: "Resist the devil, and he will flee from you. Draw near to God, and He will draw near to you" (James 4:7-8).

NOT MY HOME

. . . .

They were strangers and pilgrims on the earth.
For those who say such things declare plainly
that they seek a country...a better country,
that is, a heavenly.

HEBREWS 11:13-16

We need to bear in mind that we are sojourners. This world is not our home. Unless we are mindful of this obvious fact, we may become so attached to this world that we lose sight of the distant land to which we are going.

Thus it is fitting that we consider some facts about our pilgrimage:

§ *There is no inheritance in the land we now occupy.* So why should we fix our affections on earthly things? They are unsatisfactory and must be left behind.

§ *This pilgrimage is fleeting.* We are passing through for a purpose—to reach a certain destination. There is work to do. Failures will sadden. Victories will gladden. Pleasantries will be enjoyed. Suffering will be endured. But time is short and our pilgrimage will soon end.

§ Accordingly, *let us be faithful to the duties involved in the journey.* We pass through this life only once; we shall not come this way again. Let's be true and helpful while we can.

§ Also, *let's be content.* It's too much to expect to have all the comforts and joys of heaven while we're here on earth. As we face a few hardships, let's remember that in the land beyond we shall rest from our labors and no heart shall ever ache and no tear shall ever be shed.

THE WORD IS NOW

. . . .

For now we live, if you stand fast in the Lord.

1 THESSALONIANS 3:8

The knowledge we possess today is an accumulation of yesterday's lessons. This being true, we are smarter now than we have ever been before. Being more experienced and wiser, we should be able to do more.

Now is the time for life to be used, lived and enjoyed. Precious time is wasted by using the now to get ready to live tomorrow. After all, as the Scriptures say, "You know not what shall be on the morrow."

Now is the watchword of the wise. The foolish, however, say that they will do this or that tomorrow. This takes no working of the brain, no activity of the hands, no moving of the feet...just a little wagging of the tongue.

Sometimes it's *now or never* for two reasons: first, time may run out and there will be no more "nows"; second, tomorrow we may no longer have the desire. Good intentions don't always linger. Quench them enough times and they will die.

Now

Never mind about tomorrow—
It always is today;
Yesterday has vanished,
Wherever none can say.

Each minute must be guarded—
Made worth the while somehow;
There are no other moments;
It's always Just Now.

Then never mind tomorrow—
'Tis today you must enjoy
With all that's true and noble;
And the time for this is—
NOW.

A Good Today and a Better Tomorrow

· ·

For you do not know what a day may bring forth.

HEBREWS 10:25

An elderly brother often prayed at church: "Forgetting the things which are behind, give us strength and wisdom to press onward to a brighter future. May we be a progressive, improving people. May our tomorrow (if there be a tomorrow) be a little better than today and a lot better than yesterday."

Isn't that good? He was elderly...but not too old to dream.

Our future is waiting on the doorstep, and it's brighter if God is the keeper at the door. No one can tell what the future holds for us, but there are many things that we can forecast with considerable accuracy.

For instance, if we want our house—literally and figuratively—to stand the ravages of time, we must be thoughtful and visionary enough to build it on the Rock, Jesus Christ. It doesn't go up as fast, but it lasts longer.

Furthermore, if we would drink pure water from our well tomorrow, we can't throw garbage into it today. And if we would have a harvest in the fall, we can't eat the seed corn in the winter. If we want a high credit rating in the future, we must pay our present bills.

Moreover, we can't waste our bread today if we're going to have an appetite tomorrow. We can't be ugly to people now if we would have them as helping friends in times to come. We musn't sow wild oats in the spring if we would have a better harvest in the fall.

HIS LAWS WERE MADE FOR US

And He said to them,
"The Sabbath was made for man,
not man for the Sabbath."

MARK 2:27

Jesus and His Disciples walked through a cornfield on the Sabbath and plucked some of the ears. This "work" on the Sabbath irritated the more-concerned-with-law-than-people Pharisees. So they charged the Disciples with violating the Sabbath. But the Lord of the Sabbath came to His Disciples' defense, as seen in Mark 2:27 above.

The Sabbath law was made to bless man. But if a circumstance should arise whereby the keeping of it would produce the opposite effect, then its observance would counteract the very purpose for which it was given. Jesus determined that in this case man's welfare came first. This proves that the Lord really, really loves us. We are very special to the heart of God. *Everything* He has provided for us is for our good, whether it's the benefits of nature or the laws in the Bible regulating our relationships to one another and to God.

Every law God ever gave was for our welfare. He never gave a single commandment just to "boss" us, but to bless us. The highest motive prompted it.

Moreover, God's laws have always applied equally to all people. Even the law on tithing applied to all alike. God never eased this requirement for some to put a heavier burden on others. For laws to be fair they must treat everybody the same way. Fairness is so important in legislation, and God is one to be copied.

MAKE HAY WHILE THE SUN SHINES

. . . .

To every thing there is a season, and a time to every purpose
under the heaven: a time to be born, and a time to die;
a time to plant, and a time to pluck up that which is planted.

ECCLESIASTES 3:1-2

My father operated a general merchandise store in a little village. Much of my early life was spent working in it. Growing up in a village store and observing and listening to the people was a whole education within itself. I learned of their loves, their hates, their prejudices, their philosophies and their personalities. I learned about people and what made them tick.

Bright and early one morning, a farmer rushed in and bought some binder wire to use in binding hay. He commented, "I've got to make hay while the sun shines." He needed to take care of his duty before the rains came.

What he said is more than efficient farming; it's sound philosophy.

Timing has had a vital part in every success story. There is a time to act. Delay can mean failure. People who get ahead are always on top of things at the right time. By procrastinating, one can lose an important opportunity. Some people are too slow. It takes them more than two hours just to get something done that required no more than sixty minutes. Their hay will rot in the fields.

God's best gift to us is not things, but opportunities and the time to seize them. Let's make hay while the sun shines.

THE FOX AND THE CROW

· ·

A man who flatters his neighbor spreads a net for his feet.

PROVERBS 29:5

There is a valuable lesson in an old fable about a crow that took a piece of cheese out of a cottage window and flew up into a high tree. There she planned to eat the cheese.

A fox came along. When he saw the crow and the cheese, he sat down underneath the tree and began to flatter her. Knowing she was a vain bird, he said, "I never noticed it before, but your feathers are whiter and more delicate than any I have ever seen on any other crow in my life. What a fine shape and graceful turn of body you have! And your voice is so melodious and sweet. I don't believe there's a bird anywhere that could compare with you."

The blarney tickled the crow, and she strutted and wriggled about. She was so pleased, she felt like cawing. That was exactly what the fox wanted her to do, because the instant she opened her beak, the cheese dropped out. The fox snapped it up and trotted away, laughing at the credulity of that old crow.

The love of praise is common among us. This proneness to flattery makes a person vulnerable to exploitation by self-seeking people. We must watch to see if compliments come free. They may actually come with a high price attached.

> *'Tis an old maxim in the schools,*
> *That flattery is the food of fools;*
> *Yet now and then your men of wit*
> *Will condescend to take a bit.*

WHO AM I?

. . . .

Who has woe?
Who has sorrow? Who has contentions?
Who has babbling? Who wounds without cause?
Who has redness of eyes?... At the last it bites
like a serpent, and stings like an adder.

PROVERBS 23:29-32

Guess who I am.

I get a person to take me, and then I take the person. I enter lives and chase wisdom out. I am a chief destroyer of homes, have made countless numbers of orphans. I am the greatest murderer, have killed more people than all the wars of the world.

I have done more to destroy the human brain than anything else. I produce hangovers and decrease efficiency. I am the undertaker's roundup of business. I have knocked a world of people from the peak, but have never lifted any up. I have turned ambitious, industrious youths into irresponsible bums.

I weaken the strong and destroy the weak. I have made unconscionable brutes out of sensitive, high-grade people. I bleed the hearts of parents whose child likes me so much. I have bankrupted thousands of businesses. I dull the sense of people and give them a don't-care attitude.

I am something the Bible permits for medicinal purposes (1 Timothy 5:23). I am also something of which the Bible severely warns (Proverbs 20:1).

Who am I? I'm *alcohol!*

THE MOUSE

. . . .

It is a land that devours
its inhabitants...and there we saw the giants...
and we were in our own sight as grasshoppers,
and so we were in their sight.

NUMBERS 13:32-33

When the weak-kneed scouts reported to their comman-der, Joshua, they exaggerated.

In a more modern time and in another country, the mountains echoed with strange noises. Residents of the area gathered in anxious wonder to learn what was causing the peculiar sounds. After awhile, out crept...a mouse!

The moral is, *Do not make much ado about nothing.*

Fear is one of the most devastating adversaries of man, one that he himself feeds and nurtures. The most frighten-ing agonies of mankind come from dread rather than from actual trouble. Fear will cause people to think the noise of a mouse is volcanic rumblings about to erupt. Fear exagger-ates every danger. It makes mountains out of anthills. Fear kills our expectancy of better days, breaks down our defenses and unfits us for triumphant living.

The problem is not the mouse, the mountains, the land, nor is it other people. The problem is fear. More faith and trust in God will arm us with a more fearless spirit. Truly,

God hath not given us the spirit of fear;
but of power, and of love, and of a sound mind.

2 TIMOTHY 1:7

THE VICTOR'S STRENGTH

. . . .

They go from strength to strength,
every one of them in Zion appears before God.

PSALM 84:7

In Indian lore, when a man kills an enemy the strength of the slain foe passes into the victor's body. In that weird fancy lies a truth concerning man and his struggles. Each conquest makes us stronger for the next combat, but each defeat leaves us weaker for the next battle. Truly, victory heralds victory and defeat follows defeat.

Victory gives confidence, which is a most needed quality in facing opposition. This was exemplified in David's courage. He had tangled with the lion and the bear, and had slain them. This gave him confidence to go up against the giant.

Victory, however, can undo us, particularly if it makes us over-confident and we drop our guard.

Anybody can win if there is no opposition. Moreover, anybody can act bravely when there is no combatant to lift a dagger or when the opponent has fallen. When the brave lion is dead, even the scared donkeys switch to theatrical bravery, come out of hiding and kick him.

It's the hard-fought victories that prove our heroic nature. Battles easily won add little to glory. Hard-fought battles leave us bruised, scarred and hurt, but they're not so painful when we win.

No group can struggle, endure and take the blows like those who fight out of conviction. Mercenaries never do as well in the pulpit, in the classroom, in medicine, in business, in the factory or on the field of battle as those who are energized by a commitment that says, "Keep up the fight."

THE GHOST OF MIGHT-HAVE-BEEN

How shall we escape,
if we neglect so great a salvation?

HEBREWS 2:3

Neglect

Miss Meant-to has a comrade
And her name is Didn't-do.
Have you ever chanced to meet them,
Did they ever call on you?
These two girls now live together
In the house of Never-win,
And I'm told that it is haunted
By the ghost of Might-have-been.

THE SUNDAY SCHOOL JOURNAL

It was some time ago, but I remember it like yesterday. I went by an old, country cemetery that had suffered the ravages of neglect. Weeds and bushes were as high as my head. Some monuments had fallen. Others with cherished epitaphs were leaning, including one which said, "Gone but Not Forgotten." Not forgotten? It appeared that all the dead there had been erased from memory.

On the way back to town I passed an old farmhouse that was falling apart, leaning and tumbling to the ground. It was a crumbling reminder of the havoc wrought by neglect. The old house had perhaps been a sacred place to a happy family. There diligence had seen dreams fulfilled and hopes realized. Then neglect, creeping in like the hand of death, mocked the dreams and dashed the hopes. And now the house is the ghost of Might-have-been.

SIN AT THE DOOR

If you do well, will you not be accepted?
And if you do not do well, sin lies at the door.

GENESIS 4:7

One thing the human family has in common is sin. "For all have sinned, and come short of the glory of God" (Romans 3:23). It's the attitude we have toward sin that differentiates us. "Fools make a mock at sin" (Proverbs 14:9). "But a prudent man foresees the evil, and hides himself" (Proverbs 22:3).

Because of our own vulnerability to sin we should be merciful toward those who have succumbed to this common foe of man. Jesus said to the accusers of the sinful woman, "He that is without sin among you, let him first cast a stone at her" (John 8:7). Not a stone was thrown.

One of the damaging effects of sin is that it leaves sinners with an insensitive conscience. If we allow ourselves to commit a sin a few times, it won't be long before we deem it permissible.

Much of the history of the world has been written in the annals called *Sin*, and it's not a pretty tale. Of course sin has always promised something beautiful, or at least desirable in a perverted sense. Unquestionably, sin is the great deceiver of all time. The Bible speaks of "the deceitfulness of sin."

Philosopher and patriot Benjamin Franklin said:

> *Sin is not hurtful because it is forbidden,*
> *but it is forbidden because it is hurtful.*

Since "the wages of sin is death," it behooves every person to get his sins rubbed out before payday comes. Thank God for Jesus, who makes it possible.

CALL THE DOCTOR

. . . .

But when Jesus heard that, He said to him,
"Those who are well have no need of a physician,
but those who are sick."

MATTHEW 9:12

What about the health of your soul? It's of great concern to the Great Physician. This is His wish: "I wish above all things that you may prosper and be in health, even as your soul prospers" (3 John 2). To keep our souls healthy, we need to diagnose and re-diagnose our spiritual condition.

These are some of the illnesses of the soul to which we are subject:

❧ *Eye trouble.* Vision is bad. Can't see very far—only self.

❧ *Heart trouble.* The heart is the source of all conduct. When it is wrong, everything goes wrong.

❧ *Consumption.* Inwardly we become weaker and weaker. We scarcely feel it. We do not know it. We think everything's all right and that we will be better tomorrow.

❧ *Creeping paralysis.* It leaves us with no religious feelings at all. We feel neither happiness nor unhappiness. Our vital power is passing away, but we neither know nor care.

❧ *Fever.* There are different degrees of it. In lesser degrees there is foolish and wild talk. Words are extravagant and difficult to restrain. In higher degrees there's explosive conduct and uncontrollable behavior.

❧ Finally, there is *mortification.* Now there's no pain at all. This is *death!*

There's only one remedy for all these diseases. Call the Great Physician.

BURNING HEARTS

. . . .

And they said to one another,
"Did not our heart burn within us,
while He talked with us on the road,
and while He opened the Scriptures to us?"

LUKE 24:32

At first the two disciples did not recognize the resurrected Jesus who was walking with them. At times we, too, fail to recognize Him as He walks with us in trials and blessings.

His talking and opening the Scriptures for them caused their hearts to burn. This is understandable, for the word of God is spoken of as a fire. "His word was in my heart as a burning fire" (Jeremiah 20:9). It melts the coldness of indifference and worldliness, burns up the dross of selfishness and manifests itself in warm words and actions.

Devoid of burning hearts, we can assemble to worship without worshiping. We can say our prayers without praying. We can sing a hymn without making melody in our hearts to God. We can be exposed to a sermon without hearing it. And we can give money without giving ourselves.

We need glowing hearts—burning hearts—to give us power for life and service. Why do we have still hands, silent tongues and leaden feet? Why should one sermon on the day of Pentecost convert three thousand souls while today it takes almost three thousand sermons to witness the conversion of one soul? At least one answer is the lack of burning hearts.

INFLUENCING FUTURE GENERATIONS

. . . .

I call to remembrance the genuine faith that is in you,
which dwelt first in your grandmother Lois,
and your mother Eunice; and I am persuaded is in you also.

2 TIMOTHY 1:5

As seen in the above Bible verse, parents affect children for good or bad and they in turn affect their children, and on it goes generation after generation.

It has been revealed that an investigator of New York prisons ran across the Jukes family. Max Jukes, a Dutch settler in New York, had two sons. Each chose disreputable women for wives. Their homes had no regard for religion and the Bible. Their genealogical stream was traced five generations. Of the 709 descendants investigated, these were the findings: One fifth of them were criminals, having spent a total of 140 years in prison—a number of them murderers. Nearly one fourth had been paupers. One out of six of the women was a prostitute. My only point in giving these sickening facts is to show what a lack of religious and moral influence can do to hundreds yet unborn.

But now consider Jonathan Edwards and what real religious and moral influence can accomplish. Edwards spent the most of his life preaching in and serving the little New England village of Northampton. In morals he was strict; he stood four-square for the higher things of life. His descendants include 265 college graduates, 12 college presidents, 65 college professors, 60 physicians, 100 ministers, 75 army officers, 60 prominent authors, 100 lawyers, 30 judges, 80 public officers (including governors, state officials and mayors), 3 congressmen, 2 senators and 1 vice-president of the United States.

We are now! *now!* shaping the destinies of generations!

STAIRS OF OPPORTUNITY

. . . .

And truly if they had called to mind that country
from which they had come out,
they would have had opportunity to return.

HEBREWS 11:15

Stairs of *opportunity*. Just before a man reaches them, he has to open a closed gate that bears the sign "Push." Not pull. *"Push."* When he goes through the gate, he sees a stairway of stones that will bruise his feet or be steppingstones, depending upon his attitude. He cannot turn back on this one-way passage marked "Go." No opportunities are behind him; they're all ahead.

When we have the choice between waiting for the unreliable elevator of fortune or taking the stairs of opportunity, let's go for the stairs. Let's make the most of our lives beginning right now. When we push the gate marked "Push" and begin to climb the one-way stairs, we mustn't think there are no opportunities ahead because they're in the form of struggle, hard work, sweat and tears. Let's climb and keep climbing until we reach the top.

> *The stairs of opportunity*
> *Are sometimes hard to climb;*
> *And that can only be well done*
> *By one step at a time.*
>
> *But he who would go to the top*
> *Ne'er sits down and despairs;*
> *Instead of staring up the steps*
> *He just steps up the stairs.*

Precious opportunities come to all. The trouble is, many people don't recognize them when they see them. Opportunity seldom comes labeled "Opportunity: Take this."

HELPING ANOTHER

. . . .

For we are to God the fragrance of Christ
among those who are being saved...
the aroma of life to life.

2 CORINTHIANS 2:15-16

After paying the fees to enter the engineering school of a university, I attended a revival meeting and realized that I was in spiritual trouble. The evangelist was also a scientist and the head of the chemistry department in a Christian college. I was converted and subsequently packed my bags and went to the Christian college. Four months later I preached my first sermon.

Years passed, and then I had a tonsillectomy. I was in physical trouble. Down deep where the needles had been injected, an infection set up. My fever grew higher and higher. I was soaked with perspiration. The doctor told my family that I was going to die. But the Great Physician always has the last say. He wasn't ready for my work to end. He was sending a cure for my recovery.

A doctor of chemistry came to Forth Worth and spoke to the physicians about an amazing new sulfa drug and its ability to kill infection. My doctor was present. (Just think. What if he had not been there?) After the meeting, my doctor asked the chemist for some of this medicine, explaining that he needed it to help a dying man. He got the drug, rushed to the hospital and started giving it to me. It worked, and my life was saved. The almost-unbelievable circumstance was that the very man who helped to save my soul had a small but significant part in developing this new drug.

One person can make a world of difference. *Let's do what we can whenever and wherever we can.*

THEY GAVE UP

. . . .

And this is the victory
that overcomes the world, even our faith.

1 JOHN 5:4

A man who applied for a job with our company said that he had prepared himself for the ministry. He wanted to be a preacher. But when he got into the field, he met many discouraging situations. So he decided to get another job, and that's why he was at our door.

He said that he had preached for a church the Sunday before and learned that they had drained the baptistry and filled it with chairs. Not people. Empty chairs. Their reason was that they seldom ever baptized anyone and never used the extra chairs. If they maintained that attitude, pretty soon they wouldn't need the pews either. Might as well hang a black crepe on the door. Death was upon them.

Pessimists like that remind me of the person who blew out a candle because it was dark in the room. The room just got darker.

The kind of faith that overcomes obstacles and achieves victory is the kind that leaves no room for pessimism. How can you be pessimistic when you believe that somehow you are going to come out on top? Maybe not today, but eventually and at the proper time. God's timing is better than ours.

The one place where you should never, never find pessimism is in the church. For God has said, "So shall My word be that goes forth out of My mouth: it shall not return unto Me void, but it shall accomplish that which I please, and it shall prosper in the thing to which I sent it" (Isaiah 55:11).

THE WRONG CUE

. . . .

Let no one deceive himself.

1 CORINTHIANS 3:18

The master of ceremonies had been informed by the speaker that he would be talking about the three young Hebrew boys, Shadrach, Meshach and Abednego, from the book of Daniel. But the emcee just could not remember their names. Then he had an idea. Not wanting to hold notes, he wrote the names on a slip of paper and pinned it inside his coat lapel. Then at the proper time in the introduction, he would make a grand gesture, open his coat and take a look at the paper.

And that's what he did. At the height of his enthusiastic eloquence he said, "Our intelligent and scholarly speaker will discuss the three brave and courageous Hebrew children— (then he quickly glimpsed at the inside of his lapel) *Hart, Schaffner and Marx!*"

The wrong cue can be bewildering. As you see, this can happen to a speaker. Similarly, the football player can be given the wrong signal. Confusion results.

A farmer can fall victim to hurtful advice, and as a result failure is his harvest. Likewise, the stock buyer can be exploited with misleading tips and bankruptcy ensues. The voter may be fed vote-getting, vote-buying promises, but disappointment follows.

Therefore, closely examine everything that affects you. Weigh it carefully. Be not deceived. And above all, deceive not yourself.

BLEST BE THE TIE THAT BINDS

. . . .

And they continued steadfastly in the apostles' doctrine
and fellowship, and in breaking of bread, and in prayers.

ACTS 2:42

John Fawcett, the minister of a poor country church in
Wainsgate, Yorkshire, received such a meager salary that
it barely supported his family. Hence, he accepted a call
to a London church with a substantial compensation.

The day came for the wagons to be loaded with family
goods and furniture. Soon the house was surrounded by sorrowing, weeping people, who begged their beloved preacher
to remain. Mrs. Fawcett was overcome by the outpouring of
grief and called to her husband, "Oh, John, we cannot go!"

"No," he replied, "We cannot go. We will stay." Everything was taken back into the house.

The story goes that the gifted Dr. John Fawcett stayed
with the country church, poor but rich, on $125-a-year sup-
port and the devotion and attachment of its members. In
celebration of the event, he wrote the hymn which accentu-
ates human closeness and fellowship:

Blest be the tie that binds
Our hearts in Christian love;
The fellowship of kindred minds
Is like to that above.

Before our Father's throne
We pour our ardent prayers;
Our fears, our hopes, our aims are one,
Our comforts and our cares.

We share each other's views,
Each other's burdens bear;
And often for each other flows
The sympathizing tear.

FEED THEM

. . . .

Jesus said to him, "Feed My sheep."

JOHN 21:17

The local minister called a meeting to discuss "How to Get People to Attend Church." A representation of various occupations attended...with their advice.

The manager of the Little Theater suggested, "The church needs to be more theatrical."

"Drop some of the spiritual activities and introduce athletics. In season we play a game every Friday night and the bleachers are packed," recommended the football coach.

The psychologist said, "If we could just find some way to call everybody's name.... People like attention." A novel idea came from the head of a thrift association: "It would be appealing to have some free services. Take no collections on certain Sundays."

A young man, fresh out of a school of modernism, stated, "I have learned that the church has become too churchy. Let's use some word other than *church*. Using another word would appeal to those who don't want to be too churchy."

But it an the old farmer who came up with some practical advice we sometimes don't like to acknowledge. He said, "Last week I was at a farmers' convention. I never heard a single address on how to get cattle to come to the rack. We spent our time discussing the best kind of *feed*."

Christ's solemn command to Peter in the beginning verse of Scripture, John 21:17, is still relevant. It will do more to increase attendance than all other things combined.

THE COWBOY AND THE CACTUS

. . . .

Where there is no counsel the people fall;
but in the multitude of counselors there is safety.

PROVERBS 11:14

I recall the story of the cowboy, tormented with a rash, who ran and jumped into a cactus plant. His explanation was, "Well, at the time it seemed like it was the thing to do."

We laugh at the cowboy because we are actually laughing at ourselves. Most of us at times have jumped too fast. It is, therefore, a mark of wisdom to seek counsel. However, unless the counselors are wise and knowledgeable, one is no better off—maybe even worse. It is easy to get the wrong advice, especially up and down the streets. So do not listen to failures, or near failures, or mediocre achievers.

After consulting counselors, in the last analysis you will have to make the decision yourself. So think it through. Personally, I like to sleep on a proposition; it may have a different look in the morning. This gives me a little more time before I leap.

You certainly need a little more time before answering those who call and say, "You have been selected…." More than half the time you had better run the other way as fast as you can. I can say this because I have been selected. More than once.

GOSSIPER OR GOSSIPEE?

A talebearer reveals secrets;
but he who is of a faithful spirit conceals a matter.

PROVERBS 11:13

A college freshman class was asked to define *gossip*. One student said, "Gossip is quietly going after a person behind his back." Another answered, "It's an effort to build one up by lowering another." A third replied, "It's a secretive pastime for some that others have to pay for." A fourth stated, "It's telling something bad on another that usually begins with 'They say,' or 'Have you heard?' or 'Don't tell I told you, but.'" Those freshmen were doing some thinking.

The crowd of talebearers is large in number but short on respectability. Nobody trusts them; for if they will gossip *to* you, they will gossip *about* you.

The talebearer, having overrated his importance but with no more talent than the ordinary, with a temperament unrefined by grace, has gone underground with his activities and whispers in hush-hush tones that build up, reverberate and become roaring thunders.

Just being an observer in talkative society has taught me that gossip is mischievous, juicy and easy to swallow, easy to share, but grievous to bare. It spreads on vulture's wings and feeds on the death it carries.

There are two classes of people in the world: gossipers and gossipees. As much as I dislike being talked about, God help me to belong to this class instead of the other.

JUST BE GLAD

Why are you cast down, O my soul? And why are you disquieted within me? Hope in God; for I shall yet praise Him.

PSALM 42:11

Longfellow told of going out into his garden after a devastating storm. He saw a bird's nest ripped from the tree and scattered on the ground. As he beheld the wreckage and thought of all the apparently wasted labor, he felt sorry for the little birds. But then he heard a chattering overhead and looked up. He saw that the birds, far from being discouraged, had already begun to build another nest. They could sing and work and try again when things went wrong.

The bravest and strongest have their bad and sad days. But God can drive out dismay and make us glad again.

Just Be Glad

Oh, heart of mine, we shouldn't
Worry so!
What we've missed of calm we couldn't
Have, you know!
What we've met of stormy pain,
And of sorrow's driving rain,
We can better meet again
If it blow.

For we know, not every morrow
Can be sad;
So forgetting all the sorrow
We have had,
Let us fold away our fears,
And put by our foolish tears,
And through all the coming years
Just be glad.

JAMES WHITCOMB RILEY

WHAT DID YOU DO WITH THE SHIP?

Give no offense, either to the Jews or to the Greeks,
or to the church of God.

1 CORINTHIANS 10:32

Shortly after World War II a magician was entertaining on a ship just off the English coast. The passengers were astounded by his taking eggs from ears, pickles from noses, rabbits from hats and sawing through a box containing a woman. Also, there was a haughty parrot in the show. Each time the magician performed a feat, the parrot would squawk, "Faker! Faker!" and the people would roar.

Finally the magician promised that he would do a trick that not even Houdini had ever been able to perform. The parrot blabbed, "Faker! Faker!" while the sleight-of-hand artist sprinkled some hocus-pocus dust and waved his hand. Suddenly the ship hit a floating mine and was blown to pieces.

When dawn came there was the parrot sitting on one end of a makeshift raft and the magician sitting on the other end. After a pause, the parrot hopped over and said, "Okay, Smarty, you win. But what did you do with the ship?"

Often we refer to the church as "The Ship of Zion." It too has suffered from...shall we say, *fakers*? At least the church has suffered from incompatible behavior. It has been blasted by compromise, torpedoed by infiltration of uncommitted members, mined by lukewarmness, gunned by worldliness, shelled by humanism, bombed by ritualism and missiled by commercialism.

All of this has been hurtful—so injurious, in fact, that religion has been on the decline. If it continues, *we* may be asking, "What did you do with the ship?"

IMA MESS

. . . .

The prudent man foresees evil, and hides himself;
the simple pass on, and are punished.

PROVERBS 27:12

A woman made this startling statement: "If they had
named me in keeping with the life I've lived, my given
name would be *Ima* and my last name would be *Mess.*"

We get ourselves into so many messes that our status
quo can be defined as the mess we're in. Come to think of it,
that isn't a bad description of a big portion of our population.

We fail to figure our expenses versus our income— especially the probability of the unknown arising—and then we
have debts that smother us. This puts us in another bind. As
Solomon said, "The borrower is servant to the lender."
Sometimes we talk when we should listen. This gets us into
difficulty, too. Alienates friends or offends strangers who
might have become friends. At other times we get into a
mix-up by signing notes and becoming surety for another
person's debts.

The most heartbreaking messes, however, come from
getting caught up in a web of sin and evil. People don't plan
to go very far down the downward path, but it's hard to stop
anything going downhill. At the bottom is the crash.
Nevertheless, this caution can spare one the first step which
ends in the smash-up: "Abstain from all appearance of evil."

No matter what mess we're in, we caused it. Maybe some
others helped, but in the last analysis we made the decision
that put us there. Man's problems are man-made, but let's
take heart. They can be God-solved, and He is saying, "Your
iniquities will I remember no more."

CUT WOOD AND LET THE CHIPS FLY

. . . .

For do I now persuade men, or God?
Or do I seek to please men? For if I still pleased men,
I would not be a servant of Christ.

GALATIANS 1:10

When I was a boy we burned wood, and those cold winters required a lot of it. A hired hand and I had to cut it from standing trees. My helper was an old man, wise and overflowing with practicality. His name was Fred.

One day as we were getting ready to fell a tree, Fred said, "You see that tree? You see that axe? Just cut wood and let the chips fly."

That's what I did that day, and that's what I've tried to do ever since—"cut wood and let the chips fly."

This philosophy requires us to preach the gospel, or to do our job whatever it is; to speak the truth and uphold the right, and let the consequences take care of themselves. It requires fearlessness and forthrightness without compromise. These qualities are essential if we would have the respect of people around us. For the world is not going to follow a person who is not seen in this light. Wishy-washy people are never esteemed. Nobody can lead others while riding a merry-go-round, for that sort of person hardly knows where he wants to go himself.

SEEING OUR OWN FAULTS

And why do you look at the speck in your brother's eye,
but do not perceive the plank in your own eye?

LUKE 6:41

A strange story has come out of a village in Scotland. It's about a half-witted man who had a coat that provoked comment whenever people saw it. All down the front it was covered with patches of various sizes, mostly large. When asked why his coat was patched in such an uncommon way, he would answer that the patches represented his neighbors' shortcomings. He would point to each patch and relate the sin of some neighbor, then on to another, until he had rehearsed the sins of practically everyone in the village.

On the back of his coat there was a small, gray patch about the size of a penny. When asked what that one represented, he would reply, "That's my sin and I can't see it!"

This is a fair picture of many people today, though they would never make and wear such a coat. But what can we do to overcome this common problem?

§ *We can recognize our own faults.* "I do remember my faults this day" (Genesis 41:9).

§ *We can overcome evil with good.* "Be not overcome with evil, but overcome evil with good" (Romans 12:21).

§ *We can watch.* "Be vigilant" (1 Peter 5:8).

§ *And we can pray.* "Watch and pray, that you enter not into temptation: the spirit indeed is willing, but the flesh is weak" (Matthew 26:41).

Somewhere, some way, sometime each day,
I'll turn aside, and stop and pray.
My own sins, dear Lord, let me see,
And that will be a victory.

Unexpected Trouble

You do not know what will happen tomorrow.

JAMES 4:14

When Job was enjoying health, happiness and prosperity, he did not expect his children to be slain, his property to be taken, his body to be afflicted with boils from head to foot and his friends to deride him.

Today we all know that illness can come, but we don't expect it to strike when it does. We are susceptible to accidents, but we're not looking for them when they arrive. The dismissal slip comes. When it does, you suddenly belong to the unemployed. You're caught unaware.

Burglars strip your house. Precious valuables are gone. You had not planned to cope with this loss. A storm rips off your roof. Much damage is done. You weren't expecting this. Some of your supposed friends misjudge you and it hurts. You never thought it would happen.

What, then, what can we do to manage trouble that we cannot foresee and wouldn't think probable?

First, let's learn from Job. He maintained his faith and trust in God. He said, "Though He slay me, yet will I trust in Him" (Job 13:51). Let's leave the future and its circumstances to Him.

Second, let's meet our problems with grit. We've learned from experience that we have strength in times of need. Had circumstances been more favorable, we wouldn't have learned that. When the occasion comes, let's draw on that God-given strength.

LONGING TO RUN AWAY

Oh that I had in the wilderness a lodging place
for wayfaring men; that I might leave my people,
and go from them.

JEREMIAH 9:2

When we suffer demoralizing disappointment, bitter sorrow or agonizing failure, we may feel like fleeing to find refuge.

This was the mood of the prophet Jeremiah, as recorded in the verse above. Jeremiah's sensitivity subjected him to the despondency that so often accompanies a responsive temperament. And certainly the conduct of his people was enough to distress him or any other impressionable person. In his gloom, he longed to escape from the burden of responsibility. He wanted to run away.

For Jeremiah, as for any of us, running away is not an appropriate solution to distress. It is not the heroic thing to do. It nurtures neither self-respect nor personal strength. What it does do is weaken a person until running becomes the automatic response to problems. And because of this, some people have spent their lives on the run.

We mustn't flee. For it is our role to be stewards, and a necessary duty of a steward is to be faithful and responsible. And, it is also our calling to be soldiers, not deserters. We honor God, family, friends and ourselves when we trust on, hold on and fight on. Not in some distant place, but where the conflict needs us most.

BETRAYED BUT NOT BEATEN

The Lord Jesus on the same night in which
He was betrayed, took bread;
and when He had given thanks, He broke it.

1 CORINTHIANS 11:23-24

Betrayed!

Jesus was prepared to deal with the unfair and hateful treatment of a wishy-washy, degenerate, traitorous people. He knew all about them—their weaknesses, passions and prejudices. He understood the cowardice of His friends and the hate of His foes. He knew the weakness of Peter and the treason of Judas. Nothwithstanding, He continued with His plans. Every step took Him closer to a cross on which a bloodthirsty mob would nail Him. Yet He did not refuse His destiny in a terribly evil world.

But how did all this affect Him? He continued to pray and be thankful. "The Lord Jesus on the same night in which He was betrayed," prayed and gave thanks. Even in the shadow of the cross He found much for which to be thankful. In that trying hour, with death so close, He spoke to His Twelve about the future of the Church and gave instructions about a memorial to Him. Serenity and hope—not frustration and desperation—ruled His heart. This feeling was based upon a knowledge of *all* the facts.

In contrast, in our partial knowledge and incomplete faith we often doubt and despair. Good people are disillusioned by their fellowmen and become downhearted. This presents a danger, not only to their spirit but to their future. For a victorious life, let's look to the Master. He says, "Take up your cross and follow Me."

STAY IN THERE

· ·

For as he thinks in his heart, so is he.

PROVERBS 23:7

After being in a scuffle, a little boy ran away. When asked if he'd lost, he said, "No! I just ran away for awhile."

I like that. There is no defeat until a person admits it. Let's train ourselves not to accept defeat, but to stay in there.

Nine times out of ten defeat was due to the mind's raising a white flag when it should have shouted, *"Charge!"*

Defeat

If you think you are beaten, you are;
If you think you dare not, you don't;
If you'd like to win but you think you can't,
It's almost a cinch you won't.

If you think you'll lose, you're lost;
For out of the world we find
Success begins with a fellow's will,
It's all in the state of mind.

Life's battles don't always go
To stronger or faster men,
But soon or late the man who wins
Is the one who thinks he can.

Defeat is not so bad *if* it does not become a vocation. Not so tragic *if* it's a preparation for continued effort. In this latter case, defeat is not defeat, just a temporary setback that gives stimulus to a new and better start.

CHEATED AND BLESSED

Yet your father has deceived me,
and changed my wages ten times,
but God did not allow him to hurt me.

GENESIS 31:7

After a lady and her five little children started attending church, she appealed to me for help. Her husband was in the penitentiary, and she wanted me to get him released. That wasn't easy back then, and especially since he was a bricklayer who was needed in the construction work going on at the prison. But I told her I would help.

After several calls to the governor and other officials, it was agreed that he would be released if I found him a job. Now that *was* difficult—getting a job for an unseen, unknown convict. After much effort, however, I did find employment for him.

Still more had to be done. He needed clothes, and I furnished them. He needed transportation to get to and from his job, and to carry his tools. I loaned him $100 (worth about $500 now) to make a down payment on an old car. He promised to reimburse me $10 a week. All I ever got from him was $30, and that wasn't easy to get.

Still, under the same circumstances I would do it again. I didn't help him, for people who fail to respond to kindness are not helped; but maybe I did help his poor wife and the even poorer children. Whether the effort helped them or not, it helped me. For God blesses givers regardless of the merit of the receivers.

A LIFETIME OF LEARNING

· ·

And besides this, giving all diligence,
add to your faith virtue; and to virtue, knowledge.

2 PETER 1:5

The college senior, feeling his importance, said, "Listen, I know a *few* things."

The freshman answered, "You don't have anything on me. *I* know as *few* things as anybody!"

After a senior finished the semester and received his degree, he rushed out and shouted, "O world, how you'd have suffered if I hadn't been born. Here I am! *I have an A.B.*"

The world shouted back, "Son, it will take you a *lifetime* to learn the rest of the alphabet!"

When a person is educated beyond his intelligence, the world has a way of adjusting his position from High Brow to Low Brow. He'll get the shock of his life when he sees how many people with so little classroom schooling know so much that he doesn't know. *Education is where one finds it*, and they continued to find it where they were, on a day-to-day basis.

God wants us to learn and to keep on learning. The Christian's calling includes a lifetime of increasing knowledge. And if older people have lived up to this command, they know more than the younger ones, all other things being equal. "Days should speak, and multitude of years should teach wisdom" (Job 32:7).

EARS THAT DON'T HEAR
. . . .
They have ears, but they do not hear.

PSALM 115:6

Little Bobby received permission from his mother to play with a friend in a nearby park. His mother warned him, however, not to go to the other boy's home. She insisted, "Don't go home with Jimmy, because I wouldn't know how to get in touch with you."

When night was beginning to come on and Bobby hadn't returned home, his mother and father went looking for him. He wasn't at the park. The neighbors didn't know where he was. After many calls and searching, they found the other boy's home and there was their wandering boy.

After sighs of relief, hugs and kisses, Bobby's father said, "Didn't you hear your mother say you weren't supposed to go to Jimmy's house?" "Yes, but barely," came the scarcely audible answer.

Bobby's hearing describes a world of adults. They hear, but barely. They hear, but don't heed.

Bobby heard with his ears but not with his heart. Jesus linked the ears and heart together—closed ears and hardened heart (Mark 8:17-19). To hear, we must use more than our ears; we must also use our heart.

THE BEAUTY OF HOLINESS

· ·

Charm is deceitful, and beauty is vain,
but a woman who fears the Lord,
she shall be praised.

PROVERBS 31:30

A church member who had a disfigured face was visiting the minister's wife. The preacher's boy (and we all know how children can speak their feelings) blurted out, "You're ugly."

The embarrassed mother scolded him. When the boy apologized he said, "I only meant it for a joke." Too confused to think, the mother replied, "Well, dear, the joke would've been much better if you'd said, 'How pretty you are!'"

Some of us do have a special talent for opening our mouth and sticking our foot in it.

And it's said that beauty is only skin deep. If we're thinking of physical beauty, that's right. Obviously physical beauty is only skin deep, and that's why it's so short-lived.

But spiritual beauty is different; it becomes more attractive as the years go by. In a counseling session I asked a woman to write down the most beautiful qualities a person could have. She came up with this list: tolerant, forgiving, merciful, unrevengeful, courteous, polite, thankful, kind, helpful, affectionate, understanding, humble, mild, faithful, trusting, unselfish, enthusiastic, cooperative, prayerful, not self-willed, not easily provoked.

Nobody could say a person with these qualities is ugly. We can all be beautiful when we clothe ourselves with the beauty of holiness.

WE ARE NOT ALONE

. . . .

And the Lord God said,
"It is not good that man should be alone."

GENESIS 2:18

*L*ast year little Jimmy went to summer camp. It was his first time away from home alone. He wasn't known for his letter writing, but one day he did write a card. It contained only twenty-one words:

Dear Mom and Dad,

There are sixty boys in camp this week,
but I sure wish there were only fifty-nine.

Jimmy

Jimmy was lonely even though there were fifty-nine other little boys around him. The most lonely I've ever been was in the midst of seven million people. I was in New York City and knew nobody. Other people were lonesome, too, because I could see the stamp of loneliness on their faces. So it takes more than people to save you from the feeling of loneliness. You need people you know and enjoy and with whom you have a communion of spirits.

Of course, there is one comforting thing about loneliness: it's better to be alone than to be in bad company.

However, there are ways to prevent loneliness even if you are separated from people. When you're with a pleasant and helpful book, you're not alone. When you're engaged in prayer, you're not alone. When you permit God's Holy Word to speak to your heart, you are not alone.

HORSE SENSE

. . . .

Let your yea be yea; and your nay, nay.

JAMES 5:12

*A*t dinnertime, a boy asked his father, "What does it mean when they say a fellow has horse sense?"

"It means he can say *Nay!*" replied the father.

It's horse sense to learn to say *No*. Power for daily living and success demand it. We face a barrage of requests from every side that requires us to say *Yes* or *No*. It's easy to say *Yes*. It's the *No* that's harder to say.

Mankind has suffered immeasurably because frail humans have found it difficult to say *No*. The trail of tears leads all the way back to Adam and Eve. Eve couldn't say *No* to the serpent. Adam couldn't say *No* to Eve.

Many a failure and predicament has come because *No* was too hard to utter. The alcoholic, the dope addict, the playboy, the criminal, the idler, the beguiled, the holder of bad debts, the school dropout, the compromiser, all failed to say *No*.

Today a world that groans in misery says, "My unhappiness is the unhappiness of not saying *No*."

But many *Yes*es are needed in life. No person should be all negative. So my definition of *greatness* is "the courage to speak *Yes* and *No*, and the discernment to know when to speak each."

PLAYING ON ONE STRING

. . . .

Thus says the Lord:
"Refrain your voice from weeping, and your eyes
from tears; for your work shall be rewarded...
and there is hope."

JEREMIAH 31:16-17

As the story goes, a distraught man was about to jump from the Brooklyn Bridge. But a policeman laid hand on him and pulled him back. The man who was bent on suicide protested, "I'm miserable. My life is hopeless! Let me go!"

"I'll make you a proposition," stated the officer. "You take five minutes to tell me why life is *not* worth living, and I'll take five minutes to tell you why life *is* worth living. Then if you still feel like jumping, I won't stop you." After ten minutes they both jumped.

Whether this story is true or not, I don't know. But this I *do* know: hope is the "anchor of the soul" (Hebrews 4:19). Without hope a person is free to drift or jump or give up. When hope is gone, there is nothing left.

There is a lesson in Frederic Watt's famous painting of "Hope." A young woman is sitting on a globe with her head bowed and eyes bandaged. In her hand is a harp with only one string; all of the others are broken. Interestingly, she is strumming that last string.

When everything is broken, gone, and the harp of life is left with only one string and it pressed to the breaking point, hope plays on it a sweet melody. When fortune is gone, health broken, opportunity fled, then hope takes up life's harp and plays on the one remaining string.

LAUGH A LITTLE

. . . .

God has made me laugh,
so that all who hear will laugh with me.

GENESIS 21:6

One of the very effective resources of creative people is their sense of humor, adaptability and playfulness. Their comments on unexpected ideas are entertaining to them and to others. Laughter comes easily to such people, like the bubbling waters of a flowing well. Anything is to them the starter for a bit of wit.

Care drives nails in our coffin. Laughter pulls them out.

Care to our coffin adds a nail, no doubt;
And every grin, so merry, draws one out.

JOHN WOLCOT

The person who has not cultivated a sense of humor is to be pitied. For laughter is one of those blessings, like music and flowers, that God has given to relieve the tensions of life.

The day we can laugh at ourselves is the day we have grown up. And when we do, there is little chance that we shall be proud and pompous.

When we are faced with serious, difficult and trying situations, we can clear our burdened heads and think better if we can laugh a bit.

LOUDER!

. . . .

But there are some who trouble you.

GALATIANS 1:7

Grandfather held a revival in a community where some profane men decided to break up his meeting. As he got up to speak, one of the men stood up and shouted, "Speak up *loud* so we can hear you!" Accordingly, there being no public address system, Grandpa spoke loud and clear. A little later the man stood up and yelled again, *"Louder!"* And louder Grandpa got until surely everybody could hear. But shortly the man stood again and roared, *"Louder!"*

It was then that Grandpa stopped his sermon and said, "Ladies and gentlemen, the day will come when this old world will quit turning, the sun will cease to shine, the stars will fall and explode, and Gabriel will blow the trumpet so loud that it will be heard around the world; and at when that happens, I'm sure that one in this crowd will stand up and holler, *'Louder!'* "

It doesn't take oratorical talent to interrupt a speech or stir up strife in a crowd. It doesn't take the skill of a seamstress to needle somebody. Being human, we are more sensitive than a piece of cloth, but *smarter;* so we needn't let the pricks show. Let's try to remain calm. Let's keep cool. Let's keep our head; for if it gets to be a battle of wits, we'll need it.

We have no control over hecklers, needlers and agitators, but we can control ourselves and refuse to allow bitterness to spring up within us and trouble us even more than what someone does and says.

LIFE IS NOT A HUNDRED-YARD DASH

The plans of the diligent lead surely to plenty,
but those of everyone who is hasty, surely to poverty.

PROVERBS 21:5

Solomon states that haste leads to want—yes, to *many* wants. Hurry wreaks its damage in stress, strain and unproductivity. It leaves many victims along the way of life.

Some people hurry while sitting down and doing nothing. When sitting down, waiting for a plane, they're in a hurry. Of course their sense of urgency doesn't hurry the plane. Waiting for their meal at the restaurant, they hurry; but their steaming doesn't cook the meal any quicker. They feel hurried because they've had their foot on the accelerator of their nervous system so long that now they can't let up and coast.

We must wait for some things to run their course. For this reason some who live in a frenzied hurry wouldn't make good obstetricians or midwives.

We should not allow external circumstances to set our tempo in life. Each individual is different and must set his own pace. The great Finnish runner Paavo Nurmi illustrated this principle. He always carried a watch with him in his races. He referred to that watch, not to the other runners. He ran his own race, kept his own tempo, regardless of competition.

Life is not a hundred-yard dash. It's more like a cross-country run. Since life is not a short dash, victory doesn't necessarily go to the swift but rather to the persevering.

WHEN EVIL IS PRAISED

. . . .

The memory of the just is blessed.

PROVERBS 10:7

It is not uncommon for justice to be flouted and for evil to be enthroned. The wicked often take advantage of the righteous. There is much unfairness. But the prosperity of the wicked is only a seeming success. Evil on a throne is still evil, and right in a dungeon is still right; and in time, their places will be reversed.

In their struggles for right, good people may have been tempted to think that their labors were in vain. But their warfare has not been for naught. Their heroic stand has made the battles easier for others, and it is in grateful memory of them that we pay tribute to their accomplishments.

For the most part, history is on the side of right. Time has a way of correcting wrongs. History usually blesses the just person instead of the glory-seeking faker. No one thinks of Ahab and Nero as he thinks of Moses and Paul. By some standards, all four men were great; but only the memories of the Moses and Paul are blessed today.

It gives us optimism to keep in mind the glorious truth that "the memory of the just is blessed." It renews our hopes when we live not only for today, but for our works that will follow after us when we rest from our labors (Revelation 14:13).

REMEMBER THE GOAL

. . . .

The Lord had called us to preach the gospel to them.

ACTS 16:10

A young preacher went to an older preacher and asked him what to do to draw a crowd and make a congregation grow. He said, "I have tried philosophy, history, book reviews and even politics, but the people won't come. What should I do now?"

The old man kindly responded, "Preach the gospel and pray. It will make a difference in you and touch hearts around you."

In writing, pick up the pen and write. In farming, plant the seed. In merchandising, sell. In sheep ranching, shepherd the sheep. In mechanics, wield the wrench. In transportation, move. In banking, get money in and lend it out. In social work, help somebody. In baseball, hit the ball. In education, teach. In building and maintaining the church, preach the gospel.

The point is, no matter what the cherished reason for a group's existence is and the major goal they have, *unless they are watchful* they may be diverted and become bogged down in so many other matters that they lose sight of the original intent. This is one reason why people fail in various endeavors. It was said of a man whose business failed, "He became so involved in other interests that he neglected his business." If a school becomes so entangled in new projects that it gives only minor attention to the basics, the result will be a new crop of students who can barely read, write and figure. And if a church, which is a spiritual body, becomes so absorbed in material matters that it assigns the gospel to a back pew, in time the other pews will go empty.

LOSE OR USE OPPORTUNITY

. . . .

After the reading of the law and the prophets, the rulers
of the synagogue sent to them, saying, "Men and brethren,
if you have any word of exhortation for the people, say on."
Then Paul stood up, and motioning with his hand said,
"Men of Israel, and you who fear God, listen."

ACTS 13:15-16

The name of William Jennings Bryan has gone down in
the annals of time as one of the greatest orators that ever
graced a platform. A few years before his death, a friend was
riding with him across Chicago. They passed close to the
coliseum where he made a forceful speech at the Democratic
Convention, 1896—the very speech which catapulted him
to become the presidential nominee of his party in three
elections. It was the speech in which Bryan concluded by
saying, "You shall not press down upon the brow of labor
this crown of thorns. You shall not crucify mankind upon a
cross of gold."

The friend said, "Mr. Bryan, I suppose many times
before you had made just as able a speech as that, and it was
never heard of."

"Yes," he replied, "I suppose so. But that convention was
my opportunity, and I made the most of it." Then after a
moment of silence he said, "And that's about all we do in
this world—lose or use our opportunity."

Grabbed opportunity is the key that opens the door of
success. Seized occasion is the ladder by which we climb to
usefulness and achievement. The answered call is the victory
over slumber. He who seizes the right moment becomes the
man of the hour.

So, "strike while the iron is hot." This is what the Apostle
Paul did when he went into the synagogue.

OPEN HOUSE FOR FRIENDS

. . . .

And Julius treated Paul kindly and gave him liberty
to go to his friends and receive care.

ACTS 27:3

*A*lways keep an open heart, open house, open hands and open time for friends. George W. Childs has said, "Do not keep the alabaster box of your love and tenderness sealed up until your friends are dead. Speak approving, cheering words while their ears can hear them. The kind things you mean to say when they are gone, say before they go. The flowers you mean to send for their coffin, send to brighten and sweeten their homes before they leave them.

"Let us learn to anoint our friends while they are yet among the living. Postmortem kindness does not cheer the burdened heart; flowers on the coffin cast no fragrance backward over the weary way."

Of what shall a person make room in his house, if he has not room for friends? And of what shall he have time, if he has not time for friends?

We just shake hands at meeting
With many that come nigh;
We nod the head in greeting
To many that go by—

But welcome through the gateway
Our few old friends and true;
Then hearts leap up, and straightway
There's open house for you,
Old friends,
There's open house for you.

GERALD MASSEY

WHISPERS OF HOPE

. . . .

For our sakes, no doubt, this is written, that he who plows
should plow in hope; and he who threshes in hope
should be partaker of his hope.

1 CORINTHIANS 9:10

*C*all them the whispers of fancy if you wish, but I prefer to
call them the whispers of *hope*...and to listen to them.
Hope is an energizing voice. When you feel like dropping
dead in your tracks, hope helps you to take another step and
somehow, some way, keep going.

Living expectantly changes the tune of life. It makes the
night less dark, the solitude less lonely, the hurt less painful
and the fear less acute. It gives broad dimensions to life.

But for many people this charming and winsome trait—
the zest of life—is gone. Instead of a growing expectancy and
excitement as the years go by, their lives have shrunk into
dull routines and dumb acceptances of the status quo. Here
they are in a big, wonderful world with just one try at it, and
they are allowing their days to be little more than the ticks
of the ever-moving hands of time. It could be their world of
adventure, savor, enjoyment and expectation. It *should* be.

Why do they live with no dream of the future?

❧ *One reason is they're asleep*—yes, asleep and satisfied.
They are satisfied to eat three meals a day, read the evening
paper, watch a favorite television program, sleep eight
hours, go to work and start the same type of day all over
again. No expectancy!

❧ *Another reason is they have practiced caution and
timidity for so long* that anything different would be discon-
certing. It would break into their routine of habits.

For these reasons they assign themselves to the hum-
drums of life.

TIME WITH GOD

. . . .

And when He had sent the multitudes away,
He went up on a mountain by Himself to pray.
And when evening had come, He was there alone.

MATTHEW 14:23

Although God the Father saw that it was not good for man to live alone, His own Son saw that sometimes being alone was a great relief. And if Jesus felt the need to seek relief from the strain and stress of life, how much more should that feeling sometimes exist in us. If He could find needed relief in solace and prayer, so can we.

Gaius Glenn Atkins aptly stated: "Twice in each twenty-four hours the tides of the ocean—soiled and discolored through contact with our shores—withdraw themselves into the bosom of the deep to be cleansed and rebaptized in the clean and salt immensity of the sea. There they hear again the call of the sun, the moon and the stars, and come back cleansed with a blessed power upon the coasts which are unlovely without them and are kept sweet only by their healing contact.

"Life is like that. For we too are much stained through our contact with occupation or pleasure through all the coast of reality. The withdrawing tides of our souls need to be gathered again into the clean, the vast, and the unfailing; there to be rebaptized in goodness and vision; there to hear the voice of the eternal, to answer to the compulsion of the Unseen.

"Out of such a communion as this we shall return again to our duties and our relationships—healed and recollected—to achieve some vaster advance, some new victory and to release some deepened measure of love and power."

THE BRIDGE NOT CROSSED

The earth is full of the goodness of the Lord.

PSALM 33:5

*A*fter an old recluse had passed this life, some interesting pieces of paper were found in his cheap room, destitute of comforts. On those papers were written estimates of how long his money would last if he spent $50 a week and how much longer if he could squeeze by on $40, including rent. The startling fact was that he could have lived another sixty years on the first figures.

He was haunted by fear of the future and lived on the basis that he might never make another penny, that his present pile might never earn a cent and that his miserable, paltry existence might extend many more years than the normal span. While he denied himself peace of mind and necessities of body, his gold cankered. He spent a life in building a bridge he never crossed.

This is an illustration of many people who are torn by needless worry. The futility of this lifestyle is obvious. Once we set our own cheerless thoughts on ourselves, they'll incessantly attack and enfeeble us. Anxiety about some imaginary difficulty makes us less able to meet today's actualities.

It's no use to invest in and build bridges never to be crossed. So...

Distinguish gold from dross;
Waste neither time nor thought about
The bridge you'll never cross.

KEEP IT SIMPLE
. . . .
Come, let Us go down, and there confuse
their language, that they may not understand
one another's speech.

GENESIS 11:7

A man received a letter from an out-of-town attorney. He didn't understand it, so he took the letter to a local lawyer, who said, "Go ahead and read it to me."

This was the message: "Your uncle James, having come to advanced years, having suffered reverses, being debilitated by the encroachment of senility, in a moment of temporary dementia, perpetrated his own demise."

The lawyer said, "You want to know what it means? Well, in simple language it means this: Your uncle James grew old, lost his wad, went nuts, and bumped himself off."

I don't know that we have to speak quite so plainly, but we do need to speak simply. There's not much sense in using speech that doesn't communicate.

Jesus communicated with simple words and common examples. To shed light on His thoughts, He talked about a vine and its branches, a shepherd and the sheep, a watchman, light, salt, leaven and a sower. He used ordinary matters to teach the deepest and most profound lessons. An extraordinary point can be expressed in ordinary words.

No one is blessed by a message he does not understand.

PLUCK MAKES ITS OWN LUCK

. . . .

Be of good courage,
and He shall strengthen your heart,
all you who hope in the Lord.

PSALM 31:24

*F*ortune favors the brave. The bells of success toll for the gritty. The person with pluck definitely has better luck than the person without it.

Pluck is the bulldog spirit of bravery and tenacity one exemplifies in facing opposition or an adverse circumstance. All of us at times are called upon to wrestle with failure, disappointment, miscalculation or outright opposition. The question is, *Do we have the grit to bravely meet the threat and to triumph over it?* If we do, there's a good chance that our pluck will turn to luck.

For any struggle to be won,
Must be determined, dared and done.

A person's grit, however, is never fully known until he's fully tested. Then the hidden heroic quality has a chance to come out. Those who are thought to be ordinary people rise to extraordinary heights when the challenge comes. A common cat can prove to have a lion's heart when backed into a corner. How much more this valiant spirit is seen among people...and in the simple, ordinary affairs of life, as in the case of a wife with a sick husband, three children and a mortgage.

The harder the match, the greater the victory. The more strenuous the struggle, the more satisfaction in winning.

LOGICAL DEDUCTION

He answered them,
"I told you already, and you did not listen.
Why do you want to hear it again?"

JOHN 9:27

Some of the clearest and most irrefutable logic I have ever heard was expressed many years ago by an old farmer. It was down-to-earth logic from a man of the soil. He said that he had learned from experience (now get this: had learned from *experience*) that when cholera breaks out among his hogs and one takes it and lingers on and on and on, that hog has a much better chance of getting well than one that takes it and dies right straight.

I never did question his logic.

Jesus made an appeal to logic in teaching a lesson on the wise and foolish builders (Matthew 7:24-27). Actually, it is a story of the logical thinker in contrast to the illogical one. The wise man built his house on the rock, and it withstood the storms. But the foolish man built his house on the sand, and the storms swept it away. In his defiance of logic and common sense, he tried a shortcut. His logic went to pieces, and so did his house.

The lives that stand are the workmanship of sound, logical thinking. The lives that lie in heaps of wreckage along the pathway of life are the results of unsound reasoning. They thought they could get without giving, play with fire and not be burned, sow one thing and reap something else. But they couldn't.

It's tragic to disregard facts or to try to suppress them. We should never abdicate logic and common sense.

LOOPHOLES

· ·

Those who received the temple tax came to Peter
and said, "Does your Teacher not pay the temple tax?"
He said, "Yes."

MATTHEW 17:24-25

While I was eating breakfast in a local restaurant, I couldn't help overhearing a conversation between three men at a table nearby. They were discussing federal income taxes, and it was their unanimous view that all loopholes should be closed. Yes, *all* of them. They thought some taxpayers were getting breaks. And the more they thought about it, the louder and more indignant they became.

Finally I couldn't take it any longer. I went over to the table and introduced myself and said, "You say you don't want any loopholes at all. Let's consider the loopholes. You get a tax deduction for you, your wife and your children. Do you want *that* loophole closed? You have another loophole on the deduction of interest you pay on your home and other debts. Do you want *that* loophole closed? You get a deduction on contributions to church and charitable institutions. Do you want *that* loophole closed, too?"

They responded, "Certainly not." Then they said what they really meant: "We want all the loopholes closed *for the rich.*"

That seems to be the consensus of a fair tax—one that taxes the other fellow. God commanded the tithe—ten percent. This was a flat rate and God's view of fairness. The more one made the more he gave, but the rate was the same. Jesus paid taxes, and surely it was not out of His abundance.

As citizens we enjoy the benefits of government, and thus have a fair and divine obligation to "Render therefore to Caesar the things which are Caesar's" (Matthew 22:21).

THANKSGIVING

. . . .

Giving thanks always for all things to God and the Father in
the name of our Lord Jesus Christ.

EPHESIANS 5:20

Our forefathers' desire to have a special day of thanksgiving is indeed a laudable quality. While they were poor in many respects, they were rich in thanks. We are blessed to be the descendants of such robust, grateful people. We are the privileged children of a glorious heritage.

It is not what a person gets that makes him truly great; it is what he is thankful for. This shows the nobler side of his soul.

Thanks are justly due for favors and blessings bestowed. And the person who feels no compulsion to say *Thanks* for the courtesies, considerations and blessings given him is unworthy to receive more.

Even a dog will wag its tail at the person who gives it a bone. So don't expect happiness if you live below the level of a dog. Indeed, our degree of happiness depends much upon the depth of our gratitude. Have you ever noticed that a grateful mind is a joyful mind?

If life is sweet, *give thanks.* If bitter, give thanks that you still have life, which gives you another chance.

> *My God, I thank Thee who hast made*
> *The earth so bright,*
> *So full of splendor and of joy,*
> *Beauty and light;*
> *So many glorious things are here,*
> *Noble and right.*

ADELAIDE A. PROCTER

BE THANKFUL

. . . .

Know that the Lord, He is God; It is He who has made us,
and not we ourselves; we are His people and the sheep
of His pasture. Enter into His gates with thanksgiving,
and into His courts with praise. Be thankful to Him,
and bless His name.

PSALM 100:3-4

"Every good gift and every perfect gift is from above, and comes down from the Father of lights, with whom is no variableness, neither shadow of turning" (James 1:17). This is visibly evident in His supplying the needs of His creatures. Year by year earth's inhabitants are fed, watered, clothed and warmed. Generations come and go, nations rise and fall, yet God continues to live and keeps this old earth turning and the sun shining, and sends seedtime and harvest, day and night.

This Thanksgiving season may we recognize the God from whom all blessings flow—either directly or indirectly—and offer Him the praise of our lips, the love of our hearts and the consecration of our lives.

Such gratitude can deepen character and spark personality. One of the chief requisites for making an optimist is a grateful memory, yet how often we forget! And how devastating forgetting is to personality and outlook on life! The person who constantly complains that nothing goes right, that everything is against him, invariably has a good "forgettery" rather than a good memory. But the optimist—the winner—sees his blessings and counts them with appreciation. It centers his days on the positives of life.

"It is a good thing to give thanks unto the Lord."

PSALM 92:1

A GREAT PERSON IS THANKFUL

And be thankful.

COLOSSIANS 3:15

A Sunday School teacher began her class by saying that everyone had been blessed and should be thankful. Then she asked one little boy what he was especially thankful for.

"My glasses," he replied. "They keep the boys from hitting me and the girls from kissing me."

In time he would outgrow the latter cause for thankfulness, but he would never, never outgrow—no matter how old he became, or how much he amassed, or how much he accomplished—the many other reasons for gratitude that are visited upon all people in every nation and circumstance of life. Whether all are thankful or not, there are reasons to be *thankful.*

We can be thankful for the earth that gives a place to stand, for the sun that gives us warmth and light, for the tree that gives us shade, for the air that lets us breathe, for the animals in our subjection, for the sprouting seeds that give us food, for friends who walk by our side and hold our hands, for the God who loves us, for the Bible that gives us direction and hope, for the fellowship of the church that gives us strength, for the hope of immortality that takes tragedy out of death, and for countless other blessings.

We will never outgrow the *reasons* to be thankful. May we never outgrow the *desire* to be thankful.

SHE READ TO ME

. . . .

Blessed is he who reads and those who hear....

REVELATION 1:3

I know parents who are always buying books to read to their children. Their favorites are Bible story books, books with high morals that shape the mind and mold the character. They would gladly sacrifice food for their own stomachs to have books (mental food) for their children. Every purchase is a matter of priority, and they place the cultivation of the mind at the top.

Napoleon said, "Show me a family of readers, and I will show you the people who move the world."

Reading will open up new worlds—real and imaginary—for our children. Let's read for information, read for character formation, read for inspiration and read for pleasure.

By reading to our children we write on their hearts. Moreover, we write what water and soap can't wash away. Many things we do for our children may change with the shifting sands of time, but reading to them engraves on their hearts a record that time changes not. Actually, the children become books themselves, known and read by others.

If we want our children to have scholastic and wholesome minds, we must start shaping their minds while they are young. In so doing, we give these precious ones the richest riches. Here are the closing lines of one of my favorite poems, "The Reading Mother," by Strickland Gillilan:

> *You may have tangible wealth untold;*
> *Caskets of jewels and coffers of gold.*
> *Richer than I you can never be—*
> *I had a mother who read to me.*

KEEP AN OPEN MIND

. . . .

What further need do we have of witnesses?

MARK 14:63

The judge's decision left them astonished and bewildered. One morning as he was shaving, dressing, getting ready to go to his court, his wife insisted that he meet her on a certain street corner at eleven o'clock. At first he refused. But after reconsidering, he decided it shouldn't take too long to hear the morning case, so he agreed.

After the trial got underway, it was evident that it would take longer than he had estimated. As it got near the critical time for him to leave, lo and behold, the two opposing attorneys asked for an hour each to argue the case further. The judge ruled: "Requests granted. But I promised to meet my wife at eleven o'clock, and when you get through arguing, you will find my decision in this little drawer. I wrote it out last night before I went to bed."

The judge's mind was in a straitjacket.

Too many decisions are made on no truths, half-truths, one-sided presentations or preconceived ideas.

Prejudice is a slave to error, a lid on open-mindedness and an obstacle in the way of progress. May we keep an unbiased mind. Let's hear a matter fully, listening to both sides. We need to investigate, compare and analyze. Factual decisions can't be made without all the facts.

We should follow the noble example of the Bereans, who "received the word with all readiness of mind, and searched the Scriptures daily, whether those things were so" (Acts 17:11).

AMBITIOUS GOALS

· ·

There remains very much land yet to be possessed.

JOSHUA 13:1

Edward Gibbon's epic, *The Decline and Fall of the Roman Empire*, is a classic example of a pursuing ambition. The author began this work in Rome on October 11, 1764. Twenty-three years later, on June 27, 1787, at Lausanne, he wrote the last line of the last page. The price had been great: it had absorbed his attention; he had given up much of his freedom; he had sacrificed many calls and joys of life. And now at last, though old age was coming on, his astonishing work was accomplished. His fame was secure. He had aimed high. He had "hitched his wagon to a star," as Ralph Waldo Emerson had suggested that we should do.

The urge to *go forward,* to *attain,* to *succeed,* to *improve* and to *master* is a fundamental law of human nature and of Christianity. It is a law of growth and development. The Apostle Paul is a great example. He counted not himself to have apprehended, but reached for the things that were ahead. And that showed him to be a great Christian.

Frederick Watts is also a noteworthy pattern. At eighty years of age he felt that his best pictures were yet to be painted. No wonder he became historic.

Joshua is another glorious example of high seeking. At the age of 110 he went down to death with these words of the Lord ringing in his ears: "There remaineth yet very much land to be possessed" (Joshua 13:1).

He who shoots at the stars will shoot higher than he who aims at a bird's nest. Ambition is a necessary condition of success. It has no substitute.

IF WE KNEW EACH OTHER

Then hear in heaven Your dwelling place, and forgive,
and act, and give to every man according to his ways,
whose heart You know (for You, only You,
know the hearts of all the sons of men).

1 KINGS 8:39

While some of us claim to have an open mind, we still shut it to people we don't like. This could be because we don't really know them.

If we understood the causes of a person's failures or shortcomings, we would be less critical. Let us, therefore, be more eager to find an explanation of the person's faults.

If we knew each other better, we would love each other more. We would be more tolerant, more forgiving and more helpful. There are so many hidden causes we don't know. All we see are the effects. It's easy to jump to conclusions. But before we do, we should try wearing the other person's shoes for awhile. Oh, how those shoes might pinch and chafe!

To Know All Is to Forgive All

If I knew you and you knew me,
As each one knows his own self, we
Could look each other in the face
And see therein a truer grace.
Life has so many hidden woes,
So many thorns for every rose;
The "why" of things our hearts would see,
If I knew you and you knew me.

NIXON WATERMAN

FATIGUED FROM FANNING

· ·

Therefore, since we have such hope,
we use great boldness of speech.

2 CORINTHIANS 3:12

"When you deal with something, don't mince words," was the view of Grandfather, who was an unusual preacher.

At a preachers' conference that was held to discuss the merits or demerits of preaching on hell, the chairman pointed him out and asked, "Do you preach on hell very often?"

"No."

"Why not?" inquired the chairman. "Is it because you feel that you aren't effective on the topic?"

"No. I don't often preach about hell because it disrupts the service."

"How's that?" continued the chairman.

"It's like this," explained Grandpa. "The audience becomes so fatigued from *fanning* that I have to declare a recess about every five minutes."

Being plain and bold gives one a chance to be recognized as either a sharp intellectual or a blundering fool. On the other hand, speech that hides one's views is to no purpose— unless the purpose is to be politically right by riding the fence, and that's no feather in any person's cap.

As we speak honestly, however, let us follow the common decency of courtesy, consideration, kindness and helpfulness. Then we shall be welcomed as speakers worthy of an audience, whether it be one person or a million.

Free the Slaves

Stand fast therefore in the liberty by which Christ
has made us free, and do not be entangled again
with the yoke of bondage.

GALATIANS 5:1

The cruelest and most rigorous slavery is self-enslavement. We put ourselves in harsh bondage by picking and serving the wrong masters. In doing this we become:

❧ *Enslaved to self-satisfaction.* This takes away the freedom to advance and make progress. This slavery is usually rationalized by saying, "Oh, I'm holding my own." But the world is bigger than hold-your-own parameters. There are still rivers to cross, plains to traverse and mountains to climb. Where there is no ambition there can be no climb.

❧ *Enslaved to hate.* Love opens the world to us, but hate is restricting. Hate builds a fence around the hated one. The trouble is, once the fence is completed the hated one is not within it, only the fence builder.

❧ *Enslaved to vengeance.* Whoever digs a pit shall fall in. He who rolls a stone in vengeance shall be hit by it himself and become a crippled, imprisoned slave. Instead, "If your enemy is hungry, feed him; if he is thirsty, give him drink."

❧ *Enslaved to restlessness.* Our world is troubled. Every newspaper we pick up screams scary headlines at us. Disorder can easily unsettle our nerves and trouble our brow. Why are people so frenzied and frustrated? Why can't they handle their lives? It may sound simplistic, but the basic reason is that they have gotten away from the One who said, "Come unto Me and I will give you rest."

WHAT A FRIEND WE HAVE IN JESUS

. . . .

If you ask any thing in My name, I will do it.

JOHN 14:14

This popular hymn was written by Joseph Scriven, who was born in Ireland in 1820. He emigrated to Canada at age twenty-five and there he found life hard and trying. His heart was big, and he freely helped the poor and needy, giving away most of his own clothes.

Though Scriven was kind and sympathetic, he was a lonely man. His only link with his family in his native land was the slow-traveling mail. His mother became ill in 1857. Besides illness, there was her sorrow over Joseph's being away. He would write and comfort her as best he could. On one occasion he wrote and sent to her this renowned hymn to dispel her fears and give her courage:

> *What a friend we have in Jesus,*
> *All our sins and griefs to bears!*
> *What a privilege to carry*
> *Everything to God in prayer!*
> *Oh, what peace we often forfeit,*
> *Oh, what needless pain we bear,*
> *All because we do not carry*
> *Everything to God in prayer!*
>
> *Have we trials and temptations?*
> *Is there trouble anywhere?*
> *We should never be discouraged,*
> *Take it to the Lord in prayer:*
> *Can we find a friend so faithful*
> *Who will all our sorrows share?*
> *Jesus knows our every weakness,*
> *Take it to the Lord in prayer.*

MAKING ADJUSTMENTS
· ·
Do not boast about tomorrow,
for you do not know what a day may bring forth.
PROVERBS 27:1

*C*onfucius stated it this way: "The grass must bend when the wind blows across it."

We are forced to react to such changes as ill health, loss of a job, financial reverses, coming of a baby, misunderstandings, misplaced confidence, new assignments, a move to a strange city, the marriage of a child, and even death.

Let me tell you about one woman's adjustment to death. After years of happy marriage, her husband passed this life and went on to the next and better. They had been together a long time. When he died, it seemed that half of her had died. A big change had come, and she heroically made it. She resigned herself to the unchanging fact that her lover had been taken, that she was left behind and that life for her would have to continue. There was no bitterness, no resentment. She sought no sympathy. She would simply remark, "The Lord gave, and the Lord has taken away; blessed be the name of the Lord" (Job 1:21). She knew she could not roll the calendar back. She would have to start a new life from where she was.

She found these words of David (who lost his son) a soothing balm for the heartache she thought would never end: "Why should I fast? Can I bring him back again? I *shall* go to him, but he shall not return to me" (2 Samuel 12:23). Such a fixed purpose gave her a triple blessing: hope, direction and courage.

If she at her age could make such a major adjustment, don't you think that we can make the more minor adjustments we are called upon to make?

What an Honor to Be Called "Chicken"

. . . .

You shall not follow a crowd to do evil.

EXODUS 23:2

If we refuse to go along with the crowd, we're apt to be called "chicken." But those who conform have nothing to crow about.

The word is used to slur and belittle the person who refuses to fall in line with the group. It takes strength and iron will to stand for convictions when they're contrary to what the crowd demands. When one brave soul of conviction was told that the whole crowd was against him, he replied, "Then I guess I'm against the whole crowd!"

If the slur causes us to give up our persuasion and conform, it is then that we actually become chicken, so weak that we can be scared and handled like a chicken.

All truly great people have learned to be different from the run-of-the-mill type of humanity. It takes much more courage to stand alone than it does to run with the crowd.

Pilate, the governor who tried Jesus, let the crowd control him. He had some conviction but not enough. During the trial his wife sent a message to him, warning him not to listen to the multitude's clamor. But he was afraid the mob would say, "Pilate's chicken!" so he sided with the crowd. His wife had tried to get him to hear another voice—the voice of right. Most of us have someone who is trying to get us to hear the voice of right. Our major concern should not be the smear from the smearers, but the possibility of becoming one of them.

GODLINESS MAKES FOR PROSPERITY

Now the Lord was with Jehoshaphat because he walked
in the former ways of his father David; he did not seek
the Baals.... Therefore the Lord established the kingdom
in his hand... and he had riches and honor in abundance.

2 CHRONICLES 17:3-5

Jehoshaphat began his reign as king of Judah when he
was thirty-five, and he reigned twenty-five years. Since it
was one of the most prosperous reigns, it gives insight to
the true way of prosperity. Jehoshaphat was a peaceful king
and a godly one. He was a teacher, sending out princes and
priests to instruct the people in the Scriptures. God honored
him because he honored God.

*Being on God's side is the best way to avoid the pitfalls of
evil and to secure our footing.* Those on sinking sand or
questionable ground are the most vulnerable to attack.
Moreover, they are unhappy, and unhappiness invites the
assaults of temptation.

*There is a great lift of heart in the consciousness of doing
right.* It lifts us above discouragements, doubts and temptations toward an unworthy life. This sort of elevation and
self-image gives courage, hope and cheer.

Thus piety is the best friend of prosperity. The Bible states
this: "Godliness is profitable unto all things," even for "the life
that now is" as well as for "that which is to come" (1 Timothy 4:8). It pays here and now to do right.

No kingdom or government that does not make room
for the law of the Lord is on a solid and lasting foundation.
"Righteousness exalts a nation: but sin is a reproach to any
people" (Proverbs 14:34). A fact of life!

TRIBUTE TO A DOG

. . . .

The dogs came and licked his sores.

LUKE 16:21

One of the most beautiful tributes ever paid a dumb animal came from the lips of George Graham Vest. The occasion was a court trial pertaining to the killing of a boy's dog. He said:

"Gentlemen of the jury...the one absolutely unselfish friend that man can have in this selfish world, the one that never deserts him, the one that never proves ungrateful or treacherous is his dog. A man's dog stands by him in prosperity and in poverty, in health and in sickness. He will sleep on the cold ground, where the wintry winds blow and the snow drives fiercely, if only he may be near his master's side.

"He will kiss the hand that has no food to offer; he will lick the wounds and sores that come in encounter with the roughness of the world. He guards the sleep of his pauper master as if he were a prince. When all other friends desert, he remains. When riches take wings, and reputation falls to pieces, he is as constant in his love as the sun in its journey through the heavens.

"If fortune drives the master forth an outcast in the world, friendless and homeless, the faithful dog asks no higher privilege than that of accompanying him, to guard him against danger, to fight against his enemies. And when the last scene of all comes, and death takes his master in its embrace and his body is laid away in the cold ground, no matter if all other friends pursue their way, there by the graveside will the noble dog be found, his head between his paws, his eyes sad, but open in alert watchfulness, faithful and true even in death."

When he concluded there were but few dry eyes in the audience. The jury promptly returned a verdict for the plaintiff.

SIXTY YEARS AGO

. . . .

I remember the days of old.

PSALM 143:5

How lasting is a precious memory; and, as Alexander Pope stated, "How vast a memory has love." Moreover, it gives the heart something to feed on.

From the heartstrings of memory there comes the swelling of a sweet and precious melody.

Reliving the happy past can put zest in the present. We need a memory that does more than take us backward. We need one that also turns us around and pushes us forward with hope.

Memory. Oh! how many days and worlds you encompass! Within that one word lies the quickened poetry of humanity's emotions.

I've wandered to the village, Tom,
I've sat beneath the tree
Upon the schoolhouse playground
That sheltered you and me;
But none was there to greet me, Tom,
And few were left to know
Who played with us upon the green,
Just sixty years ago.

Well, some are in the churchyard laid,
Some sleep beneath the sea,
But none is left of our old class,
Excepting you and me;
And when our time shall come, Tom,
And we are called to go,
I hope we'll meet with those we loved
Some sixty years ago.

OVERCOME EVIL WITH GOOD

· ·

Do not be overcome by evil,
but overcome evil with good.

ROMANS 12:21

There is a fascinating story about a wealthy farmer. A poor man whose house had burned and who had no provisions came to him for help. The farmer, moved with compassion, decided that he would give the man a ham from his smokehouse. On the way to get it, the tempter whispered to him, "Give him the smallest." The farmer struggled over that. Should he give him a large or a small ham. Finally he took down the largest one.

"You're a fool," the tempter said.

"If you don't keep still," the farmer replied, "I'll give him *every* ham I have!"

It seems that practically every time a person is about to do something good, he's struck with a satanic thought to prevent the good or to lessen it.

This conclusion is fully borne out in the following verse: "Now there was a day when the sons of God came to present themselves before the Lord, and Satan came also among them" (Job 1:6). Satan came not to aid, but to hinder! It's a little shocking that the old devil was in heaven among the sons of God, but isn't that a logical place for him to work?

When our good intentions are bombarded with selfish, evil and diverting thoughts, there is only one thing to do: answer with a big, emphatic *NO!* Jesus said, "Get behind Me, Satan; you are an offense to Me" (Matthew 16:23).

LYING LIPS ARE NOT BECOMING

The truthful lip shall be established for ever,
but a lying tongue is but for a moment.

PROVERBS 12:19

Mrs. Jones got an awful shock when she learned that little Junior had told a fib. In her confrontation with him she hammered away at the ugliness, vileness and danger of telling a lie.

She said, "A big, mean man—looking like an ape with long, scrawny fingers and bloodshot eyes and with a horn growing out of each side of his head—grabs little boys who tell lies and stuffs them in a big bag and carries them off to the dark side of the moon and makes them work in a coal mine and gives them nothing to live on but bread and water." Satisfied with her graphic presentation, she gave it the final punch: "Now you won't ever tell another lie, will you, sweetie pie?"

"No, Mom," answered Junior. "I could *never* match your whopper!"

It's easy to tell a lie, but it's not easy to tell just one lie.

Still we hear it said, "Maybe it's not so bad to tell *white* lies." Before long, the tellers become colorblind.

It's also said, "This world would be a boring, dull place if all we had was truth." Wait a moment! I don't take that view of another habitation where liars shall not dwell—*heaven.*

Another thing: most people don't have good-enough memories for them to be successful liars. And still another thing: because he is a liar, the liar believes nobody.

LOOK THE OTHER WAY

. . . .

If I am being poured out as a drink offering
on the sacrifice and service of your faith,
I am glad and rejoice with you all.

PHILIPPIANS 2:17

Surface and momentary delights are easily found because they have a thousand sources, but they are all fleeting. Time takes them away. The fun of youth and the enjoyment of health, the joys of success and the gratification of recognition are perpetually passing away. The joy of each is exhausted by its consumption. Our hearts cry out, therefore, for a joy that is more satisfying and lasting.

After exhausting the world's ideas to achieve joy in life, we understand why Jesus said that true and lasting joy will only come when we look in the opposite direction. If we look for happiness in pleasing ourselves, we won't find it. Happiness comes from giving up self with all of its cheap and shoddy traits to find one's self again in a sweeter and nobler character.

For this is peace, —to lose the lonely note
Of self in love's celestial-ordered strain;
And this is joy, —to find one's self again
In Him whose harmonies forever float
Through all the spheres of song, below, above, —
For God is music, even as God is love.

WAS IT A COMPLIMENT?
· ·
Woe to you, when all men shall speak well of you,
for so did their fathers to the false prophets.
LUKE 6:26

Recently I attended a funeral in which the minister said of the deceased, "No one ever spoke an ill word of our beloved." He meant that sentence as a compliment, but *was it?*

This could not be said of the Apostle Paul. He was called a babbler and a troublemaker. At the end of his life, he was led outside the gates of Rome and beheaded because of his unyielding faith and uncompromising convictions.

Neither could this compliment be paid to Jesus. He was accused of working with Beelzebub, the prince of devils. Public favor so turned against Him that He was crucified.

When a person has the praise of everybody (there are many kinds), he has been so flexible and wiggly as to bend out of true form. As seen in Luke 6:26 above, it places a person under the condemnation of the Bible and tags him as one we should avoid.

Paul knew enough about people also to know that his expressed belief could precipitate ruffled feelings and strong opposition. He spoke out anyway. However, he tempered his message by asking, "Have I become your enemy because I tell you the truth?" (Galatians 4:16).

When no one ever speaks a harmful word against you, it indicates that you haven't done much...or you have no convictions... or you are afraid to speak up. In any case, it is *not* complimentary.

SHEEP THIEF

. . . .

You have put off the old man with his deeds;
and have put on the new man.

COLOSSIANS 3:9-10

It has been reported that two brothers were convicted as sheep thieves. In keeping with their crime, their recognizable and humiliating punishment consisted of branding on the forehead the letters *ST*, which meant "Sheep Thief."

One of the brothers was unable to bear the brand of shame, so he ran away and buried himself among strangers in a foreign land. Still he was asked the meaning of the letters, which agonized him to the degree that he fled from land to land. At last he died, embittered and friendless, and was buried in a forgotten grave.

The other brother, who was penitent, decided to stay at home and stick it out. He told himself, "I can't run away from the truth that in a time of weakness I gave way to temptation and stole sheep. Running away won't change the fact. Whether people know it or not, *I* will know it. So, I will remain here until I win back the respect and goodwill of my neighbors." As the years passed, he gained a reputation for respectability, integrity, dependability, helpfulness and godliness. No one questioned his living on the highest plane. He had established himself.

One day a stranger in the little town saw the old man with the letters *ST* on his forehead and curiously asked a villager what they indicated.

After thinking a little while the neighbor replied, "It happened a long time ago and I have forgotten just what occurred, but I think the letters are an abbreviation of *Saint*."

THE TRAGEDY OF BELIEVING SOMETHING FALSE

. . . .

And for this reason God will send them strong
delusion, that they should believe the lie.

2 THESSALONIANS 2:11

On the western part of our county a lady was faced with a very perplexing problem. Her husband went to the battlefields of World War I. She lived in fear that he would not survive, and in this concern she herself died a thousand deaths. Finally the dreaded letter from the War Department came, stating that he had died in battle. Believing the report, she grieved. With the passing of time, however, her broken heart began to heal and she remarried. More time passed and then, one day, her first husband appeared on the scene. He was alive. Her believing a false report had not made it true. Believing he was dead did not make him dead.

In all the affairs of life—government, business, marriage, war, religion—the belief of a proposition does not guarantee its truthfulness or safety. Many a bad move has been made by legislators who believed they were doing right. Many a person has lost money by believing a fraudulent investment was sound. Many a battle has been lost because the commanders believed a lie. Many a person has blindly followed man instead of God because he did not investigate.

Thus it is incumbent upon us to *look* before we leap, to *think* before we move, and to *investigate* before we align. John commanded this wise course: "Beloved, believe not every spirit [every person who claims to be under the influence of the Holy Spirit], but try [prove] the spirits whether they are of God: because many false prophets are gone out into the world" (1 John 4:1).

MORE FAITH AND LESS WORRY

. . . .

Which of you by worrying can add one cubit to his stature?

MATTHEW 6:27

I remember seeing my grandmother in her old rocking chair, and I can still hear the profound bits of philosophy she shared with me as she rocked, slowly, thoughtfully. One was, "Worry is like a rocking chair; it gives you something to do, but it doesn't get you anywhere."

There is a world of difference between worry and concern. A worried person frets over a problem even if it's not there, while the concerned person calmly solves problems. The worried person crosses rivers before he reaches them, and if there isn't one to cross, he makes one; but the concerned person goes ahead and when he gets to a river, detours or swims it or takes a ferry or builds a bridge.

Worry is the payment of a debt before it's due, a debt which in most cases never comes due. Most of our worries are over troubles that never happen. Life requires thought, planning, arrangement, rearrangement, adjustment, readjustment. But we can do it without worrying about it.

Faith in God's care prevents fretful anxiety. Worry can't get started if we believe that everything will work out all right, some way, somehow.

> *Said the robin to the sparrow,*
> *"I should really like to know*
> *Why these anxious human beings*
> *Rush about and worry so."*
>
> *Said the sparrow to the robin,*
> *"I think that it must be*
> *They have no Heavenly Father*
> *Such as cares for you and me."*

THE LAST TOKEN

· ·

There is no fear in love; but perfect love casts out fear.

1 JOHN 4:18

There is a impressive painting by Max Gabriel that tells a touching love story. It is called "The Last Token." The original is in Paris, but copies of it are found in many galleries.

It portrays a scene from long ago, when Christians were the objects of fierce persecution and ghastly martyrdom. It pictures a beautiful and slender maiden about to be gnashed and torn to pieces by wild animals. She is standing on the ground of an amphitheater crowded with a cruel mob ready to make sport while she dies. The iron grating of the cage has been lifted, and an enraged tiger has crept out of its steel confines. With the glaring eyes of an instinctive killer, the animal faces its helpless victim.

The maiden is clothed all in white, except for the dark mantle covering her head and shoulders. Though she stands only a few feet from the tiger's cage, she heeds him not, but seems to be caught up in another thought. At her feet lies a white rose, thrown into the arena by some lover or relative or friend who isn't afraid to be loyal to the very end. Her upturned eyes eagerly scan the crowd for the face of the one who cast the rose.

One single rose with one loving, unfailing heart behind it has changed the whole spectacle. She is oblivious to the hungry beasts and jeering mob. All that matters is a white rose and triumphant love. Perfect love has cast out fear.

Knowing that God and others love us, plus our reciprocal love for them, casts out fear. It is impossible to be brave if we love no one and think no one loves us. Love gives the assurance that we do not stand alone, and this strengthens the heart.

EVERY LIFE NEEDS A CENTER

When Christ, who is our life, shall appear,
then you also will appear with Him in glory.

COLOSSIANS 3:4

There is an interesting story concerning Rear Admiral Richard E. Byrd's first expedition to the South Pole. He left his small, isolated hut one day for a brief trip of exploration and then in a sudden storm became hopelessly lost. In that barren whiteness there was nothing to give him a sense of direction. If he had struck out blindly to find his hut and had failed, chances are he would have become lost in the storm and perished.

He had a long pole he always carried to probe for holes in the ice. He stuck it in the snow and tied a scarf to it. He said later, "That was my center. If I failed to find my hut, I could return to the center and try again. Three times I tried and failed, but each time I returned to my center, without which I would have been lost and would have died. In the fourth attempt I stumbled upon my hut."

To be safe, every life must have a center, a point of reference, a point of return. Everything must have a center around which it revolves. In mathematics the center is established in the decimal point. In literature the center is in the basic rules of grammar. In Christianity the center is Christ. Our standards come from Him. "To live is Christ" (Philippians 1:21).

If we should lose our bearings when life's storms beat upon us, we can return to our center and start all over again. This assures us that we shall not lose our directions for long. Indeed, it is a comforting thought to live in the Land of Beginning Again, where all our mistakes and all our heartaches can be left behind.

Do It NOW

· ·

Behold, now is the accepted time;
behold, now is the day of salvation.

2 CORINTHIANS 6:2

Whatever you need to be saved from—sin, dismay, disillusionment, fear, boredom and hopelessness—behold, *now* is the time.

Whatever we need to do for God, country, others and ourselves, *now* is the time to do it. If all postponed intentions were placed in caskets and buried, this old world would be crowded for space. And in burying those good but never-performed intentions, the procrastinators would have buried their might-have-beens.

What greater grief is there than to look back on the wasted past? One *Now* is worth a hundred *Laters*. There is no better philosophy than *Live today*. He who doesn't get full value from today's living is not apt to get a better bargain tomorrow. Concerning real living, it almost boils down to this: *now or never*. There are some exceptions, but not many.

NOW

If you have hard work to do,
Do it now.
Today the skies are clear and blue,
Tomorrow clouds may come in view,
Yesterday is not for you;
Do it now.

If you have kind words to say,
Say them now.
Tomorrow may not come your way,
Do a kindness while you may;
Loved ones will not always stay;
Say them now.

THE HARDER FENCE TO PULL DOWN

· ·

Love your enemies, bless those who curse you....

MATTHEW 5:44

*T*wo farmers became bitter enemies because of a fence that separated their farms. That fence of posts and wire could have been pulled down easily. But there was another fence between them much harder to remove than the one made of wood and metal; it was the barrier of hate. At first hate harassed their peace of mind. Then it upset their production. Gradually it sickened their bodies.

Finally one of them called in his minister and told him about the fence and his neighbor. The preacher responded, "You don't like that man, do you."

"Like him!" he stormed, "He's a stinkin' skunk with no principles!"

The minister said gently, "George, that fence out there on the farm is really not very important, but that fence in your heart *is.* Unless you overcome your animosity it is going to destroy your living, your peace of mind, your health and soul. To get over it, you'll have pray for your neighbor every night *and* for yourself. Ask God to bless him and his farm. And then ask God to help *you* rid yourself of hate."

Naturally the man objected. But then, after much persuasion, he agreed to try. That night he prayed, "Dear God, I promised the preacher I'd pray for that dirty excuse of a man. You know I have mixed feelings, that I want him to be blessed and I don't want him to be blessed. But if You think it's best, go ahead and bless him."

The next night it was easier to pray for his neighbor, the next night even easier. In time they became the best of friends and a new life opened up for both of them.

CAN'T STOP TO CHASE OFF EVERY DOG

Therefore you shall be careful to do
as the Lord your God has commanded you:
you shall not turn aside to the right hand or to the left.

DEUTERONOMY 5:32

When I was a boy we had one possession that not every family had. It was our pride and joy. An automobile—a Model T Ford.

Occasionally we made the trip into town in that Model T. It was a luxurious, pleasurable ride. It certainly beat walking or even riding in a buggy or wagon. But the ride over the narrow, bumpy, dirt road was slow.

It was so slow, in fact, that we were subjected to the harassment of all the dogs along the way. They would run out and bark at us. Of course their bark was worse than their bite. I'll never forget my father's philosophy on this point. He said, "If we stop to run off all the dogs that bark at us, we'll never get where we're going."

That principle, learned at an early age, has stuck with me. I have tried to live by it. If I had stopped every time somebody barked at me, I never would have accomplished anything. There are many things to divert our attention. Pulls from every source and direction. Therefore, to reach our goals, we must:

 look ahead.

 go on and keep going.

We may not completely reach them, but there's one thing sure: we'll get closer to them and put on muscle for the effort.

GO ONE WAY

. . . .
And they…ate their food with gladness
and simplicity of heart.
ACTS 2:46

For singleness of heart, go one way.

A farmer, while driving down a street in a Texas town, heard a pedestrian shout at him, "Hey! This is a *one*-way street!"

Unshaken, he yelled back, "I *am* going one way!"

Though it was unintentional, the farmer had expressed a very profound principle of life—singleness of direction. Go one way. If we follow this principle, we will save ourselves a world of frustrations, nervousness, unhappiness and defeat.

One Sunday afternoon a distraught woman came to our house, seeking help. She was a bundle of raw nerves, thinking she couldn't wait until Monday for consultation. She said, "I'm being pulled to pieces. It's killing me. I haven't had a peaceful day in three years." She was trying to travel in opposite directions—north, south, east and west—at the same time. The conflict was tearing her apart.

Our peace of mind is dependent upon one-directional living. The reason we cannot have peace of mind is that we have too many minds. Those opposing minds need to be unified into a singleness of mind.

The Apostle Paul, as great as he was, had to deal with the opposing pulls of life. He said, "I find this law, that, when I would do good, evil is present with me" (Romans 7:21). He, like all successful and happy persons, got himself sufficiently organized to travel in one direction. He could say, "This *one* thing I do" (Philippians 3:13). It gave him peace and satisfaction, two qualities everyone wants.

As Brooks Make Rivers

· ·

He came to Nazareth where He had been brought up.
And as His custom was, He went into the synagogue
on the Sabbath day, and stood up to read.

LUKE 4:16

*Y*ears ago a rural mail carrier who drove a buggy told me
that his horse would go the right way out of habit. The
horse had gone over the mail route so many times that
he needed no guidance. When they came to a crossroad,
there was no need to pull on either rein. The horse knew
which turn to take. Habit had prepared him for the trip.

Habit begins so small and becomes so big.

Ill habits gather by unseen degrees—
As brooks make rivers, rivers run to seas.

JOHN DRYDEN

Habits, both good and bad, have a powerful hold on the
human family. Habit is first just a cobweb, but when cultivated it becomes a cable hard to break. We have the first say;
we make the habits. But the habits have the last say; they
make us. We cannot sow bad habits and reap a good life. We
can't pick sweets from bitter weeds.

When evil habits make their play,
Give it no ear nor glance its way,
Touch not, taste not, when it first nears,
Stop the slavery when it appears.

Since habit is such a dominating power, it should be
made to work *for* us. All we have to do is develop the right
kinds of habits.

THE PROTECTIVE POWER OF THE LITTLE WORD "NO"

My son, if sinners entice you, do not consent.

PROVERBS 1:10

In other words, learn to say *No.*

As long as there is breath there must be the everlasting *Yes* and the everlasting *No.* This is because all of us are caught between truth and error, right and wrong, love and hate, accomplishment and failure, sin and sanctification.

The courts, jails, penitentiaries, clinics, unemployment lines—all the territory of the unhappy and the heaped-up pile of failures is filled with people who could not say *No.*

No is a little word, but it takes big people to say it and hold to it. It is so easy to grant requests and to move along with the crowd.

There is aggressive power in positive thinking, but there is also *protective* power in negative thinking. In our society the former has been lauded and the latter lambasted, but both are needed. Both are essential to a successful life.

Eight of the Ten Commandments are in negative form: *No, No, No, No, No, No, No, No.* Only two are in the positive: *Yes, Yes.* If you don't want to be putty in the hands of a world that would mold you into its shape, then you must say *No* when the hurtful call comes.

When we say *Yes* to God, we must say *No* to the world. Furthermore, our *No* must be stronger than the exploiter's, the tempter's and the sinner's *Yes.*

WHAT MAKES ACHIEVERS
· ·

They went forth to go into the land of Canaan
and into the land of Canaan they came.

GENESIS 12:5

Genesis 12:5 is a favorite Bible verse among achievers. It is well suited to all who have ambition, drive, determination and perseverance.

There are two qualifications for success in life:

❧ *Start with a definite goal in mind.* "They went forth to go into the land of Canaan." They knew where they wanted to go. A limousine is no better than an oxcart if a person doesn't know where he wants to go. We ought to ask ourselves, "What do I want *from* the world? What do I want to contribute *to* the world?"

The problem some people have is setting goals too low. This is what makes ordinary people *ordinary.* They need to raise their sights. Of all the goals we may have, let's be sure we include these: to walk with God, enjoy life to the fullest, serve our fellowmen and leave the world better than we found it.

The words of Napoleon are very appropriate:

Great ambition is the passion of a great character.

❧ *Get going and continue.* A person needs to know what he or she wants to do and then want that so much that the goal is tirelessly pursued. *Move!* And *keep moving!* No turning back! No letting up! Once we're headed in the right direction, our responsibility is to go forward with confidence. "Be strong and of a good courage...for the Lord your God, He goes with you; He will not fail you, nor forsake you" (Deuteronomy 31:6).

Benefits From the Christmas Season

Suddenly there was with the angel a multitude of the heavenly host praising God, and saying, Glory to God in the highest, and on earth peace, goodwill toward men.

Luke 2:13-14

*A*t this season of the year when our minds are turned toward peace and goodwill toward men, it is an excellent time for personal improvement. We should:

❧ *Think first of someone else.* Be kind. Be gentle. Gladden the lives of others. Appreciate our friends and what they do for us. Express gratitude for all favors.

❧ *Examine our demands of others.* Think more about giving than receiving, more about serving than being served.

❧ *If trouble has come between us and another, let's mend it.* Overcome malice. Replace suspicion with trust. Give a soft answer. Dismiss a grudge. Forgive a wrong. Flee envy. Listen. Try to understand. Apologize if we are wrong.

❧ *Contact a friend we have not seen or heard from for a long time.* Relive some of the joys we have had with that one in the past.

❧ *Be a friend to strangers.* Do something for the down-and-out.

❧ *Enjoy the wonder and beauty of the earth.* Lift our eyes to the heavens and see the glory of God.

These are but a few of the large number of helpful things we can do. They are simple. They are old but ever relevant. Their influence is immeasurable.

I REMEMBER

. . . .

Remember the days of old, consider the years
of many generations. Ask your father, and he
will show you; your elders, and they will tell you.

DEUTERONOMY 32:7

By rewinding the past, we can gain momentum for the future. As this occurs at Christmastime, we find ourselves joyously rejuvenated.

Eleanor Arnett Nash has stated: "Yesterday I wasn't a woman at all, but a little girl with a plump face and fat round black curls, a red sash tied about my cozy tummy, and a crisp white dress. For I've captured the spirit of Christmas. You see, I've recaptured it through the memory of Christmases of my childhood....

"*The sights of Christmases gone by:* Tinsel. Icicles. Red ribbon and white tissue. Flaming candles on a full branched tree. My mother, unbelievably beautiful for seven o'clock on Christmas morning. My father, a six-foot-two with the reddest hair, pretending to feel no emotion over our excitement.... Broken candies you can't get nowadays, hanging from bough tips. Red bound volumes of *St. Nicholas* magazine. Toys— and the wax angel with the silver trumpet, topping the tree.

"*The smell of Christmas:* Cedar. Pine cones. Oranges. The crisp unmistakable odor of snow. Wood smoke from the huge open fire.

"*The taste of Christmas:* Peppermint. Maple sugar. Raisins. Yams all sugary....

"As I remember I wonder.

"Are all the children of today being given memories to store up and bring out in much later years?"

ONE SOLITARY LIFE

. . . .

Unto you is born this day in the city of David a Savior,
who is Christ the Lord.

LUKE 2:11

An anonymous writer once penned this classic summation of the life of Christ:

"Here is a young man who was born in an obscure village, the child of a peasant woman. He grew up in another village. He worked in a carpenter shop until he was thirty, and then for three years he was an itinerant preacher. He never wrote a book. He never held an office. He never owned a home. He never had a family.

"He never went to college. He never put his foot inside a big city. He never traveled 200 miles from the place where he was born. He never did one of the things that usually accompany greatness. He had no credentials but himself.

"While he was still a young man the tide of public opinion turned against him. His friends ran away. He was turned over to his enemies. He went through the mockery of a trial.

"He was nailed to the cross between two thieves. While he was dying, his executioners gambled for the only piece of property he had on earth, and that was his coat.

"When he was dead he was laid in a borrowed grave through the pity of a friend. Nineteen centuries wide have come and gone, and today he is the central figure of the human race and the leader of the column of progress.

"All the armies that ever marched and all the navies that ever sailed, and all the parliaments that ever sat, and all the kings that ever reigned, put together, have not affected the life of man upon this earth as has that one solitary life."

THE MAN IN THE MIRROR
· ·
I myself always strive to have a conscience
without offense toward God and men.
ACTS 24:16

When I first began to shave it was a first-class comedy. If Hollywood had known about it, I'm sure they would have paid a big price just for the film rights.

As you can guess, there wasn't much to shave, just a little peach fuzz. Maybe three or four longer whiskers. By the time I finished I was nicked, cut and sliced like I had been through a storm of flying glass. My father said, "Son, it's not the whiskers you see, but the man in the mirror that counts."

Through the years I have remembered those words. He was right. Let others think and say and do as they please, it's the man in the mirror that makes the difference. If I have his respect and approval, I have the friendship of the one person on earth who can help me most, other than God.

When you get what you want in your struggle for self,
And the world makes you king for a day,
Just go to a mirror and look at yourself,
And see what that man has to say.

He's the fellow to please, never mind all the rest,
For he's with you clear up to the end.
And you've passed your most dangerous, difficult test,
If the guy in the glass is your friend.

You may fool the whole world down the pathway of years,
And get pats on the back as you pass.
But your final reward will be heartaches and tears,
If you've cheated the man in the glass.

MOCKERY CHANGES NOTHING

Let them be turned back for a reward
of their shame that say Aha, aha.

PSALM 70:3

Derision is a shameful thing. And useless. It changes nothing.

The grasshopper mocks the ant, but alters neither the fortune of the grasshopper nor the ant. Winter will find them out, and then the little ant that stuck with its job all summer can say:

Where be your gibes now?

WILLIAM SHAKESPEARE

What difference does it make if the owl hoots at the dog's bark? The dog still has its job to protect the house, and its bark continues to sound a warning. Neither does the parrot's mockery change the sweet melody of the canary.

When reason is against a person, he or she may resort to ridicule. But ridicule is a low, backhanded stroke that flattens nobody who is willing to stand up to it and go about his or her business. God made us, so let's be determined that mockers shall not unmake us. Mockery should be regarded only as an unkind sport that mocks the mocker and feeds on itself, so sneerers must be content to live on their own dish.

The important thing is for us to live as we should and leave the reaction to others, whether it be applause or mockery. It is ours to act, theirs to react. Let us stick to our purpose, do the best we can and say in the words of Job, "Suffer me that I may speak; and after that I have spoken, mock on" (Job 21:3).

IT DOES NO GOOD TO GRUMBLE

· ·

When the people complained, it displeased the Lord.

NUMBERS 11:11

Constant grumblers are not appreciated. For the public knows the worst wheel of the cart creeks the most. No matter what anyone says, nagging isn't horse sense; it's just plain nonsense.

> *Grumble? No, what's the good?*
> *If it availed, I would.*
> *But it doesn't a bit,*
> *Not it.*
>
> *Laugh? Yes, why not?*
> *'Tis better than crying a lot;*
> *We were made to be glad,*
> *Not sad.*
>
> *Sing? Why, yes to be sure;*
> *We shall better endure,*
> *If the heart's full of song*
> *All day long.*

Not everything can always go our way. Sometimes it's our fault. Sometimes it's the fault of others. Regardless of the cause, we can handle the aggravation in a way that spares our friends the fire and smoke of the occasion. It's wise to consume our own smoke lest our friends become annoyed by the fumes and soot of our complaints. When we feel wronged, let's file our complaint with the proper one in a gentle tone of voice. Let's hold our temper. Let's not make enemies.

NOT LIVING IN VAIN

. . . .

I was hungry and you gave Me food;
I was thirsty, and you gave Me drink;
I was a stranger and you took Me in.

MATTHEW 25:35

This well-known and encouraging Scripture means we do not have to live in vain.

> *If I can stop one heart from breaking,*
> *I shall not live in vain.*
> *If I can ease one life the aching,*
> *Or cool one pain,*
> *Or help one fainting robin*
> *Into his nest again,*
> *I shall not live in vain.*

EMILY DICKINSON

If I give a cup of cold water to a thirsty traveler, my life is not in vain. If I lift up a child who has stubbed his toe and dry a tear, my life is not for naught. If I am only one tiny, flickering light in a world of darkness, my life is not a failure. If I weep with one who weeps and rejoice with another who rejoices, my life is not purposeless.

If I guide and mold a child into honorable manhood or womanhood, my life is not useless. If I cast a ray of sunshine wherever I go, my life is not unimportant. If I set in motion one little bit of influence for good, my life is not futile.

If I bear the burden of a friend weighted down, my life is not unavailing. If I lift one fallen person, my life is not ineffectual. If I read one Scripture verse to a soul who hungers and thirsts for righteousness, my life is not unfruitful.

I SHALL NOT BE MOVED

· ·

They who trust in the Lord shall be as Mount Zion,
which cannot be removed, but abides for ever.

PSALM 125:1

The ancient people of God beheld Mount Zion as stable and immovable. But they saw more than the mountain and did more than relate to it. They perceived that trust in God would give them a fixed purpose and stability like the mountain in the distance. Mount Zion, always there, always unchanged, conveyed a message to them, one that all of humanity needs to heed. *Stability! Solidity!*

Indeed, trust in God provides the firm foundation that prevents us from slipping and tottering. It gives the fixed heart which brings the whole man into the effort, uniting and coordinating all his labors, and thus raises a mountain of stability within him. On the other hand, distrust changes the solid mountain into quicksand, where the soul sinks lower and lower. When our trust in God is full and undivided, we stand as immovable as the mountain and can declare with confidence, "The Lord is my rock...in whom I will trust" (Psalm 18:2).

I Shall Not Be Moved

Though the tempest rage round me,
Through the storm, my Lord, I see;
Standing like a mountain holy,
I shall not be moved from Thee.
I shall not be moved,
Anchored to the Rock of Ages,
I shall not be moved.

ALFRED H. ACKLEY

PRAISE THE LORD

· ·

Praise the Lord...let everything that has breath
praise the Lord. Praise the Lord.

PSALM 150:1-6

"Praise the Lord" is chosen as the last devotional and guide in this series of 365. In making this decision, I am following the example of the Psalmist. For in the last five psalms (including Psalm 150), each begins and ends with praise: "Praise the Lord." This was the fitting ending to the wondrous and superb Book of Psalms. It is also appropriate that this volume ends with an expressive laudation of the majesty of God.

As pilgrims, we have kept up the march and come to the end of another year. Our days have been beset by trials, temptations, conflicts, disappointments, sufferings, troubles, defeats, sorrows and tears. But we've also had steps of faith, climbs to greater heights, glorious victories, abundant blessings, overflowing joys, renewals of confidence and beckoning hopes. All of these vicissitudes and blessings have accompanied us on our journey through life. Our experiences, we hope, have made us smarter, stronger, better, kinder, more helpful and more dependent upon God and each other. Thus it is fitting that we exclaim, *Praise the Lord!*

Praise the Lord, ye heavens adore Him!
Praise Him, angels, in the height;
Sun and moon rejoice before Him;
Praise Him, all ye stars of light.
Praise the Lord, for He is glorious;
Never shall His promises fail;
God hath made His saints victorious:
Sin and death shall not prevail.

LOWELL MASON